SUPREME COURT JUDGMENTS ON INDIAN CONSTITUTION

Mukesh Kumar Suman

Contents

Preface   XI

UNION & ITS TERRITORY

1. IN RE : THE BERUBARI UNION AND EXCHANGE OF ENCLAVES   1

2. IN RE: ARTICLE 370 OF THE CONSTITUTION   4

CITIZENSHIP

3. DR. PRADEEP JAIN VS UNION OF INDIA   8

DEFINITION OF STATE

4. PRADEEP KUMAR BISWAS VS INDIAN INSTITUTE OF CHEMICAL BIOLOGY   12

AMENDABILITY OF FUNDAMENTAL RIGHTS

5. SANKARI PRASAD DEO VS UNION OF INDIA   15

6. SAJJAN SINGH VS. STATE OF RAJASTHAN   18

7. I. C. GOLAK NATH VS STATE OF PUNJAB   21

8. KESVANAND BHARATI VS STATE OF KERALA   24

9. MINERVA MILLS LTD VS UNION OF INDIA   29

10. I R COELHO VS STATE OF TAMIL NADU   31

RIGHT TO EQUALITY : REASONABLE CLASSIFICATION

11. THE STATE OF WEST BENGAL VS ANWAR ALI SARKAR   35

RIGHT TO EQUALITY : NON - ARBITRARINESS

12. E. R. ROYAPPA VS. STATE OF TAMIL NADU   37

RIGHT TO EQUALITY : RESERVATION

13. STATE OF MADRAS VS SRIMATHI CHAMPAKAM DORAIRAJAN   40

14. M. R. BALAJI VS STATE OF MYSORE   42

15. INDRA SAWHNEY VS UNION OF INDIA   44

16. E. V. CHINNAIAH VS STATE OF ANDHRA PRADESH   48

17. M. NAGARAJ VS UNION OF INDIA   50

18. PRAMATI EDUCATIONAL AND CULTURAL TRUST VS UNION OF INDIA   54

19. JARNAIL SINGH VS LACHHMI NARAIN GUPTA   57

20. JANHIT ABHIYAN VS UNION OF INDIA   60

21. STATE OF PUNJAB VS DAVINDER SINGH   64

RIGHT TO EQUALITY : GENDER RIGHTS

22. VISHAKA VS STATE OF RAJASTHAN   67

23. SHAYARA BANO VS UNION OF INDIA (TRIPLE TALAQ JUDGMENT)   69

24. JOSEPH SHINE VS UNION OF INDIA   72

25. INDIAN YOUNG LAWYERS ASSOCIATION VS THE STATE OF KERALA (SABARIMALA JUDGMENT)   75

RIGHT TO FREEDOM

26. ROMESH THAPPAR VS. THE STATE OF MADRAS — 78

27. UNION OF INDIA VS NAVEEN JINDAL — 80

28. SHREYA SINGHAL VS UNION OF INDIA — 82

29. ASSOCIATION OF DEMOCRATIC REFORMS VS UNION OF INDIA (ELECTORAL BOND JUDGMENT) — 85

30. S RANGARAJAN VS P JAGJIVAN RAM — 88

31. KAUSHAL KISHOR VS STATE OF UTTAR PRADESH — 91

32. EXCEL WEAR ETC VS UNION OF INDIA — 94

33. DAMYANTI NARANGA VS. UNION OF INDIA — 97

34. KHARAK SINGH VS STATE OF U.P. — 99

RIGHT AGAINST SELF-INCRIMINATION

35. SELVI VS STATE OF KARNATAKA — 102

RIGHT TO LIFE AND LIBERTY : WIDER INTERPRETATION OF ARTICLE 21

36. MANEKA GANDHI VS. UNION OF INDIA — 105

RIGHT TO LIFE AND LIBERTY : RIGHT TO DIGNITY

37. FRANCIS CORALIE MULLIN VS. THE ADMINISTRATOR, UNION TERRITORY OF DELHI — 109

38. SHANTISTAR BUILDERS VS NARAYAN KHIMALAL TOTAME — 112

RIGHT TO LIFE AND LIBERTY : LBGTQ RIGHTS

39. NATIONAL LEGAL SERVICES AUTHORITY VS UNION OF INDIA — 114

40. SUPRIYO @ SUPRIYA CHAKRABORTY VS UNION OF INDIA — 117

RIGHT TO LIFE AND LIBERTY : REPRODUCTIVE RIGHTS

41. SUCHITA SRIVASTAVA VS CHANDIGARH AD-MINISTRATION ... 120

RIGHT TO LIFE AND LIBERTY : PRIVACY RIGHTS

42. JUSTICE K. S. PUTTASWAMY VS UNION OF IN-DIA (PRIVACY JUDGMENT) ... 122

43. JUSTICE K. S. PUTTASWAMY (RETD.) VS UNION OF INDIA (AADHAAR JUDGMENT) ... 125

RIGHT TO LIFE AND LIBERTY : UNDERTRIAL/CON-VICT RIGHTS

44. HUSSAINARA KHATOON VS HOME SECRETARY, STATE OF BIHAR ... 128

45. M. H. HOSKOT VS STATE OF MAHARASHTRA ... 130

46. PREM SHANKAR SHUKLA VS DELHI ADMINIS-TRATION ... 132

47. RUDUL SAH VS STATE OF BIHAR ... 134

48. SHEELA BARSE VS STATE OF MAHARASTRA ... 136

49. D. K. BASU VS STATE OF WEST BENGAL ... 138

RIGHT TO LIFE AND LIBERTY : RIGHT TO EDUCA-TION

50. MISS MOHINI JAIN VS STATE OF KARNATAKA ... 142

RIGHT TO LIFE AND LIBERTY : RIGHT TO DIE

51. COMMON CAUSE VS UNION OF INDIA ... 145

RIGHT TO LIFE AND LIBERTY : ENVIRONMENTAL RIGHTS

52. SUBHASH KUMAR VS STATE OF BIHAR ... 149

53. VELLORE CITIZENS WELFARE FORUM VS UNION OF INDIA ... 151

54. M C MEHTA VS UNION OF INDIA (OLEUM LEAK CASE) ... 153

55. M C MEHTA VS KAMAL NATH ... 156

56. IN RE : NOISE POLLUTION ... 159

RIGHT TO RELIGION

57. BIJOE EMMANUEL VS. STATE OF KERALA ... 162

58. S P MITTAL VS UNION OF INDIA ... 165

59. REV. STAINISLAUS VS STATE OF MADHYA PRADESH ... 168

MINORITY RIGHTS

60. TMA PAI FOUNDATION VS STATE OF KARNATKA ... 170

61. ALIGARH MUSLIM UNIVERSITY VS. NARESH AGARWAL ... 174

PUBLIC INTEREST LITIGATION

62. DR. ASHWANI KUMAR VS. UNION OF INDIA ... 177

63. STATE OF UTTARANCHAL VS BALWANT SINGH CHAUFAL ... 180

DIRECTIVE PRINCIPLES OF STATE POLICY

64. MOHD AHAMAD KHAN VS SHAH BANO ... 183

65. PROPERTY OWNER ASSOCIATION VS STATE OF MAHARASHTRA ... 185

FUNDAMENTAL DUTIES

66. AIIMS STUDENTS UNION VS AIIMS ... 188

PRESIDENT/GOVERNOR AND COUNCIL OF MINISTERS

67. RAI SAHIB RAM JAWAYA KAPUR VS STATE OF PUNJAB — 191

PARDONING POWERS OF PRESIDENT/GOVERNOR

68. MARU RAM VS UNION OF INDIA — 193

69. SHATRUGHAN CHAUHAN VS STATE OF UP — 196

DISQUALIFICATION OF MEMBER OF PARLIAMENT

70. JAYA BACHCHAN VS UNION OF INDIA — 199

71. KIHOTO HOLLOHAN VS ZACHILLHU AND OTHERS — 201

72. KEISHAM MEGHACHANDRA SINGH VS THE HON'BLE SPEAKER MANIPUR LEGISLATIVE ASSEMBLY — 204

73. SUBHASH DESAI VS PRINCIPAL SECRETARY, GOVERNOR OF MAHARASTRA — 207

PARLIAMENTARY PRIVILEGES

74. PANDIT M. S. M. SHARMA VS SRI KRISHAN SINHA — 211

75. IN RE : KESHAV SINGH — 214

76. RAJA RAM PAL VS HON'BLE SPEAKER , LOK SABHA — 217

77. THE STATE OF KERALA VS. K. AJITH — 221

78. SITA SOREN VS UNION OF INDIA — 224

ORDINANCE

79. DR D. C. WADHWA VS. STATE OF BIHAR — 227

SUPREME COURT

80. SUPREME COURT ADVOCATE-ON-RECORED ASSOCIATION VS UNION OF INDIA (FOURTH JUDGES CASE) — 230

GOVERNOR

81. B. P. SINGHAL VS UNION OF INDIA — 233

82. STATE OF PUNJAB VS. PRINCIPAL SECRETARY TO GOVERNOR OF PUNJAB — 237

COLOURABLE LEGISLATION

83. K C GAJAPATI NARAYAN DEO VS STATE OF ORISSA — 240

REPUGNANCY OF LAWS

84. INNOVENTIVE INDUSTRIES VS ICICI BANK — 243

INTERSTATE TRADE AND COMMERCE

85. JINDAL STAINLESS LTD VS. STATE OF HARYANA — 245

TRIBUNALS

86. ROJER MATHEW VS SOUTH INDIAN BANK LTD — 248

87. MADRAS BAR ASSOCIATION VS UNION OF INDIA — 253

ELECTION & CRIMINALISATION OF POLITICS

88. ANOOP BARANWAL VS UNION OF INDIA — 256

89. UNION OF INDIA VS ASSOCIATION OF DEMOCRTIC REFORMS — 258

90. PUBLIC INTEREST FOUNDATION VS UNION OF INDIA — 261

PRESIDENT RULE

91. S R BOMMAI VS UNION OF INDIA — 263

About the author — 266

Preface

Indian Constitution is fundamental law of the land. The Supreme Court is the ultimate interpreter of the provisions of the Constitution. Essence of the Constitution can not be comprehended in totality without understanding the essence of several landmark judgments delivered by the Supreme Court.

The second edition of this book comprises of summaries of ninety-one landmark judgments on the Constitution. These judgments have been arranged topic wise so that readers can easily comprehend development of constitutional jurisprudence.

It is a great pleasure to share this book with readers. I hope that this book will be useful for students preparing for civil service examinations, judicial service examinations, students of law, lawyers and many others who have interest in Constitution and its development.

I am thankful to family and friends for supporting me in writing this book.

IN RE : THE BERUBARI UNION AND EXCHANGE OF ENCLAVES

The Supreme Court in **In Re : The Berubari Union And Exchange of Enclaves, 1960 3 SCR 250** was of the opinion that India as a sovereign country can cede part of national territory but for giving effect to any such cession Constitution has to be amended under Article 368.

Case Title : In Re : The Berubari Union And Exchange of Enclaves
Date of Decision : 14.03.1960
Bench : Justice B.P. Sinha, Justice A.K. Sarkar, Justice J.C. Shah, Justice K.C. Das Gupta, Justice JK. Subba Rao, Justice M. Hidayatullah, Justice P.B. Gajendragadkar, Justice S.K. Das

---

FACTS OF THE CASE

Boundary Commission under Chairmanship of Sir Cyril Radcliffe was appointed under Section 3 of the Indian Independence Act, 1947 for drawing boundary between India and Pakistan. Boundary Commission made an award known as Radcliffe Award. Certain disputes arose out of interpretation of award. With mutual consent of Dominion of India and Dominion of Pakistan, a Tribunal under chairmanship of Hon'ble Lord Justice Algot Bagge was set up to resolve the disputes, which delivered awards known as "Bagge Awards".

Dispute arose between Government of India and Government of Pakistan in respect of Berubari Union No. 12 in District of Jalpaiguri and certain other territories. To resolve these disputes Government of India and Government of Pakistan entered into Indo-Pakistan Agreement.

Dr. Rajendra Prasad, the President of India, referred the matter to the Supreme Court under Article 143 of the Constitution of India for opinion on following issues in respect of Berubari Union No. 12 and Cooch Behar enclaves.

(1)Is any legislative action necessary for the implementation of the Agreement relating to Berubari Union ?

(2) If so, is a law of Parliament relatable to Article 3 of the Constitution sufficient for the purpose or is an amendment of the Constitution in accordance with Article 368 of the Constitution necessary in addition or in the alternative ?

(3) Is a law of Parliament relatable to Article 3 of the Constitution sufficient for implementation of the Agreement relating to Exchange of Enclaves or an amendment of the Constitution in accordance with Article 368 of the Constitution necessary for the purpose, in addition or in the alternative?

FINDINGS OF THE SUPREME COURT

The Supreme Court observed that parties to the agreement came to conclusion that the most expedient and reasonable way to resolve the dispute would be to divide the area in question in half and half. There was no trace in the Agreement of any attempt to interpret the Radcliffe Award or to determine what the Award really meant. The Agreement says that though the whole of area of Berubari Union No. 12 was within India, India was prepared to give half of it to Pakistan in spirit to give and take in order to ensure friendly relations between the parties and remove causes of tensions between them. The Supreme Court noted that it was difficult to accept argument that the agreement amounts to no more than ascertainment and delineation of the boundaries in the light of the award.

The Supreme Court held that the Agreement in respect of Berubari Union No. 12 and Cooch-Behar enclaves involve cession of territory.

It was contended before the Supreme Court that Parliament does not have power to cede any territory in favour of foreign state relying on Preamble and Article 1 (3) (c) of the Constitution. The Supreme Court rejected this argument. Supreme Court observed that Preamble is not part of the Constitution and it can not be regarded as the source of any substantive power.

The Supreme Court observed that it is universally recognized that one of attributes of sovereignty is the power to cede parts of national territory if necessary.

The Supreme Court concluded that it would not be competent for the Parliament to make a law relatable to Article 3 of the Constitution for purpose of implementing of agreement involving cession of territory. Law necessary to implement the agreement has to passed under Article 368 of the Indian Constitution.

IN RE: ARTICLE 370 OF THE CONSTITUTION

The Supreme Court in **In Re: Article 370 of the Constitution, (2023) 16 SCC1** held that order issued by the President for abrogation of Article 370 was constitutionally valid.

Case Title : In Re: Article 370 of the Constitution
Date of Decision : 11.12.2023
Bench : Chief Justice D.Y. Chandrachud, Justice B.R. Gavai, Justice Surya Kant, Justice S.K. Kaul, Justice Sanjiv Khanna

FACTS OF THE CASE

Article 370 of the Constitution incorporated special arrangements for the governance of the State of Jammu and Kashmir. The President vide Constitution Orders 272 and 273 abrogated Article 370 during subsistence of a proclamation under Article 356 (1) (b). Parliament also enacted Jammu and Kashmir Reorganization Act, 2019 which bifurcated the State in two Union Territories. The constitutionality of these actions was challenged before the Supreme Court.

State Government in Jammu and Kashmir was formed by an alliance of People's Democratic Party (PDP) with Bhartiya Janata Party (BJP) in 2015 and Ms. Mehbooba Mufti of PDP became Chief Minister. BJP withdrew its support and thereafter proclamation was done under Article 92 of Constitution of Jammu and Kashmir and Governor assumed power and functions of Government of the State. Governor dissolved the Legislative Assembly on 21st November, 2018. On recommendation of Governor, President Rule was imposed under Article 356 on 19th December, 2018. President Rule was extended by approval of Parliament.

On 5th August, 2019 the President issued CO 272, the Constitution (Application to Jammu and Kashmir) Order, 2019 whereby all the provisions of Constitution of India were made applicable to Jammu and Kashmir either with or without modifications. The term "Constituent Assembly" in the proviso to Article 370 (3) was changed to "Legislative Assembly".

Subsequently, the Jammu and Kashmir Reorganization Bill, 2019 was also passed by Parliament bifurcating Jammu and Kashmir into Union Territory of Jammu & Kashmir with Legislature and Union Territory of Ladakh without Legislature.

On 6th August, 2024 Parliament discharged function as Legislature of Jammu and Kashmir and Lok Sabha recommended to the President under Article 370 (3) that special provision under Article 370 (3) shall cease to operate and provisions of Constitutions will apply to Jammu and Kashmir.

On 6th August, 2019 the President pursuant to recommendation of Lok Sabha issued Constitutional Orders, whereby Article 370 ceased to apply with effect from 6th August, 2019.

FINDINGS OF THE SUPREME COURT

Sovereignty of Jammu & Kashmir

It was contended by Petitioners that State of Jammu and Kashmir retained an element of sovereignty. It was argued that the Instrument of Accession ceded "external sovereignty" to the Union of India by ceding control over the subjects of defense, foreign affairs and telecommunication but the State retained "internal sovereignty". The supreme Court held that the State of Jammu and Kashmir does not retain any element of sovereignty after the execution of Instrument of Accession and the issuance of the Proclamation dated 25th November, 1949 by which the Constitution of India was adopted. The State of Jammu and Kashmir does not have "internal sovereignty" which is distinguishable from the powers and privileges enjoyed by other States in the Country. Article 370 was a feature of asymmetric federalism and not sovereignty.

Temporary Nature of Article 370

The Supreme Court observed that it can be garnered from the historical context for the inclusion of Article 370 and placement of Article 370 in Part XXI of the Constitution that it is a temporary provision. The power under Article 370 did not cease to exist upon the dissolution of the Constituent Assembly of Jammu and Kashmir. When the Constituent Assembly was dissolved, only the transitional power recognized in the proviso to Article 370 (3) which empowered the Constituent Assembly to make its recommendations ceased to exist. It did not affect the power held by the President under Article 370 (3).

Procedural Irregularity

The Supreme Court held that Article 370 cannot be amended by exercise of power under Article 370 (1) (d). Recourse must have been taken to the procedure contemplated by Article 370 (3) if Article 370 is to cease to operate or is to be amended or modified in its application to the State of Jammu and Kashmir. Paragraph 2 of CO 272 by which Article 370 was amended through Article 367 is ultra vires Article 370 (1) (d) because it modifies Article 370, in effect, without following the procedure prescribed to modify Article 370. An interpretation clause cannot be used to bypass the procedure laid down for amendment.

Power of President under Article 370 (1) (d)

The Supreme Court held that the exercise of power by the President under Article 370 (1) (d) to issue CO 272 is not *mala fide*. The President in exercise of power under Article 370 (3) can unilaterally issue a notification that Article 370 ceases to exist. The President did not have to secure the concurrence of the Government of the State or Union Government acting on behalf of the State Government under the second proviso to Article 370 (1) (d) while applying all the provisions of the Constitution to Jammu and Kashmir because such an exercise of power has the same effect as an exercise of power under Article 370 (3) for which the concurrence or collaboration with the State Government was not required. CO 272 issued by the President in exercise of power under Article 370 (1) (d) applying all the provisions of the Constitution of India to the State of Jammu and Kashmir is valid. Such an exercise of power is not *mala fide* merely because all the provisions were applied together without following a piece-meal approach.

The President had the power to issue a notification declaring that Article 370 (3) ceases to operate without the recommendation of the Constituent Assembly. The continuous exercise of the power under Article 370 (1) by the President indicates that the gradual process of Constitutional integration was ongoing. The declaration issued by the President under Article 370 (3) is a culmination of the process of integration and as such is a valid exercise of power.

The Supreme Court held that the views of the Legislature of the State under the first proviso to Article 3 are recommendatory. Thus, Parliament's exercise of power under the first proviso to Article 3 under the proclamation was valid and not *mala fide*.

The Supreme Court did not find it necessary to determine whether the reorganization of the State of Jammu and Kashmir into two Union Territories of Ladakh and Jammu and Kashmir is permissible under Article 3. The Supreme Court upheld that validity of the decision to carve out the Union Territory of Ladakh in view of Article 3 (a) read with Explanation I, which permits forming a Union Territory by separation of a territory from any State.

The Supreme Court directed for conduct of elections to Legislative Assembly of Jammu and Kashmir constituted under Section 14 of the Reorganization Act by 30th September, 2024.

DR. PRADEEP JAIN VS UNION OF INDIA

The Supreme Court in **Dr. Pradeep Jain Vs Union of India (1984) SCR (3) 942** held that there is only one domicile under Constitution of India i.e. domicile in India.

Case Title : Dr. Pradeep Jain Vs Union of India
Date of Decision : 22.06.1984
Bench : Justice P. N. Bhagwati, Justice Ranganath Mishra, Justice Amarendra Nath Sen

FACTS OF THE CASE

Several Petitions were filed before the Supreme Court challenging residential qualifications and institutional preferences in admission to Medical Colleges in several States. The Supreme Court noticed that it was consistent and uniform practice in almost all states to provide for such residential qualification and institutional preference. Notices were issues to several states and matter was heard by the Supreme Court.

FINDINGS OF THE SUPREME COURT

The Supreme Court observed that Preamble emphasizes that the people who have given themselves to this glorious document are the people of India. Article 1 declares that India shall be a Union of States. It is as yet one nation with one citizenship. Articles 14 and 15 are intended to strike against discrimination and arbitrariness against state action, whether legislative or administrative. Article 19 (1) again recognizes the essential unity and integrity of the nation and reinforces the concept of one nation by providing in clauses (d) and (e) that every citizen shall have the right to move freely throughout the territory of India and to reside and settle in any part of the territory of India. Article 301 declares that subject to other provisions of Part XIII, trade, commerce and intercourse throughout territory of India shall be free. There are situations envisaged in certain Articles of the Constitution such as Article 353 and 356 where the executive power of State forming part of Union is exercisable by the Central Government or subject to the direction of the Central Government.

The Supreme Court observed that entire country is taken as one nation with one citizenship. Every effort of the Constitution makers is directed towards emphasizing, maintaining and preserving the unity and integrity of the nation. Now if India is one nation and there is only one, citizenship, namely citizenship of India and every citizen has a right to move freely throughout the territory of India and to reside and settle in any part of India, irrespective of the place where he is born or the language which he speaks or the religion which he professes and he is guaranteed freedom of trade, commerce and intercourse throughout the territory of India and is entitled to equality before the law and equal protection of the law with other citizens in every part of territory of India, it is difficult to see how a citizen having his permanent home in Tamil Nadu or speaking Tamil Language can be regarded as an outsider in Uttar Pradesh or a citizen having his permanent house in Maharashtra or /speaking Marathi Language regarded as outsider in Karnataka. He must be held entitled to the same rights as a citizen having his permanent home in Uttar Pradesh or Karnataka, as the case may be. To regard him as an outsider would be to deny him his constitutional rights and to derecognize the essential unity and integrity of the country by treating it as if were a mere conglomeration of independent states.

The Supreme Court observed that Article 15 bars discrimination on grounds not only of religion, race, caste, or sex but also of place of birth. Article 16 (2) goes further and provides that no citizen shall on grounds only of religion, race, caste, sex, descent, place of birth, residence or any of them be ineligible for or discriminated against in State Employment. Residential requirement would be unconstitutional as a condition of eligibility for employment or appointment to an office under the State.

The Supreme Court observed that Article 16 (3) provides an exception to this rule by laying down that Parliament may make a law prescribing in regard to a class or classes of employment or appointment to an office under the Government of or any local or other authority, in a state or union territory, any requirement as to residence within that state or union territory prior to such employment or appointment. Parliament alone is given the right to enact an exception to the ban on discrimination based on residence and that too only with respect to position within the employment of a State Government. Despite the same Several State Governments were following policies of localism.

The Supreme Court noted that at present there are no Parliamentary enactment permitting preferential policies based on residence requirement except in the case of Andhra Pradesh, Manipur, Tripura and Himachal Pradesh where the Central Government has been given the right to issue directions setting residence requirements in the subordinate services. Yet in face of Article 16 (2), some of States are following sons of soil policies giving preference to domicile or residence requirements.

The Supreme Court noted that as far as admission to educational institutions are concerned, Article 16 (2) has no application. Any requirement of "residence" for admission in educational institutions cannot be challenged on ground of "place of birth" under Article 15 or Article 16 (2) as place of birth and place of residence are two distinct concepts. Such requirements can only be tested on anvil of Article 14.

The Supreme Court noted that in several states there are domicile requirements for admission in Medical Colleges. Domicile is basically a legal concept for the purpose of determining what is the personal law applicable to an individual and even if an individual has no permanent home, he is invested with a domicile by law. There are two main classes of domicile – domicile of origin that is conferred by operation of law to each person at birth, that is the domicile of his father or his mother; and domicile of choice which every person of full age is free to acquire in substitution for what which he presently possesses.

The Supreme Court observed that Constitution of India recognizes only one domicile i.e. domicile in India. India is not a federal state in traditional sense of the term. It has only one citizenship i.e citizenship of India. It has only one single legal unified system which extends throughout the territory of India. The concept of "domicile" has no relevance to the applicability of municipal laws whether made by the Union or by the States.

It was contended before the Supreme Court that State Governments prescribing requirement of domicile for admission to medical colleges situated within their territories is used not in its technical sense but in a popular sense as meaning residence and is intended to convey the idea of intention to reside permanently or indefinitely. The Supreme Court also interpreted word "domicile" used in rules regulating admissions to medical colleges framed by some of the States in the same loose sense of permanent residence and not in the technical sense in which it is used in private international law. The Supreme Court urged State Governments to stop wrong use of word "domicile" in respect of admission to medical colleges.

The Supreme Court condemned wholesale reservation made by some of the State Governments on the basis of "domicile" or residence requirements within the state or on the basis of institutional preference for students who have passed qualifying examination held by the University or the State excluding all students not satisfying the requirements, regardless of merit. Such wholesale reservation was declared unconstitutional by the Supreme Court. The Court was of the opinion that reservation on the basis of residence should not be more than 70% of total open seats.

The Supreme Court was also of the view that so far as admission to postgraduate courses, such as , M.S. , M.D. and the like are concerned, it would be eminently desirable not to provide for any reservation based on residence requirements within the State or on institutional preference. But having regard to broader considerations of equality of opportunity and institutional continuity in education which has its own importance and value, the Supreme Court directed that residence requirements within state should not be a ground for reservation in admissions to Post Graduate courses, a certain percentage of seats may in the present circumstances be reserved on the basis of institutional preference. Even reservation on such institutional preference should not be more than 50%. But even in regard to admission to the post-graduate courses, so far as super specialties such as neuro-surgery and cardiology are concerned, there should not be any reservation even on the basis of institutional preference.

PRADEEP KUMAR BISWAS VS INDIAN INSTITUTE OF CHEMICAL BIOLOGY

The Supreme Court in **Pradeep Kumar Biswas Vs Indian Institute of Chemical Biology** (2002) 3 SCR 100 held that whether an authority is "state" under Article 12 will depend on extent of financial, functional and administrative domination or control of Government.

Case Title : Pradeep Kumar Biswas Vs Indian Institute of Chemical Biology
Date of Judgment : 16.04.2022
Bench : Justice Ruma Pal, Justice S. P. Bharucha, Justice S. S. M. Quadri, Justice N. Santosh Hegde, Justice Arijit Pasayat, Justice R. C, Lahoti, Justice D. Raju

FACTS OF THE CASE

The appellants in this case had challenged their termination in a Writ Application before the Calcutta High Court. The Writ Application before Calcutta High Court was rejected on the ground that CSIR was not covered under "authority" as defined under Article 12 in light of judgment of the Supreme Court in **Sabhajit Tewary Vs Union of India 1975 SCC(1) 485.** Aggrieved by the dismissal by Calcutta High Court, Appellants filed appeal before the Supreme Court. The matter was referred to Constitution Bench to reconsider the judgment in Sabhajit Tewary.

The issue before the Supreme Court was whether CSIR was covered under definition of State ?

FINDINGS OF THE SUPREME COURT

Article 12 defines State. State includes the Government and Parliament of India, Government and Legislature of each state and all local and other authorities within the territory of India or under the Control of Government of India. The Supreme Court noted that definition of "state" is inclusive and not exhaustive.

The Supreme Court noted that earlier "authorities" were interpreted *ejusdem generis* with the authorities mentioned in Article 12. The next stage was reached when the definition of State was understood in light of remedies available against it.

In **Rajasthan Electricity Board vs Mohan Lal (1967) 3 SCR 377,** the Supreme Court held that "other authorities" will include all constitutional or statutory authorities on whom powers are conferred by law.

In **Praga Tools Corporation Vs Sri C A Imanual, (1969)3SCR773,** the Supreme Court held that no mandamus will be issued against Praga Tools Corporation as there was neither statutory nor public duty imposed on it by a statute in respect of which mandamus could be enforced.

In **Sukhdev Singh Vs Bhagatram Sardar Singh Raghuvanshi , (1975) 3 SCR 619** the issue was whether Oil and Natural Gas Commission, Industrial Finance Corporation and Life Insurance Commission were covered under definition of State. The Supreme Court scrutinized the formation of these organisations, financial support given to them, nature of services rendered and held that they are covered under "authorities" as defined under Article 12.

The Supreme Court noted that there has been drastic changes in approach of perception of "State" in Sukhdev Singh and **Ramana Vs International Airport Authority of India (1979) SC 1628.** The form of an organization is immaterial, what is relevant is whether such organization is acting as instrumentality of state.

The test formulated by Mattew Judge in Sukhdev Singh was reformulated in **Ajay Hasia Vs Khalid Mujib Sehravardi (1981) 1 SCC722.** The Supreme Court reiterated the view that concept of instrumentality or agency of state is not limited to corporations created by statute but also companies and society if it is covered under term "authority".

In **Som Prakash Rekhi vs Union of India AIR (1981) SC 212** again Ramana was followed and Bharat Petroleum Corporation was held to be State.

In **P. K. Ramchandra Iyer Vs. Union of India (1984) 2 SCC 141** it was held that Indian Council of Agricultural Research and Indian Veterinary Research Institute are covered under "other authorities". The Supreme Court in this case noted that ratio of Sabhajit tewari has considerably watered down.

Subsequently in several judgments Indian Statistical Institute, Central Inland Water Transport Corporation, Sainik School Society were covered under definition of "State".

The Court concluded that test propounded in Ajay Hasia are not rigid set of principles. The question in each case would whether in light of cumulative facts, the body in question is financially, functionally and administratively dominated by or under the control of Government.

The Supreme Court analyzed the objects, functions, management, control and finances and held that CSIR is covered under the definition of State.

SANKARI PRASAD DEO VS UNION OF INDIA

The Supreme Court in **Sankari Prasad Deo Vs. Union of India** (1951 **AIR** 458) held that Fundamental Rights can be amended Parliament under Article 368 of the Constitution. This judgment was overruled in **I. C. Golak Nath Vs. State of Punjab** (1967 AIR 1643) and finally culminated in "basic structure" doctrine in **Kesavananda Bharati Vs. State of Kerala** (1973) 4 SCC 225.

Case Title : Shankari Prasad Deo Vs. Union of India
Date of Judgment : 05.10.1951
Bench : Chief Justice Harilal Kania, Justice Patanjali Sastri, Justice Mukherjea, Justice Das, Justice Chandrasekhara Aiyar

---

FACTS OF THE CASE

After Independence the Union Government and State Government initiated several agrarian reforms. Many States passed Zamindar Abolition Acts. These acts were challenged in several states before respective High Courts on the ground that they violated Right to Property under Article 31 of the Constitution. The High Court of Bihar held Zamindari Abolition Act unconstitutional while Highs Courts of Uttar Pradesh and Madhya Pradesh found them valid.

Parliament responded by passing the 1st Amendment of the Constitution. Parliament introduced Article 31 A, 31B and Ninth Schedule. Article 31A provided that laws providing for acquisition of estates cannot be challenged on the ground of inconsistency with the Fundamental Rights. Article 31 B provided that Acts and Regulations specified in Ninth Schedule cannot be invalidated on the ground of inconsistency with Fundamental Rights. Ninth Schedule was unique innovation of the Parliament to save any enactment from Judicial Review.

FINDINGS OF THE SUPREME COURT

Whether Provisional Parliament Can Amend Constitution

One of the argument raised before the Supreme Court was that the power of amending the Constitution provided for under Article 368 was conferred not on Parliament but on the two Houses of Parliament as a designated body and, therefore, the provisional Parliament was not competent to exercise that power under Article 379. It is pertinent to mention that at that time constituent assembly was functioning as provisional parliament. Parliament has yet not been constituted on the basis of fresh elections. The Supreme Court held that the framers were well' aware that such a Parliament could not be constituted till after the first elections were held under the Constitution. It, thus, became necessary to make provision for the carrying on, in the meantime, of the work entrusted to Parliament under the Constitution. Accordingly, it was provided in article 379 that the Constituent Assembly should function as the provisional Parliament during the transitional period and exercise all the powers and perform all the duties conferred by the Constitution on Parliament. Article 379 should be viewed and interpreted in the wider perspective of this scheme and not in its isolated relation to article 368 alone. The Petitioners' argument that the reference in article 368 to "two Houses" makes that provision inapplicable to the provisional Parliament would equally apply to all the provisions of the Constitution in regard to Parliamentary action and, if accepted, would rob article 379 of its very purpose and meaning.

Amendability of the Fundamental Rights

Insertion of Article 31 A and Article 31 B was also challenged on the ground that it purports to take away or abridge Fundamental Rights which fall within the prohibition of Article 13(2). Article 13 (2) provides that State shall not make any law which takes away or abridges the rights conferred by this Part and any law made in contravention of this clause shall, to the extent of the contravention, be void. It was argued before the Court that "State" Includes Parliament and "law" includes "amendments" under Article 368. It was submitted before the Court that it is not uncommon to find in written constitutions a declaration that certain Fundamental Rights conferred on the people should be "eternal and inviolate" as for instance article 11 of the Japanese Constitution. Article 5 of the American Federal Constitution provides that no amendment shall be made depriving any State without its consent of its equal suffrage in the Senate.

The Supreme Court held that there is a clear demarcation between ordinary law, which is made in exercise of legislative power, and constitutional law, which is made in exercise of constituent power. The Court held that in the context of article 13 "law" must be taken to mean rules or regulations made in exercise of ordinary legislative power and not amendments to the Constitution made in exercise of constituent power, with the result that article 13(2) does not affect amendments made under Article 368.

Thus, the Supreme Court invoked the principle of sovereign constituent power of Parliament, although no such explicit provision in the Constitution exists, and held that Article 13 (2) has no application on the amendments under Article 368.

Non-Ratification by States

Article 368 (2) provides for ratification by majority of State Legislatures if amendment seeks to make changes in some specific sections. One of the grounds raised before the Supreme Court was that the amendment required ratification from states as insertion of 31 A and 31 B affected power of the High Court under 226 to entertain writs and power the Supreme Court under Article 131 and 136 to entertain appeals from such writs. The Supreme court held that It is not correct to say that the powers of the High Court under article 226 to issue writs "for the enforcement of any of the rights conferred by Part III" or of this Court under articles 132 and 136 to entertain appeals from orders issuing or refusing such writs are in any way affected. They remain just the same as they were before, only a certain class of cases has been excluded from the purview of Part III and the Courts could no longer interfere, not because their powers were curtailed in any manner or to any extent, but because there would be no occasion hereafter for the exercise of their power in such cases.

The most important finding of the Supreme Court in this judgement was that laws as defined under Article 13 (2) do not apply on amendments under Article 368. As such every Fundamental Right could have been amended by the Parliament under Article 368.

SAJJAN SINGH VS. STATE OF RAJASTHAN

The Supreme Court in **Sajjan Singh Vs. State of Rajasthan (1965 SCR (1) 933)** reiterated the view taken in **Sankari Prasad Deo Vs. Union of India (1951 AIR 458)** that Fundamental Rights can be amended under Article 368 of the Constitution.

Case Title : Sajjan Singh Vs. State of Rajasthan
Date of Judgment : 30.10.1964
Bench : Chief Justice P. B. Gajendragadkar, Justice Raghubar Dayal, Justice M. Hidayatullah, Justice J. R. Mudholkar, justice K. N. Wanchoo

FACTS OF THE CASE

Parliament vide seventeenth amendment incorporated several agrarian reform legislations passed by States in Ninth Schedule. Sajjan Singh, a former ruler of Ratlam, filed Writ Petition under Article 32 of the Constitution challenging the validity of seventeenth Amendment. Several other petitions were also filed challenging the validity of seventeenth Amendment.

FINDINGS OF THE SUPREME COURT

Whether procedure prescribed under Article 368 was followed ?

One of the grounds of challenge in this case was whether procedure prescribed under Article 368 has been followed. The Supreme Court held that in construing both the parts of Article 368, the rule of harmonious construction requires that if the direct effect of the amendment of Fundamental Rights is to make a substantial inroad on the High Courts' powers under Art. 226, it would become necessary to consider whether the proviso would cover such a case or not. If the effect of the amendment made in the fundamental rights on the powers of the High Courts prescribed by Art. 226, is indirect, incidental, or is otherwise of an insignificant order, it may be that the proviso will not apply. The proviso would apply where the amendment in question seeks to make any change, inter alia, in Art. 226.

The Supreme Court observed that if the pith and substance test is applied to the amendment made by the impugned Act, it would be clear that Parliament is seeking to amend Fundamental Rights solely with the object of removing any possible obstacle in the fulfilment of the socio-economic policy in which the party in power believes. If that be so, the effect of the amendment on the area over which the High Court's powers prescribed by Art. 226 operate, is incidental and in the present case can be described as of an insignificant order. The impugned Act does not purport to change the provisions of Art. 226 and it cannot be said even to have that effect directly or in any appreciable measure.

Whether amendment falls under jurisdiction of State ?

Another issue which was raised before the Supreme Court was that amendment was essentially related to land and fell within jurisdiction of State Legislature and Parliament was having no right to pass the Amendment. The Supreme Court held that the argument was misconceived. In dealing with this argument, again, the pith and substance test is relevant. What the impugned Act purports to do is not to make any land legislation but to protect and validate the legislative measures in respect of agrarian reforms passed by the different State Legislatures in the country by granting them immunity from attack based on the plea that they contravene Fundamental Rights. Parliament, in enacting the impugned Act, was not making any provisions of land legislation. It was merely validating land legislations already passed by the State Legislatures in that behalf.

Whether Power to amend includes power to take away Fundamental Rights ?

Another issue which was raised before the Supreme Court was that the power to amend, which is conferred by Art. 368, does not include the power to take away the Fundamental Rights guaranteed by Part III. The Supreme Court observed that it is true that the dictionary meaning of the word "amend" is to correct a fault or reform; but in the context, reliance on the dictionary meaning of the word is singularly inappropriate because what Article 368 authorizes to be done is the amendment of the provisions of the Constitution. It is well-known that the amendment of a law may in a proper case include the deletion of any one or more of the provisions of the law and substitution in their place of new provisions. Similarly, an amendment of the Constitution which is the subject matter of the power conferred by Art. 368, may include modification or change of the provisions or even an amendment which makes the said provisions inapplicable in certain cases. The power to amend in the context is a very wide power and it cannot be controlled by the literal dictionary meaning of the word "amend".

The Supreme Court expressed its full concurrence with Sankari Prasad Judgment. The Supreme Court observed that it is true that Art. 13(2) refers to any law in general, and literally construed, the word "law" may take in a law made in exercise of the constituent power conferred on Parliament; but having regard to the fact that a specific, unqualified and unambiguous power to amend the Constitution is conferred on Parliament, it would be unreasonable to hold that the word "law" in Art. 13 (2) takes in Constitution Amendment Acts passed under Art. 368. If the Constitution makers had intended that any future amendment of the provisions in regard to Fundamental Rights should be subject to Art. 13 (2), they would have taken the precaution of making a clear provision in that behalf. Besides, it seems very unlikely that while conferring the power on Parliament to amend the Constitution, it was the intention of the Constitution makers to exclude from that comprehensive power Fundamental Rights altogether. There is no doubt that if the word "law" used in Art. 13(2) includes a law in relation to the amendment of the Constitution, Fundamental Rights can never be abridged or taken away, because as soon as it is shown that the effect of the amendment is to take away or abridge fundamental rights, that portion of the law would be void under Art. 13 (2). We have no doubt that such a position could not have been intended by the Constitution-makers when they included Article 368 in the Constitution.

I. C. GOLAK NATH VS STATE OF PUNJAB

The Supreme Court with 6:5 majority in **I. C. Golak Nath Vs State of Punjab (1967) 2 SCR 762** held that Parliament has no power to amend Fundamental Rights under Part III of the Constitution. This judgment overruled **Shankari Prasad Deo Vs Union of India (1959) SCR 89** and **Sajjan Singh Vs State of Rajasthan (1965) SCR (1) 933** but itself was subsequently overruled in **Kesavananda Bharati Vs State of Kerala AIR 1973 SC 1461.**

Case Title : I. C. Golak Nath Vs State of Punjab
Date of Judgment : 27.02.1967
Bench : Chief Justice K. Subba Rao, Justice J. C. Shah, Justice S. M. Sikri, Justice M. Shelat, Justice C. A. Vaidialingam, Justice K. N. Wanchoo, Justice V. Bhargava, Justice G. K. Mitter, Justice M. Hidayatullah, Justice R. S. Bachawat, Justice V Ramaswamy

FACTS OF THE CASE

Several Acts were included in Ninth Schedule vide Seventeenth Amendment of the Constitution including Mysore Land Reforms Act, 1961 and the Punjab Security of Land Tenures Act, 1953. Three Writ Petitions were filed before the Supreme Court challenging the validity of Constitution (Seventeenth Amendment) Act, 1964.

FINDINGS OF THE SUPREME COURT

The Supreme Court noted that in the question of amendability of Fundamental Rights was considered in **Shankari Prasad Deo Vs. Union of India (1951 AIR 458)** and **Sajjan Singh Vs. State of Rajasthan (1965 AIR 845).** In Sankari Prasad decision was based on an assumption that the expression "law" in Article 13 (2) does not include constitutional law. In Sajjan Singh the ratio of Sankari Prasad was followed and it was observed that the expression amendment of the constitution plainly and unambiguously means amendment of all the provisions of the Constitution including Fundamental Rights.

The Supreme Court observed that all laws in force in the territory of India immediately before the commencement of the Constitution in so far as they are inconsistent with the said rights are to the extent of such inconsistency void. The Constitution also enjoins the State not to make any law which takes away or abridges the said rights and declares such laws to the extent of such inconsistency to be void. Thus, Fundamental Rights are given a transcendental position under the Constitution and are kept beyond the reach of the Parliament. At the same time Part III and Part IV constituted an integrated scheme forming a self-contained code. The scheme is made so elastic that all the Directive Principles of State Policy can reasonably be enforced without taking away or abridging the fundamental rights.

While recognizing the immutability of Fundamental Rights, subject to social control, the Constitution itself provides for the suspension or the modification of Fundamental Rights under specific circumstances, for instance, Article 33 empowers Parliament to modify the rights conferred by Part III in their application to members of Armed Forces. Article 34 enables it to impose restrictions on the rights conferred by the said parts while martial law is in force in an area. Article 32 makes the right to move the Supreme Court by appropriate proceedings for the enforcements of the rights conferred by the said Parts a guaranteed right. Even during grave emergencies Article 358 only suspends the provisions of Article 19 and Article 359 enables the President by order to declare the right to move any court for the enforcement of such of the rights conferred by Part III as may be mentioned in that order to be suspended, that is to say even during emergency only Article 19 is suspended temporarily and all other rights are untouched except those specifically suspended by the President.

The Supreme Court observed that the Constitution declares certain rights as Fundamental Rights, makes all the laws infringing the said rights void, preserves only the laws of social control infringing the said rights and expressly confers power on Parliament and the President to amend or suspend them in specified circumstances. If the decisions in Sankari Prasad and Sajjan Singh laid down the correct law, it enables the same Parliament to abrogate them with one stroke provided the party in power singly or in combination with other parties commands the necessary majority. While articles of less significance would require consent of the majority of the States, Fundamental Rights can be dropped without such consent. The entire super structure built with precision and high ideals may crumble at one false step. Such a conclusion would attribute unreasonableness to the makers of the Constitution, for, in that event they would be speaking in two voices. Such an intention cannot be attributed to the makers of the Constitution unless the provisions of the Constitution compel us to do so.

The Supreme Court observed that there is no distinction in the Constitution of India between ordinary law and law in exercise of constituent power.

The Supreme Court observed that an amendment of the Constitution is made only by legislative process with ordinary majority or with special majority, as the case may be. Therefore, amendments either under Article 368 of under other Articles are made only by Parliament by following the legislative process adopted by it in making other law. In the premises, an amendment of the Constitution can be nothing but "law".

The Supreme Court rejected the argument that Parliament has any implied power to amend the Fundamental Rights and held that there is nothing in the nature of the amending power which enables Parliament to override all the express or implied limitations imposed on that power. Indian Constitution had adopted a novel method in the sense that Parliament makes the amendment by legislative process subject to certain restrictions and the amendment so made being subject to Article 13 (2).

The Supreme Court concluded that Parliament has no power to amend Part III of the Constitution so as to take away or abridge the Fundamental Rights. The Supreme Court also applied principles of prospective overruling, which meant that the Parliament would not be able to amend Fundamental Rights in future. Past amendments were not disturbed.

KESVANAND BHARATI VS STATE OF KERALA

The Supreme Court by 7:6 majority in **Kesavananda Bharati Vs. State of Kerala (1973) Supp. 1 SCR 1** held that basic structure of the Constitution cannot be amended by Article 368 of the Constitution.

Case Title : Kesavananda Bharati Vs. State of Kerala
Date of Judgment : 24.04.1973
Bench : Chief Justice S. M. Sikri, Justice J. M. Shelat, Justice K.S. Hegde, Justice A.N. Grover, Justice A.N. Ray, Justice P. Jaganmohan Reddy, Justice D.G. Palekar, Justice H.R. Khanna, Justice K.K. Mathew, Justice M.H. Beg, Justice S.N. dwivedi, Justice A.K. Mukherjea and Justice Y.V. Chandrachud

FACTS OF THE CASE

Twenty Fourth, Twenty Fifth and Twenty Ninth amendments were challenged before the Supreme Court in this batch of Writ Petitions.

24th Amendment inserted clause (4) to Article 13 which provided that nothing in this Article shall apply to any amendment of this Constitution made under Article 368. Clause (3) was also added to Article 368 which provided that nothing in Article 13 shall apply to any amendment made under this Article.

25th Amendment inserted Article 31C which provided that notwithstanding anything contained in Article 13, no law giving effect to the policy of the State towards securing the principles specified in clause (b) or clause (c) of Article 39 shall be deemed to be void on the ground that it is inconsistent with or takes away or abridges any of the rights conferred by Article 14, Article 19 or Article 31 and no law containing a declaration that it is for giving effect to such policy shall be called in question in any court on the ground that it does not give effect to such policy. Provided that where such law is made by the Legislature of a State, the provisions of this Article shall not apply thereto unless such law having been reserved for the consideration of the President has received his assent.

29th Amendment inserted Kerala Land Reforms Act (Amendment) Act, 1969 and Kerala Land Reforms Act, 1971 in the Ninth Schedule.

FINDINGS OF THE SURPEME COURT

Chief justice S. M. Sikri was of the opinion that it was the common understanding that Fundamental Rights would remain in substance as they are and they would not be amended out of existence. It seems also to have been common understanding that the fundamental features of the Constitution, namely, secularism, democracy and the freedom of the individual would always subsist in the welfare state. In view of above reasons, a necessary implication arises that there are implied limitations on the power of Parliament. The expression "amendment of this Constitution" has consequently a limited meaning in our constitution and not the meaning suggested by the Respondents.

The expression "amendment of this Constitution" in Article 368 means any addition or change in any of the provisions of the Constitution within the broad contours of the Preamble and the Constitution to carry out the objectives in the Preamble and the Directive Principles applied to Fundamental Rights it would mean that while Fundamental Rights cannot be abrogated, reasonable abridgments of Fundamental Rights can be effected in the public interest.

Justice J. M. Shelat and A. N. Grover observed that the correct approach to the question of limitations which may be implied in any legislative provisions including a Constitutional document has to be made from the point of view of interpretation. It is not a novel theory or a doctrine which has to be treated as an innovation of those who evolve heterodox methods to substantiate their own thesis. The argument that there are no implied limitations because there are no express limitations is a contradiction in terms. Implied limitations can only arise where there are no express limitations.

The basic structure of the Constitution is not a vague concept and the apprehensions expressed on behalf of the respondents that neither the citizen nor the Parliament would be able to understand it are unfounded. In the historical background, the Preamble, the entire scheme of the Constitution, the relevant provisions thereof including Article 368 are kept in mind there can be no difficulty in discerning that the following can be regarded as the basic elements of the constitutional structure. These cannot be catalogued but can only be illustrated – (i) the Supremacy of the Constitution (ii)Republican and Democratic form of Government and sovereignty of the Country (iii) secular and federal character of the Constitution (iv) demarcation of power between the legislature, executive and judiciary (v) the dignity of the individual secured by the various freedoms and basic rights in Part III and the mandate to build a welfare State contained in Part IV (vi) the unity and integrity of the nation.

Justice K. S. Hedge and A. K. Mukherjee observed that it is difficult to accept the contention that Constitution makers after making immense sacrifices for achieving certain ideals made provision in the Constitution itself for the destruction of those ideals. There is no doubt as men of experience and sound political knowledge, they must have known that social, economic and political changes are bound to come with the passage of time and the Constitution must be capable to being so adjusted as to be able to respond to those demands. Our constitution is not a mere political document. It is essentially a social document. It is based on a social philosophy and every social philosophy like every religion has two main features, namely, basic and circumstantial. The former remains constant but the latter is subject to change. The core of a religion always remains constant but the practices associated with it may change. Likewise, a constitution like ours contain certain features which are so essential that they cannot be changed or destroyed. In any event it cannot be destroyed from within. In other words, one cannot legally use the Constitution to destroy itself. Under Article 368 the amended Constitution must remain "the Constitution" which means the original Constitution. When we speak of the "abrogation" or "repeal" of the Constitution, we donot refer to any form but to substance. If one or more of the basic features of the Constitution are taken away to that extent the Constitution is abrogated or repealed. If all the basic features of the Constitution are repealed and some other provisions inconsistent with those features are incorporated, it cannot still remain the Constitution referred to in Article 368. The Personality of the Constitution must remain unchanged. When a power to amend the Constitution is given to the people, its contents can be construed to be larger than when the power is given to a body constituted under the Constitution. Two-thirds of members of the two Houses of the Parliament need not necessarily represent even the majority of the people of this Country.

The word "amendment" in Article 368 carries with it certain limitations, further, that the power conferred under Article 368 is subject to certain implied limitations though that power is quite large.

Justice P. Jaganmohan Reddy observed that Article 13 (2) inhibits only a law made by the ordinary legislative agency and not an amendment under Article 368. The power of Parliament under Article 368 is wide, but it is not wide enough to totally abrogate or what would amount to an abrogation or emasculating or destroying in a way as would amount to abrogation of any of the fundamental rights or other essential elements of basic structure of the Constitution and destroy its identity.

Justice H. R. Khanna observed that amendment of the Constitution necessarily contemplates that the constitution has not to be abrogated but only changes have to made to it. The word "amendment" postulates that the old constitution survives without loss of its identity despite the change and continues even though it has been subjected to alterations. As a result of the amendment, the old constitution cannot be destroyed and done away with; it is retained though in the amended form. What then is meant by retention of the old constitution ? it means the retention of the basic structure or framework of the old constitution. A mere retention of some provisions of the old constitution even though the basic structure or framework of the constitution has been destroyed would not amount to the retention of the old constitution. Although it is permissible under the power of amendment to effect change howsoever important, and to adapt the system of the requirements of changing conditions, it is not permissible to touch the foundation or to alter the basic institutional pattern. The words "amendment of the constitution" with all their wide sweep and amplitude cannot have the effect of destroying or abrogating the basic structure or framework of the constitution. It would not be competent under the garb of amendment, for instance, to change the democratic government into dictatorship or hereditary monarch nor would it be permissible to abolish Lok Sabha and Rajya Sabha. The secular character of the State according to which the state shall not discriminate against any citizen on the ground of religion only cannot likewise be done away with. Provision regarding the amendment of the Constitution does not furnish a pretence for subverting the structure of the Constitution nor can Article 368 be so constructed as to embody the death wish of the Constitution or provide sanction for what may perhaps be called its lawful hara-kiri. Such subversion or destruction cannot be described to be amendment of the Constitution as contemplated by Article 368.

The words "amendment of this Constitution" and "the Constitution shall stand amended" in Article 368 show that what is amended is the existing Constitution and what emerges as a result of amendment is not a new and different Constitution but the existing Constitution though in an amended form. The language of Article 368 thus lends support to the conclusion that one cannot while acting under that Article, repeal the existing Constitution and replace it by a new Constitution.

Justice Khanna was of the opinion that majority view in Golak Nath case that Parliament did not have the power to amend any provisions of Part III of the Constitution so as to take away or abridge the fundamental rights cannot be accepted to be correct. Fundamental Rights contained in Part III of our Constitution can be abridged or taken away in compliance with the procedure prescribed by Article 368, as long as the basic structure of the Constitution remains unaffected.

The Supreme Court overruled **I. C. Golak Nath Vs State of Punjab (1967) SCR (2) 762** judgment but held that Article 368 does not enable the Parliament to alter the basic structure of the Constitution. The Supreme Court also upheld constitutional validity of 24th and 29th amendment. The Supreme Court also upheld Constitutional validity of Section 2 (a), 2 (b) and first part of Section 3 of 25th amendment but held second part namely "and no law containing a declaration that it is for giving effect to such policy shall be called in question in any court on the ground that it does not give effect to such policy" constitutionally invalid.

MINERVA MILLS LTD VS UNION OF INDIA

The Supreme Court in **Minerva Mills Ltd Vs Union of India (1981) 1 S.C.R. 206** declared that Section 4 and 55 of the Constitution (Forty Second Amendment) Act , 1976 are void and beyond amending power of the Parliament.

Case Title : Minerva Mills Ltd Vs Union of India
Date of Judgment : 31.07.1980
Bench : Chief Justice Y. V. Chandrachud, Justice P. N. Bhagwati, Justice A.C. Gupta, Justice N. L. Untwalia , Justice P.S. Kailasam

---

FACTS OF THE CASE

The Central Government appointed a committee under Section 15 of the Industries (Development and Regulation) Act, 1951 for complete investigation of affairs of Minerva Mills as it was opinion that there may be substantial fall in production. On the basis of report the said committee the Central Government authorized National Textile Corporation to take over management of Minerva Mills on the ground that its management is highly detrimental to national interest.

Various provisions were challenged in this batch of Petitions but Court determined Section 4 and Section 55 of 42nd Amendment Act. Section 4 amended Article 31 C to the effect that no law giving effect to the policy of the state towards securing all or any of the principles laid down in Part IV will be void on the ground it is consistent with Article 14, 19 and 21. Section 55 amended Article 368 and inserted clause (4) and (5). Clause 4 provided that no amendment to the Constitution under Article 368 will be challenged before any Court. Clause 5 provided that there will be no limitation on the constituent power of Parliament to amend the Constitution by way of addition, variation, or repeal.

FINDINGS OF THE SUPREME COURT

The Supreme Court observed that Constitution has conferred limited amending power to Parliament. Parliament can not enlarge limited power into absolute power. Parliament cannot under Article 368 repeal or abrogate the Constitution or to destroy its basic and essential features. The Supreme Court declared (5) ultra vires and void. Clause (4) was also declared void as it deprived courts of power of judicial review of constitutional amendments even in cases of infraction of basic structure of Constitution. Without this power fundamental rights conferred on people will become mere adornment because rights without remedies are writs in water.

As far as amendment to Article 31 C is concerned the same relate to primacy of Directive Principle of State Policy over Fundamental Rights. Fundamental Rights have unique place in lives of civilized societies and have been described as transcendental, inalienable and primordial. Indian Constitution is based on bed-rock of balance between Fundamental Rights and Directive Principles of State Policy. To give absolute primacy to one over the another is to disturb the harmony of the Constitution. The Supreme Court held that harmony and balance between Fundamental Rights and Directive Principles of State Policy is an essential feature of the basic structure of the Constitution. The amendment to Article 31 C leads to startling consequence that even if a law is in violation of Article 13 read with Article 14 and 19, its validity will not be open to question so long its objective to secure ends of Directive Principles of State Policy. The Supreme Court observed that only three Articles i.e. Article 14, 19 and 21 stand between heaven of freedom and the abyss of unrestrained power. Amendment of Article 31 C has removed two Articles of this golden triangle. The Supreme Court declared amendment to 31 C also ultra vires and void.

I R COELHO VS STATE OF TAMIL NADU

The Constitution Bench of Supreme Court in **I R Coelho Vs State of Tamil Nadu (2007) 1 SCR 706** held that a legislation placed in Ninth Schedule after **Kesavananda Bharati Vs. State of Kerala (1973) Supp. 1 SCR 1** judgment can be reviewed on the ground of violation of basic structure as reflected in Article 14, 19 and 21.

Case Title : **I R Coelho Vs State of Tamil Nadu**
Date of Judgment : 11.01.2007
Bench : Chief Justice Y.K. Sabharwal, Justice Ashok Bhan, Justice Arijit Pasayat, Justice B. P. Singh, Justice S. S. Kapadia, Justice C. K. Thakker, Justice P. K. Balasubramanyan, Justice Altamas Kabir, Justice D.K.Jain

FACTS OF THE CASE

The Gudalur Janmam Estates (Abolition and Conversion into Ryotwari) Act, 1969 insofar as it vested forest lands in the Janmam estates in the State of Tamil Nadu was struck down by the Supreme Court in Balmadies Plantations Ltd Vs. State of Tamil Nadu (1972) 2 SCC 133 because this was not found to be a measure of agrarian reform protected by Article 31A of the Constitution. Section 2 (c) of the West Bengal Land Holding Revenue Act, 1979 was struck down by the Calcutta High Court as being arbitrary and , therefore, unconstitutional and Special Leave Petition filed before the Supreme Court against the same was dismissed. These insertions were the subject matter of challenge before five Judge Bench. The contention urged before the Constitution Bench was that the statutes, inclusive of the portion thereof which had been struck down, could not have been validly inserted in the Ninth Schedule.

The broad question before the Court was whether it is permissible for the Parliament under Article 31 B to immunize legislations from Fundamental Rights by inserting them in 9th Schedule on or after 24th April, 1973.

FINDINGS OF THE SUPREME COURT

The Ninth Schedule

The High Court of Patna in **Kameshwar Vs State of Bihar (AIR 1951 PATNA 246)** has held unconstitutional legislation relating to land reform. Several zamindars had also filed several writ petitions under Article 32 of the Constitution of India. At this stage, Parliament inserted Article 31 B by First Amendment. By the same amendment Parliament added 9th Schedule. Article 31 B immunized laws contained therein on the ground that it violates any fundamental rights. The 1st Amendment was challenged in **Sankri Prasad Singh Deo Vs Union of India (1951 AIR 458)** wherein 1st Amendment was held valid. Validity of several acts inserted in 9th Schedule vide 17th amendment was challenged in **Sajjan Singh Vs State of Rajasthan (1965) AIR 845** wherein it was held valid and constitutional. In **I. C. Golaknath vs State of Punjab 967 AIR 1643**, the judgment of Sankari Prasad was overruled and held that Fundamental Rights can not be amended with prospective effect.

Vide 24th Amendment, Article 13 was amended to provide that it will not apply to amendment made under Article 368 of the Constitution. This was challenged before the Supreme Court in **Kesavanand Bharati Vs State of Kerala (1973) 4 SCC 225.** Supreme Court in Kesavanand Bharti held that basic structure can not be amended but what forms basis structure was not exhaustively defined.

Evolution of Basic Structure

In **Indira Nehru Gandhi Vs Raj Narayan (1975) AIR 1590** , the Supreme Court held that 39th amendment providing for barring of judicial review of election of Prime Minister was unconstitutional as it violated basic structure of the Constitution.

In **Minerva Mills Ltd Vs Union of India (1986) AIR 2030** case struck down clause (4) and (5) of the Article 368 on the ground that it violates basic structure.

In **Waman Rao Vs Union of India (1981) 2SCC362** the Supreme Court held that legislations inserted in 9th Schedule after Kesavananda Bharti judgment is not immune from judicial review.

In **L. Chandra Kumar Vs Union of India 1997 (3) SCC 261** the Supreme Court held that judicial Review is part of basic structure of the Constitution of India.

Fundamental Rights and Basic Structure

Modern democracy is based on principle of constitutionalism which requires control over the exercise of governmental power to ensure that it does not destroy the democratic principles upon which it is based.

Some of Fundamental Rights are part of doctrine of basic structure of Indian Constitution. Article 14, 19 and 21 reflect the foundational values of the Constitution which forms the basis of rule of law and judicial review.

Dr. Ambedkar has said that Article 32 is the most important provision among Fundamental Right without which constitution would be nullity. Article 32 has been held to be part of basic structure in several judgments by the Supreme Court including **L. Chandra Kumar and S. R. Bommai Vs Union of India (1994) AIR 1918.**

Fundamental Rights have to be examined in light of development of inter-pretation over the years. Fundamental Rights were earlier understood to be distinct and separate. But this view has been discarded in **Rustom Cavasjee Cooper Vs Union of India (1970) 3 SCR 530** wherein the Supreme Court disapproved the view that every Fundamental Right is separate and distinct. This view was further strengthened in **Maneka Gandhi Vs Union of India AIR (1978) SC 597.** Fundamental Rights together provide comprehensive guarantee against excess of state authorities. Thus, any abrogation of funda-mental rights has to be examined on the basis of the broad interpretation of the Fundamental Rights.

9th Schedule has been inserted to provide immunity to land reform laws. But subsequently legislations having no nexus with land reforms have been included in the 9th Schedule. Further, a number of legislations have been placed under 9th Schedule. Barring judicial review to such large number of legislations is contrary to constitutional supremacy.

Parliament has power to amend Fundamental Rights but this power is subject to basic structure of the Constitution.

A law that abrogates or abridges Fundamental Rights may violate basic structure or may not. Validity of each amendment has to be tested on its merits. An amendment made to the 9th Schedule   made after Kesavanand Bharati case can be judicially reviewed on the ground of violation of basic structure as reflected in Article 14, 19 and 21 by application of "rights test" and "essence of rights test".

THE STATE OF WEST BENGAL VS ANWAR ALI SARKAR

Justice S. R. Das in the **State of West Bengal Vs. Anwar Ali Sarkar (1952) 1 SCR 284** propounded twins tests of permissible classification under Article 14 which has been followed in subsequent judgments and has become locus classicus.

Case Title : State of West Bengal Vs. Anwar Ali Sarkar
Date of Judgment : 11.01.1952
Bench : Chief Justice Patanjali Sastri, Justice C. J. Fazl Ali, Justice Mehr Chand Mahajan, Justice Mukherjea, Justice Das, Justice Chandrasekhara Aiyar, Justice Vivian Bose

FACTS OF THE CASE

West Bengal State Legislature enacted the West Bengal Special Courts Act, 1950 to provide for speedier trial of certain offences. Section 3 of the Act empowered the State Government by notification in the official gazette to constitute special courts. Section 5 provided that a special court shall try such offences or classes of offences or cases or classes of cases, as the State Government by general or special order in writing direct. The Respondent was convicted by Special Court. The Respondent challenged the validity of the Act on the ground that it violated Article 14. Calcutta High Court quashed the conviction. The matter finally reached to the Supreme Court.

FINDINGS OF THE SUPREME COURT

The majority held that the procedure laid down by the Act for the trial by the Special Courts varied substantially from that laid down for the trial of offences generally by the Code of Criminal Procedure and the Act did not classify or lay down any basis for classification of the cases which may be directed to be tried by the Special Court, but left it to the uncontrolled discretion of the

State Government to direct any case which it liked to be tried by the Special Court.

Justice Das wrote a separate judgment wherein he propounded twin tests for permissible classification under Article 14.

Justice Das observed that Article 14 of the Constitution corresponds to the last portion of Section 1 of the Fourteenth Amendment to the American Constitution except that Article 14 has also adopted the English doctrine of rule of law by the addition of the words "equality before the law".

Justice Das observed that it is now well established that while Article 14 is designed to prevent a person or class of persons from being singled out from others similarly situated for the purpose of being specially subjected to discriminating and hostile legislation, it does not insist on an "abstract symmetry" in the sense that every piece of legislation must have universal application. All persons are not, by nature, attainment or circumstances, equal and the varying needs of different classes of persons often require separate treatment and therefore the protecting clause has been construed as a guarantee against discrimination amongst equals only and not as taking away from the State the power to classify persons for the purpose of legislation. The classification may be on different bases. It may be geographical or according to objects or occupations or the like. Mere classification, however, is not enough to get over the inhibition of the Article. The classification must not be arbitrary but must be rational, that is to say, it must not only be based on some qualities or characteristics which are to be found in all the persons grouped together and not in others who are left out but those qualities or characteristics must have a reasonable relation to the object of the legislation. In order to pass the test, two conditions must be fulfilled namely – (1) that the classification must be founded on the intelligible differentia which distinguishes those that are grouped together from others and (2) that differentia must have a rational relation to the object sought to be achieved by the Act. The differentia which is the basis of the classification and the object of the Act are distinct things and what is necessary is that there must be a nexus between them. In short, while the Article forbids class legislation in the sense of making improper discrimination by conferring privileges or imposing liabilities upon persons arbitrarily selected out of a large number of other persons similarly situated in relation to the privileges sought to be conferred or the liability proposed to be imposed, it does not forbid classification for the purpose of legislation, provided such classification is not arbitrary.

E. R. ROYAPPA VS. STATE OF TAMIL NADU

The Supreme Court in **E. R. Royappa Vs. State of Tamil Nadu (1974) 2 SCR 348** held that Equality is a dynamic concept with many aspects and dimensions and it could not be cribbed, cabined and confined within traditional and doctrinaire limits. Form a positivistic point of view, equality is antithetic to arbitrariness. In fact, equality and arbitrariness are sworn enemies, one belongs to the rule of law in republic while other to the whims and caprices of an absolute monarch.

Case Title : E. R. Royappa Vs. State of Tamil Nadu
Date of Judgment : 23.11.1973
Bench : Justice A. N. Ray, Justice D. G. Palekar, Justice Y. V. Chandra-chud, Justice P. N. Bhagwati, Justice V.R. Krishna Iyer

FACTS OF THE CASE

The Petitioner was a member of Indian Administrative Service from Tamil Nadu cadre. The Petitioner was put in selection grade with effect from 22.05.1961. On 11th July, the Petitioner was posted as Additional Chief Secretary. Sh. Ramakrishnan, who was working as chief secretary, went on refused leave for four months from 14th November, 1969. On 13th November, 1969, the Petitioner was posted as Chief Secretary of the Government.

The Petitioner was appointed as Deputy Chairman of the State Planning Commission subsequently as Officer on Special Duty, both non-cadre posts.

The Petitioner contended that the post has not been validly created. The Petitioner who was cadre post holder viz holding the post of Chief Secretary could not be posted to a non-scheduled post without a declaration that the non-scheduled post is equal in status and responsibilities to the scheduled post. Petitioner was posted in a position which is inferior to chief secretary as such violative of Article 14 and 16.

FINDINGS OF THE SUPREME COURT

The Supreme Court observed that Petitioner was promoted to Chief Secretary in substantive capacity is not well founded.

Sub-rule 1 of Rule 9 of Indian Administrative Service (Pay) Rules, 1954 provided that no member of Indian Administrative Service shall be appointed to a post other than a post specified in Schedule III or in other words non cadre posts unless government makes a declaration that such non cadre post is equivalent in status and responsibility to a post specified in the said schedule. This rule is intended for the protection of member of IAS. The making of such a declaration is a *sine qua non* of the exercise of power under Rule 1. it is not an idle formality which can be dispensed with at the sweet will of the Government. A member of IAS will be within his rights to contend that such non-cadre post is inferior in status and responsibility and in violation of Article 14 and 16, if such declaration is colorable exercise of power, or *mala fide* or without application of mind, the Court can set at naught such declaration.

The Supreme Court explored new dimensions of law of equality in interpretation of Article 14 and 16. The Supreme Court observed that Article 16 embodies the fundamental guarantee that there shall be equality of opportunity for all citizens in matters relating to employment or appointment to any office under the state. Though enacted as a distinct and independent fundamental right because of its great importance as a principle ensuring equality of opportunity in public employment which is so vital to the building up of the new classless egalitarian society envisaged in the constitution, Article 16 is only an instance of the application of the concept of equality enshrined under Article 14. In other words, Article 14 is a genus while Article 16 is a species. Article 16 gives effect to the doctrine of equality in all matters relating to public employment. The basic principle which therefore informs both Article 14 and 16 is equality and inhibition against discrimination. Now what is content and reach of this great equalizing principle? It is a founding faith and it must not be subjected to a narrow pedantic or lexicographic approach. It's all embracing scope and meaning cannot be truncated, for to do so would be to violate its activist magnitude. Equality is a dynamic concept with many aspects and dimensions and it could not be cribbed, cabined and confined" within traditional and doctrinaire limits. Form a positivistic point of view, equality is antithetic to arbitrariness. In fact, equality and arbitrariness are sworn enemies, one belongs to the rule of law in republic while other to the whims and caprices of an absolute monarch. Where an act is arbitrary it is implicit in it that it is unequal both according to political logic and constitutional law and is therefore violative of Article 14 and if it affects any matter relating to public employment it is also violative of Article 16 and Article 14. Article 14 and 16 strike at arbitrariness in State Action and ensure fairness and equality of treatment. They require the State Actions must be based on relevant principles applicable alike to all similarly situate and it must not be guided by any extraneous or irrelevant considerations because that would be denial of equality. Where the operative reason for State action as distinguished from motive inducing from the antechamber of mind, is not legitimate and relevant but is extraneous and outside area of permissible considerations, it would amount of mala fide exercise of power and that it is hit by Article 14 and 16. *Mala fide* exercise of power and arbitrariness are different lethal radiations emanating from the same vice, in fact the latter comprehends the former. Both are inhibited by Article 14 and 16.

The Supreme Court observed that Article 14 and 16 are not limited to cases where public servant affected has a right to post. Even if a public servant is in an officiating position, he can complain of violation of Article 14 and 16, if he has been arbitrarily and unfairly treated or subjected to mala fide exercise of power.

The Supreme Court observed that the office of Chief Secretary is a highly sensitive post. If for valid reasons Chief Secretary forfeits confidence of the Chief Minister, he can be shifted to another post provided his legal and constitutional rights are not violated. Petitioner has himself accepted position of deputy chairman of Planning Commission. As far as post of officer on special duty is concerned, it was not established that it was inferior to post of Chief Secretary.

The Supreme Court observed that allegation of mala fide exercise of power has also not been established. The Supreme Court dismissed the Petition.

STATE OF MADRAS VS SRIMATHI CHAMPAKAM DORAIRAJAN

The Supreme Court in **State of Madras Vs Srimathi Champakam Dorairajan (1951) AIR 226** held that Communal Order providing reservation for different communities in educational institutions was violative of Article 29 (2) of the Constitution. The Supreme Court also held that the Directive Principles of State Policy has to run subsidiary to Fundamental Rights.

Case Title : State of Madras Vs Srimathi Champakam Dorairajan
Date of Judgment : 09.04.1951
Bench : Chief Justice Harilal Kania, Justice Fazl Ali, Justice Patanjali Sastri, Justice Mehr Chand Mahajan, Justice Mukerjea, Justice S. R. Das, Justice Vivian Bose

FACTS OF THE CASE

State of Madras had certain medical and engineering colleges. Seats in these medical or engineering colleges were being filled according to Communal Order under which for every 14 seats to be filled by the selection committee six seats were reserved for Non- Brahmins, two seats were reserved for backward Hindus, two seats were reserved for Brahmins, one seat was reserved for Anglo Indian Christians and one seat was reserved for Muslims. The proportion fixed in the old Communal Order continued even after independence.

Smt. Champakam Dorairajan filed writ petition before the High Court on the ground that the communal order is violating her Fundamental Rights under Article 15 (1) and Article 29 (2). High Court allowed the Petition of the Smt. Champakam Dorairajan.

Sri Srinivasan who has applied for admission in Government Engineering Colleges also filed similar Writ Petition on similar grounds which was also allowed by the High Court.

State of Madras filed appeals before the Supreme Court.

FINDINGS OF THE SUPREME COURT

The State of Madras admitted that these two petitioners would have been admitted if selections would have been made on merit alone.

The Supreme Court noted that Article 29 (2) provides that no citizen shall be denied admission into any educational institution maintained by the State or receiving aid out of State funds on the grounds only of religion, race, caste, language or any of them. The right to get admission into educational institutions of the kind mentioned in clause (2) is a right which an individual citizen has as a citizen and not as a member of community or class of citizens. The right cannot be denied only on the basis of religion, race, caste, language or any of them. If a person has requisite academic qualifications but refused only on the ground of religion, race, caste, language or any of them, then there is clear breach of Fundamental Right.

It was contended by State that Article 46 charges the State with promoting special care and the educational interests of the weaker section of people in particular Scheduled Castes and Scheduled Tribes. It was contended that Article 46 would override the provisions of Article 29 (2).

Argument of State was completely rejected by the Supreme Court. The Supreme Court held that Directive Principles are un-enforceable by Court and cannot override provisions under Part III (Fundamental Rights) which have been specifically made enforceable by State. The Directive Principles of State Policy have to confirm to and run subsidiary to the Chapter of Fundamental Rights. So long there is no infringement of Fundamental Rights there cannot be any objection to the State acting in accordance with the Directive Principles of State Policy.

The Supreme Court observed that the Constitution intended to make provision in favour of backward class of citizens, who are not adequately represented in services, under Article 16 (4) but there are no such provision in respect of admission to colleges.

The Supreme Coury held that Communal Order being inconsistent with provisions of Article 29 (2) in Part III of the Constitution is void under Article 13.

M. R. BALAJI VS STATE OF MYSORE

The Supreme Court in **M R Balaji & Ors Vs State of Mysore, 1963 SCR SUPL. (1) 439** held that special provision made under Article 15 (4) should be less than 50% . The Supreme Court also held that caste cannot be sole criteria of reservation and there cannot be sub–classification of Backward Classes.

Case Title : M R Balaji & Ors Vs State of Mysore
Date of Judgment : 28.09.1962
Bench : Justice P.B. Gajendragadkar, Justice Bhuvneshwar P. Sinha, Justice K. N. Wanchoo, Justice K. C. Das Gupta, Justice J. C. Shah

---

FACTS OF THE CASE

Sate of Mysore issued order dated 31st July, 1962 under Article 15 (4) of the Constitution making special provision for advancement of the socially and educationally backward classes of citizens in the State of Mysore.

Prior to this order the State of Mysore had issued several orders in this regard which have been struck down by Courts. State of Mysore appointed Mysore Backward Classes Appointments Committee under the chairmanship of Dr. R. Nagan Gowda. The Report observed that caste and communities can be basis of classifying backward classes.

On the basis of report of this Committee the Government issued aforesaid order dated 31st July, 1962. Under this order the Backward Classes were divided under two categories – (i) Backward Classes and (ii) More Backward Classes. 50% was reserved for other Backward Classes out of which 28 % was reserved for Backward Classes and 22% was reserved for More Backward Classes. 15% was reserved for Scheduled Castes and 3% was reserved for Scheduled Tribes.

The result of this order was that 68% of seats were reserved and 32% of seats were only available for merit pool.

FINDINGS OF THE SUPREME COURT

It was contended by the Petitioners that classification made under Article 15(4) is irrational and 68% reservation is fraud on Article 15 (4).

It was also contended by the Petitioners that it was not competent for the State to make an order under Article 15 (4) unless a commission has been appointed under Article 340 (1) and a copy of report is laid before the Parliament. This argument was rejected by the Supreme Court. The Court observed that report by Commission is not condition precedent for issuing order under Article 15 (4). Further Union or State Government has to take action under Section 340 (1) and not the President.

It was also contended by the Petitioners that provision under Section 15 (4) can be made only by legislation and not executive order. This argument was also rejected the Supreme Court. The Court noted that Government is covered under definition of State. Wherever legislation is required to be passed, the same has been prescribed by Constitution.

The Supreme Court rejected sub-classification of Other Backward Classes in Backward Classes and More Backward Classes. Article 15 (4) provides special provision for really backward classes.

The Supreme Court also observed that caste cannot be sole criteria for making special provisions in favour of Backward Classes. Other factors have also to be taken into consideration.

It was contended by the State that there was no limitation of reserving seats under Article 15 (4). The argument was rejected by the Supreme Court. The Supreme Court noted that a provision which is in nature of exception cannot completely exclude the rest of society and the same is clearly outside scope of Article 15 (4). The Supreme Court also held that special provision should be less than 50%, how much less will depend on relevant prevailing circumstances.

The Supreme Court observed that order issued by the State was fraud on Article 15 (4) and allowed the Writ Petition.

INDRA SAWHNEY VS UNION OF INDIA

The Supreme Court in **Indra Sawhney & Ors Vs Union of India & Ors 1992 Supp 2 SCR 454** validated the Union of India memorandums providing for reservation to the extent of 27% for Other Backward Classes (OBC) in Government jobs and had held inter alia that caste can be sole factor for providing reservation. While this judgment has been held by some as giant step towards social justice, it has also drawn criticism from some quarters like Nani Palkhiwala as a regressive judgment which will revitalize casteism and cleave the nation into forward and backward.

Case Title : Indra Sawhney & Ors Vs Union of India & Ors
Date of Judgment : 16.11.1992
Bench : Chief Justice M.H. Kania, Justice M.N. Venkatachaliah, Justice S. Ranavel Pandian, Justice T.K Thommen, Justice A.M. Ahmadi, Justice Kuldip Singh, Justice P.B. Sawant, Justice R.M. Sahai, Justice B.P. Jeevan Reddy

FACTS OF THE CASE

Union of India on the basis of Mandal Commission Report issued Office Memorandum in 1990 providing for reservation to OBC to the extent of 27 % in Civil Posts and Services. This has led to wide scale protests and even few students had committed suicide. This Office Memorandum was challenged before the Supreme Court in several Writ Petitions.

FINDINGS OF THE SUPREME COURT

Whether provisions under Article 16 (4) has to be made by Parliament or State Legislature ?

The provisions of reservation has been made executive order. It was contended before the Supreme Court that provisions for reservation under Article

16 (4) can be made only by Parliament or State Legislature. This has been repelled the Supreme Court. The Supreme Court held that 16 (4) empowers State to make provision. The definition of State under Article 16 (4) includes Legislature, Executive and Local Authority also. As such the Executive is competent to make provisions for reservation under Article 16 (4) of the Constitution.

Whether Article 16 (4) is an exception of Article 16 (1) ?

The Supreme Court in **T Devadasan Vs Union of India (1964) SCR(4) 680**has held that 16 (4) is an exception to 16 (1) following judgment of the Supreme Court in Balaji wherein it has been held that 15(4) is an exception to 15 (1). The Court noted that till **M. R. Balaji Vs. State of Mysore (1963) Suppl. 1 SCR** and **Devadasan** it has not been recognised that Article 16 is a facet of Article 14 and classification is permissible under Article 16. In **State of Kerala Vs. N. M. Thomas 1976 SCR (1) 906** it was recognised that Article 16 is a facet of Article 14 and permits classification. The Court held that 16(4) is not an exception of Article 16 (1) but rather a facet of it. The Supreme Court also held that Article 16 (4) is not exhaustive of the concept of reservation in favour of OBC.

How to identify Backward Class of Citizens in Article 16 (4) ?

Backward Class of Citizens has not been defined in the Constitution. The Court noted that in pre-independence India, class and caste has been used interchangeably and caste was understood as enclosed class. In the Constitution the term "caste" may not have been used because caste does not exist in Islam, Christianity or Sikh. The Supreme Court held that "caste" used in 16 (4) is not antithetical to class. Class has been used to connote "social class" and not class as understood in Marxism. Caste is a social class as well as an occupational grouping whose membership is hereditary. Endogamy is its main characteristic. The Supreme Court recommended survey of communities for identifying Backward Classes. A caste in India can often be social class for purposes of Article 16 (4).

Whether 16 (4) applies to only socially and educationally backward classes ?

The Court noted that in Balaji it has been assumed that 16 (4) applied to socially and educationally backward classes following provisions of Article 15 (4). This assumption has no basis. Article 15 (4) has been inserted by 1st

Amendment which is qualified by socially and educationally. There is no such qualifications in 16 (4).

Whether Creamy Layer should be excluded ?

The Court held that exclusion of socially advanced members will make the class truly backward class and would more appropriately serve the purposes and object of Article 16 (4). The Supreme Court directed the Government of India for exclusion of creamy layer. This is not applicable to Scheduled Tribes and Scheduled Castes.

Whether representation should be adequate or proportion ?

Representation in services have to be given to such OBS, whose representation is inadequate. There does not exist provision for proportionate reservation. Representation has to be only adequate.

State has to determine whether representation is adequate or not. Backward class can not be determined on the basis of only and exclusively on economic criteria. It can be in addition to social backwardness. Backward class can be identified without reference to caste. Backward classes can be divided in backward and more backward classes.

What should be extent of reservation ?

The Court held reservation can be upto 50 % of posts. Only in extraordinary circumstances this limit can be relaxed. The Supreme Court differentiated between vertical reservation and horizontal reservation. Reservation for SC/ST and OBC are examples of vertical reservation. Horizontal reservation cut across vertical reservation and also called interlocking reservation. Reservation granted to physical handicapped persons are example of horizontal reservation.

Whether there can be reservation in promotion ?

The Supreme Court overruled findings in **The General Manager, Southern Railway Vs. Rangachari 1962 SCR (2) 586** to the extent that it permitted reservation in Promotion. The Supreme Court applied this aspect of judgment prospectively.

Should some services be excluded from reservation ?

The Supreme Court held that there are certain positions and duties where merit only counts. In such positions reservation will not be advisable. Such positions are technical posts in Research and Development Organizations, Specialties and Super Specialties in medicine, engineering and other such courses and defense services.

E. V. CHINNAIAH VS STATE OF ANDHRA PRADESH

The Supreme Court held in **E. V. Chinnaiah Vs. State of Andhra Pradesh (2005) 1 SCC 394** that sub-classification under Scheduled Castes is not permissible. Subsequently this judgment has been overruled in **State of Punjab Vs Davinder Singh (Civil Appeal No. 2317 of 2011).**

Case Title : E. V. Chinnaiah Vs. State of Andhra Pradesh
Date of Judgment : 05.11.2004
Bench : Justice N. Santosh Hegde, Justice S.N. Variava, Justice B.P. Singh

FACTS OF THE CASE

The State of Andhra Pradesh appointed a Commission headed by Sh. Ramchandra Raju to identify the groups among the Scheduled Castes found in the list prepared under Article 341 of the Constitution of India by the President who had failed to secure the benefits of reservation provided for Scheduled Castes in admission to professional colleges and services in the State. Based on report of Sh. Ramchandra Raju, the State vide an ordinance grouped Scheduled Castes mentioned in Presidential List in four groups as A, B,C and D based on *inter se* backwardness. 15% reservation for Scheduled Castes were divided into these groups – 1 % for Group A, 7% for Group B, 6% for Group C and 1% for Group D.

The Ordinance was challenged before the High Court which was dismissed.

FINDINGS OF THE SUPREME COURT

The Supreme Court framed three issues for determination –(i) Whether impugned Act is violative of Article 341 (2) of the Constitution? (ii) Whether impugned enactment is constitutionally invalid for lack of legislative competence? (iii) Whether sub-classification or micro-classification are violative of Article 14 of the Constitution ?

Article 341 provides that the President may with respect to any State or Union Territory after consultation with the Governor thereof by Public Notification, specify the castes, races or tribes or parts of groups within castes, races or tribes which shall for purposes of this Constitution be deemed to be Scheduled Castes or Scheduled Tribes. There can be only list of Scheduled Caste. Any inclusion or exclusion can only be done by Parliament. There is no provision for sub-divide for sub-divide, sub-classify or sub-group of these castes. Any executive action or legislative enactment which interferes, disturbs, re-arranges, re-groups, re-classifies the various castes found in Presidential List will be violative of Article 341 of the Constitution.

The Supreme Court considered whether Scheduled Caste in a Presidential List form a homogenous group. The Supreme Court noted that the Presidential List provides only for one list of Scheduled Castes. The Constitution intended that castes included under Presidential List will be deemed to be one class of persons.

The Supreme Court observed that principles laid down in **Indra Sawhney Vs. Union of India (1992) Suppl. (3) SCC 217** for sub-classification of backward classes will not be applicable for sub-classification of Scheduled Class. The very judgment itself held that sub-division of scheduled classes is not applicable to Scheduled Class and Scheduled Tribes.

The Supreme Court also held that State Legislature does not have competence to sub-classify Scheduled Castes. The Supreme Court observed that primary object of the impugned enactment is to create groups of sub-castes in the list of Scheduled Castes applicable to the State and apportionment of reservation is only secondary and consequential. State does not have competence to make a law dividing the Scheduled Castes List of the State by tracing it competence to Entry 41 of List II or Entry 25 of List III. The Supreme Court was of opinion that enactment was not in pith and substance a law governing field of education or Public Services.

The Supreme Court also held that if a class within a class of members of Scheduled Class is created the same would be amount to tinkering with the Presidential List and will be in violation of Article 14.

The Supreme Court observed that Reservation must be considered from social objective angle having regard to constitutional scheme and not as a political issue.

The Supreme Court held that impugned legislation is beyond the legislative competence of State Legislature and also held that the same violative of Article 14.

M. NAGARAJ VS UNION OF INDIA

The Supreme Court in **M Nagaraj Vs Union of India (2006) Supp. (7) SCR 336** held Eighty Fifth amendment of the Constitution providing reservation in promotion with consequential seniority valid. But the Supreme Court also directed that while making such provision the State has to collect quantifiable data showing backwardness of the class and inadequacy of representation of that class in public employment in addition to compliance of efficiency under Article 335.

Case Title : M Nagaraj Vs Union of India
Date of Judgment : 19.10.2006
Bench : Chief Justice Y. K. Sabharwal, Justice K.G.Balakrishnan, Justice S.H.Kapadia, Justice C.K.Thakker, Justice P.K. Balasubramanyan

FACTS OF THE CASE

In **Indra Sawhney Vs Union of India AIR1993SC477** it was held that reservation in appointments or posts under Article 16 (4) is confined to initial appointment and cannot extend to reservation in the matter or promotion. Prior to Indra Sawhney, reservation in promotion existed. Parliament passed 77th Amendment for introducing clause 4A in Article 16, which provided that nothing in this Article shall prevent the State from making any provision for reservation in matters of promotion to any class or classes of posts in the services under the State in favour of the Scheduled Castes and the Scheduled Tribes which in opinion of the State are not adequately represented.

In **Union of India vs Virpal Singh Chauhan (1995) SCC (6) 684,** the Supreme Court held that a roster-point promotee getting the benefit of accelerated promotion would not get consequential seniority. As such, consequential seniority constituted additional benefit and therefore his seniority will be governed by the panel position.

Parliament again amended clause 4A which now provided that nothing in this Article shall prevent the State from making any provision for reservation in matters of promotion, with consequential seniority, to any class or classes of posts in the services under the State in favour of the Scheduled Castes and the Scheduled Tribes which in the opinion of the State are not adequately represented in the services under the State.

Several Petitions were filed before the Supreme Court under Article 32 of the Constitution challenging the validity of Constitution (Eighty Fifth) Amendment inserting Article 16 (4A) retrospectively from 17.06.1995 providing reservation in promotion with consequential seniority as being unconstitutional and violative of basic structure.

FINDINGS OF THE SUPREME COURT

The Supreme Court observed that "equality" is the essence of democracy and accordingly a basic feature of democracy.

The Supreme Court observed that in the matter of application of the principle of basic structure, the twin tests have to be satisfied, namely, the "width test" and "the test of identity". The concept of "catch up" rule and "consequential seniority" are not constitutional requirements. They are not implicit in clauses (1) and (4) of the Article 16. They are not constitutional limitations. They are concepts derived from service jurisprudence. They are not constitutional principles. They are not axioms like secularism, federalism etc. Obliteration of these concepts and insertion of these concepts do not change the equality code indicated by the Articles 14, 15 and 16 of the Constitution. Article 16 (1) cannot prevent the State from taking cognizance of the compelling interests of backward classes of society. Article 16 (1) and (4) are restatements of principle of equality under Article 14. Article 16 (4) refers to affirmative action by way of reservation. Article 16 (4) however states that appropriate government is free to provide for reservation in cases where it is satisfied on the basis of quantifiable data that backward class is inadequately represented in the services. Therefore, in every case where the State decides to provide for reservation there must exist two circumstances, namely, backwardness and inadequacy of representation. Equity, justice and efficiency are variable factors. These factors are context specific. There is no fixed yardstick to identify and measure these three factors. It will depend on the facts and circumstances of each case. These are limitations on the mode of exercise of power by the State. None of these limitations have been removed by the impugned amendments. If the concerned State fails to identify and measure backwardness, inadequacy and overall administrative efficiency then in that event the provision for reservation would be invalid.

These amendments do not alter the structure of Articles 14, 15 and 16. The parameters mentioned in Article 16 (4) are retained. Clause 4A is derived from clause 4 of Article 16. Clause 4A is confined to SCs and STs alone. Therefore, the present case does not change the identity of the Constitution. The word "amendment" connotes change. The question is whether the impugned amendments discard the original constitution.

It was vehemently urged on behalf of the Petitioners that the Statement of Objects and Reasons indicate that the impugned amendments have been promulgated by the Parliament to overrule the decision of this Court. The Supreme Court did not find any merit in this argument. Under Article 141 of the Constitution the pronouncement of the Supreme Court is the law of the land. The judgment of this Court in **Union of India Vs. Virpal Singh (1995) SCC (6)685 , Ajit Singh Januja Vs. State of Punjab 1966 AIR 1189** and **Indra Sawhney** were judgments delivered by this Court which enunciated the law of the land. It is that law which is sought to be changed by the impugned constitutional amendments. The impugned constitutional amendments are enabling in nature. They leave it to the States to provide for reservation. It is well settled that the Parliament while enacting a law does not provide content to the "right". The content is provided by the judgments of the Supreme Court. If an appropriate government enacts a law providing for reservation without keeping in mind the parameters in Article 16 (4) and Article 335 then the Supreme Court will certainly set aside and strike down such legislation.

Applying the "width test" the Supreme Court did not find any alteration in the existing structure of the equality code. The Supreme Court found that none of axioms like secularism, federalism etc, which are overarching principles have been violated by the impugned constitutional amendments. Equality has two facets "formal equality" and "proportional equality". Proportional equality is equality "in fact" whereas formal equality is "equality in law". Formal equality exists in the Rule of Law. In the case of proportional equality, the State is expected to take affirmative steps in favour of disadvantaged sections of the society within the framework of liberal democracy. Egalitarian equality is proportional equality.

The Supreme Court held that there has been no violation of the basic structure of Constitution by these amendments. The impugned amendments have introduced merely enabling provisions because merit, efficiency, backwardness and inadequacy cannot be identified and measured in vaccum. Moreover, Article 16 (4A) and Article 16 (4B) fall in the pattern of Article 16 (4) and as long as the parameters mentioned in those articles are complied with by the States, the provision of reservation cannot be faulted. Article 16 (4A) and 16 (4B) are classifications within the principle of equality under Article 16 (4). The State is not bound to make reservation for SC/ST in matter of promotions. However, if they wish to exercise their discretion and make such provision, the State has to collect quantifiable data showing backwardness of the class and inadequacy of representation of that class in public employment in addition to compliance of Article 335. Even if the State has compelling reasons, the State will have to see that its reservation provision does not lead to excessiveness so as to breach the ceiling-limit of 50% or obliterate the creamy layer or extend the reservation indefinitely.

PRAMATI EDUCATIONAL AND CULTURAL TRUST VS UNION OF INDIA

The Supreme Court in **Pramati Educational and Cultural Trust Vs Union of India, (2014) 8SCC** held that Article 15 (5) of the Constitution inserted by the Constitution (Ninety Third Amendment) Act, 2005 and Article 21A of the Constitution inserted by the Constitution (Eighty Sixth Amendment) Act, 2002 are valid and does not violate basic structure of the Constitution.

Case Title : Pramati Educational and Cultural Trust Vs Union of India
Date of Judgment : 06.05.2014
Bench : Chief Justice R.M. Lodha, Justice Fakkir Mohamed Ibrahim Kalifulla, Justice Dipak Misra, Justice Sudhansu Jyoti Mukhopadhaya, Justice A. K. Patnaik

---

FACTS OF THE CASE

Article 15 (5) empowers the State to make special provisions by law for advancement of Socially and Educationally Backward Classes or SC or ST in relation to their admission to educational institutions including private educational institutions whether aided or unaided by state. The Supreme Court in **Ashok Kumar Thakur Vs. Union of India (2008) 6 SCC1** has held Article 15 (5) valid so far it related to admission to institutions run or aided by State. In this matter the applicability of 15(5) to private aided institutions was challenged. Validity of Article 21A was also challenged.

FINDINGS OF THE SUPREME COURT

Validity of Article 15 (5)

The Supreme Court noted that some classes of citizens, SC and SC have remained socially and educationally backward despite provisions made for them. They have not been able to approach educational institutions also. The Court held that Article 15 (5) is not an exception or a proviso overriding

Article 15 but rather an enabling provision to make equality of opportunity promised in the preamble in the constitution a reality. The Court relied on its judgments in **State of Kerala Vs. N. M. Thomas (1976) 2 SCC 310, Indra Sawhney Vs Union of India 1992 Supp (3) SCC 217, Ashoka Kumar Thakur Vs Union of India   (2008) 6 SCC 1.**

Parliament has stepped in and has inserted Article 15 (5). The Supreme Court noted that 15(5) has to a very limited extent affected the voluntary element under Article 19 (1) (g) of the Constitution. The Supreme Court held that the width of the power vested on the State under clause (5) of Article 15 of the Constitution by the Constitutional amendment is not such as to destroy the right under Article 19 (1) (g) of the Constitution.

The Supreme Court dispelled that argument that Article 15 (5) treats aided and unaided educational institutions in alike manner and thus violates Article 14. The Supreme Court noted that Clause (5) of Article 15 of the Constitution does not say that such a law will not comply with the other requirements of equality as provided in Article 14 of the Constitution.

The Court also rejected the argument that Article 15 (5) is violative of secularism as it excludes religious minority institutions. The Court held that none of the rights under Article 14, 19 (1) (g), and 21 have been abrogated by Article 15 (5).

Validity of Article 21A

The Court noted that Article 45 contemplated that State would provide free and compulsory examination upto age of 14 years within 10 years but the same was not achieved even after 50 years. Therefore Article 21A was introduced in the Constitution vide Eighty Sixth amendment. Under Article 21 constitutional obligation to provide free and compulsory education is on the State. However it empower state to decide the "manner" in which this constitutional obligation will be discharged. The Court noted that the law made by the State should not be such as to abrogate the right of unaided private educational schools under Article 19 (1) (g) or minority schools, aided or unaided, under Article 30 (1) of the Constitution.

The Supreme Court held that a new power has been vested in the State under Article 21 A of the Constitution to make a law determining the manner in which free and compulsory education will be provided to the children. This power is different from power of State under 19 (6) and has affected voluntariness of right under Article 19 (1) (g).

The Supreme Court also analyzed provisions of 2009 Act. Under Section 12 (1) (c) private unaided schools has to admit children to the extent of 25% in class I from weaker sections belonging neighborhood area. There is provision of reimbursement against such admissions. The Supreme Court held that such admission does not violate Article 19 (1) (g).

The Court held that 2009 Act so far it is applicable to minority schools is ultra vires as it may destroy minority character of the educational institutions.

Thus the Supreme Court held 15 (5) and 21A constitutionally valid. The Supreme Court also held that 2009 Act is also not **ultra vires** 19 (1) (g). However, the Court held that applicability of 2009 Act on aided or unaided minority institution *ultra vires* the Constitution.

JARNAIL SINGH VS LACHHMI NARAIN GUPTA

The Supreme Court in **Jarnail Singh Vs Lachhmi Narain Gupta, (2018) 10 SCR 663** held that collection of quantifiable data showing backwardness of Scheduled Castes (SC) and Scheduled Tribes (ST) is not required for providing reservation in promotion.

Case Title : Jarnail Singh Vs Lachhmi Narain Gupta
Date of Judgment : 26.09.2018
Bench: Chief Justice Dipak Misra, Justice Indu Malhotra, Justice Sanjay Kishan Kaul, Justice R.F. Nariman, Justice Kurian Joseph Justice Dipak Misra

FACTS OF THE CASE

The Supreme Court in **Indra Sawhney Vs Union of India (1992) Suppl. (3) SCC 217** has held that reservation in promotion is not permissible. To nullify the same, Parliament passed Eighty Fifth Amendment whereby it inserted clause 4A in the Article 16 providing for reservation in promotion to Scheduled Tribes and Scheduled Castes. This amendment was challenged before the Supreme Court in **M Nagaraj Vs Union of India (2006) 8 SCC 212.**

The Supreme Court in Nagaraj held Article 16 (4A) constitutional valid but directed that before giving reservation the State has to show in each case (i) backwardness (ii) inadequacy of representation and (iii) administrative efficiency before making provision for reservation. The Supreme Court observed that State is not bound to give reservation in promotion but if State decides to give reservation in promotion to Scheduled Castes and Scheduled Tribes, the State has to collect quantifiable data showing backwardness of the class and inadequacy of representation in public employment in addition to compliance with Article 335.

Several petitions were filed before the Supreme Court for revisiting the Nagaraj Judgment, which was referred to the Constitution Bench. The Supreme Court revisited Nagaraj judgment on following two aspects.

FINDINGS OF THE SUPREME COURT

Whether quantifiable data for Scheduled Castes and Scheduled Tribes is required for reservation in promotion ?

The Supreme Court held that findings in Nagaraj in respect of collection of quantifiable data is in contradiction of the Indra Sawhney Judgment. In Indra Sawhney the Supreme Court held that test of backwardness will not apply to Scheduled Castes and Scheduled Tribes which indubitably falls within the expression "backward class of citizens".

The Supreme Court noted that in **E. V. Chinnaiah Vs State of A.P. (2005) 1 SCC 394** Scheduled Castes have been referred as the most backward among backward classes. This is the reason that the Presidential List only contains those castes or groups which consist of untouchables.

The Supreme Court invalidated the finding of Nagaraj to the extent that State has to collect quantifiable data showing backwardness of Scheduled Castes and Scheduled Tribes for providing reservation in promotion being contrary to the nine judge bench judgment in Indra Sahwney.

Whether provision of Creamy Layer can be applied on Scheduled Castes and Scheduled Tribes ?

The Supreme Court in **Ashok Kumar Thakur vs Union of India (2008) 6 SCC 1** has held that "creamy layer" principle is inapplicable to Scheduled Castes and Scheduled Tribes.

The Supreme Court in this judgment differed from view taken in Ashok Kumar Thakur. The Supreme Court observed that if Court applies creamy layer principle it does not tinker with Presidential List under Article 341 or 342 of the Constitution of India. Object of reservation will not be achieved if creamy layer of Scheduled Castes and Scheduled Tribes bag all jobs and perpetuate themselves and remaining sections of the that class remain poor. The Supreme Court held that Constitutional Courts will be within their jurisdiction to exclude creamy layer while applying the principles of the equality under Article 14 and 16 of the Constitution of India. The Supreme Court disagreed with the its observation in Ashok Thakur that creamy layer principle is a principle of identification and not principle of equality.

The Supreme Court held that creamy layer test to Scheduled Caste and Scheduled Tribes propounded in Nagaraj does not interfere with Parliament's power under Article 341 and Article 342 as such this aspect need not be revisited.

JANHIT ABHIYAN VS UNION OF INDIA

The Supreme Court with 3:2 majority held in **Janhit Abhiyan Vs Union of India, (2022) 14 SCR 1** that One Hundred and Third Amendment to the Constitution empowering the State to provide for a maximum of ten percent reservation for Economically Weaker Sections (EWS) of citizens other than SC, ST and non-creamy lawyer of OBC is constitutionally valid.

Case Title : Janhit Abhiyan Vs Union of India
Date of Judgment : 07.11.2022
Bench : Chief Justice U. U. Lalit, Justice Dinesh Maheshwari, Justice S. Ravindra Bhat, Justice Bela M. Trivedi

---

FACTS OF THE CASE

The Supreme Court passed Constitution (One Hundred and Third Amendment Act, 2019) whereby the Parliament amended Articles 15 and 16 of the Constitution of India by adding two new clauses – clause (6) of Article 15 and clause (6) to Article 16. Vide this amendment State was empowered to provide for a maximum of ten per cent reservation for "Economically Weaker Sections" of citizens other than the Scheduled Castes, the Scheduled Tribes and non-creamy layer of "the Other Backward Classes". The amendment does not mandate but enables reservation for EWS and prescribes a ceiling limit of ten percent. Several Writ Petitions were filed before the Supreme Court challenging the Constitutional validity of One Hundred and Third Amendment. The matter was referred to the Constitution Bench.

FINDINGS OF THE SUPREME COURT

The findings of the Supreme Court on several issues were as under.

Amendability of the Constitution

The Supreme Court observed that the challenge is not to an executive order or to an ordinary legislation but to a Constitutional amendment. The challenge is founded on the premise that the amendment in question violates the basic structure of the Constitution in a manner that it destroys its identity. According to the principal part of challenge, the Equality Code, an essential feature of the Constitution, gets abrogated because of reservation structured only on economic criteria and because of exclusion of classes covered under Articles 15 (4), 15 (5) and 16 (4) from its benefit. Therefore, entire challenge is essentially required to be examined on the anvil of the doctrine of basic structure.

The Supreme Court surveyed several judgments and observed that there is no and, there cannot be any, cut-and-dried formula or a theorem which could supply a ready made answer to the question as to whether a particular amendment to the Constitution violates or affects basic structure. The nature of amendment and the features of the Constitution to be touched, altered, modulated or changed by the amendment would be the material factors for an appropriate determination of the question.

The Supreme Court observed that mere violation of the rule of equity does not violate the basic structure of the Constitution unless the violation is shocking, unconscionable or unscrupulous travesty of the quintessence of equal justice. If any constitutional amendment moderately abridges or alters the equality principles, it cannot be said to be a violation of the basic structure.

The need for affirmative action and Equality Code

The Supreme Court noticed that constitutional validity of One Hundred and Third Amendment is premised on the fact that it abrogated equality code and thereby destroys the basic structure of the Constitution of India.

The Supreme Court observed that equality is a feature fundamental to our Constitution. But, in true sense, equality envisaged by our Constitution is real and substantive equality. This process of striking at inequalities, by its very nature calls for reasonable classifications so that equals are treated equally while unequals are treated differently and as per their requirements.

The Supreme Court summarized that for the socioeconomic structure which the law in our democracy seeks to build up, the requirements of real and substantive equality call for affirmative actions and reservation is recognized as one such affirmative action which is permissible under the Constitution and its operation is defined by a large numbers of decisions of this Court.

The Supreme Court observed that if an egalitarian socio-economic order is the goal so as to make the social and economic rights a meaningful reality, which indeed is the goal of our constitution, the deprivations arising from economic disadvantages, including those of discrimination and exclusion ,need to be addressed by the State and for that matter every affirmative action has the sanction of our Constitution, as noticeable from the frame of Preamble as also the test and texture of the provisions contained in Part III and Part IV.

Whether Economic Criteria can be sole basis of Affirmative Action

It was contended before the Supreme Court that economic criteria cannot be sole basis of affirmative action. The Supreme Court observed that its observation in the past decisions that reservation cannot be claimed only on economic criteria, apply only to class or classes covered by or seeking coverage under Article 15 (4) and/or 15 (5) and/or 16 (4). The Supreme Court has not put a blanket ban on providing reservation for other sections who are disadvantaged due to economic conditions.

The Supreme Court observed that a simple reading of the heading together with the contents would make it clear that the broader expression "other weaker sections" in Article 46 is disjointed form the particular weaker sections (SC and ST) and is not confined to only those sections who are similarly circumstanced to SCs and STs.

The Supreme Court also observed that exclusion of the classes covered by Articles 15 (4), 15 (5) and 16 (4) from getting the benefit of reservation as EWS, being in nature of balancing the requirements of non-discrimination and compensatory discrimination, does not violate equality code and does not in any manner cause damage to the basic structure of the Constitution of India.

Breach of Fifty Percent Ceiling

The Supreme Court observed that fifty per cent ceiling would be applied only to those reservation which were in place before the amendment in question. No decision of Supreme Court could be read to mean that even if the Parliament finds the necessity of another affirmative action by the State in the form of reservation for a section of class in need, it could never be provided. In light of the possible harm of preferential treatment qua other innocent class of competitors i.e. general merit candidates, this Court had expressed the desirability of ceiling of fifty per cent for reservation in education and public employment. But all such observations are required to be read essentially in the context of the reservation obtaining under Articles 15 (4), 15 (5) and 16(4).

The Supreme Court in light of aforesaid findings held One Hundred and Third Amendment to the Constitution valid.

STATE OF PUNJAB VS DAVINDER SINGH

The Supreme Court in **State of Punjab Vs Davinder Singh, (2024) 8 S.C.R. 1321** held that sub-classification of Scheduled Castes is permissible under Article 15(4) and 16 (4) of the Constitution.

Case Title : State of Punjab Vs Davinder Singh
Date of Judgment : 01.08.2024
Bench : Chief Justice D. Y. Chandrachud, Justice B. R. Gavai, Justice Vikram Nath, Justice Bela M. Trivedi, Justice Pankaj Mithal, Justice Manoj Misra, Justice Satish Chandra Sharma

---

FACTS OF THE CASE

The State Legislature of Punjab enacted the Punjab Scheduled Castes and Backward Classes (Reservation in Services) Act, 2006. Section 4 (2) of the Act provided that reservation of twenty-five percent shall be made for members of the Scheduled Castes and twelve percent for Backward Classes while filing up vacancies by direct recruitment in services. Section 4 (5) provided that fifty percent of the vacancies of the quota reserved for the Scheduled Castes in direct recruitment shall be offered to Balmikis and Mazhabi Sikhs, if available, as a first preference from amongst the Scheduled Castes. High Court of Haryana and Punjab declared the Act unconstitutional relying on **E V Chinnaiah Vs. State of Andhra Pradesh (2005) 1 SCC.**

Similarly, initiatives for classifying Scheduled Castes by Haryana and Tamil Nadu were declared unconstitutional by respective High Courts relying on E V Chinnaiah.

The issue whether sub-classification of Scheduled Castes is permissible was referred to the Constitution Bench.

FINDINGS OF THE SUPREME COURT

The Supreme Court in E. V. Chinnaiah had held that principles laid down in **Indra Sawhney Vs. Union of India (1991) Suppl. (3) SCC 217** for sub-classification of backward classes will not be applicable for sub-classification of Scheduled Caste. Presidential List under Article 341 will be deemed to be one class of persons. State Legislature does not have competence to sub-classify Scheduled Castes.

No bar on Sub-classification of SC

The Supreme Court observed that a class which is not similarly situated for the purpose of the law can be further classified. The test that the Court must follow to determine the validity of the sub-classification of a class is – (i) If the class is homogenous, the class cannot be sub-classified. (ii) If the class is not homogenous, class can be sub-classified but there must be a yardstick to further classifying the class. The yardstick must have rational nexus with the object of the statute.

The Supreme Court observed that observations in Indra Sawhney were made in the specific context of Other Backward Classes. It is one thing to argue that the Scheduled Castes cannot be sub-categorized on account of their limited heterogeneity and common identity as opposed to the Other Backward Classes. But it is another issue to completely disregard the application of the principle of sub-classification to the Scheduled Castes on the ground that the Indra Sawhney limited its application to the Other Backward Class. The Supreme Court did not find merit in argument that the observations in Indra Sawney was to limit it to the other backward classes to the exclusion of the Scheduled Castes. The principle of classification will be applicable to the Scheduled Castes if the social position of the constituents among the caste/groups is not comparable.

Impact of Article 341

The Supreme Court observed that Article 341 (1) refers to the power of the President to specify the castes, races, tribes or parts of or groups within these three groups. In E. V. Chinnaiah it was held that Scheduled Castes, though drawn from various sources, races and tribes, attain a new status by the Presidential notification. Once notified through a Presidential Notification under Article 341 (1), Scheduled Castes attain a homogenous status.

The Supreme Court observed that the inclusion of certain castes within the Scheduled Caste category is only to demarcate them from other castes which are not included in the category. The inclusion does not automatically lead to the formation of a uniform and internally homogenous class which can not be further classified. Article 341 creates a legal fiction for the limited purpose of identification of Scheduled Castes by distinguishing them from other groups. If offers no guidance on how the Scheduled Castes fare among themselves or on heterogeneity among the Scheduled Castes for the purpose of the Constitution. The legal fiction which assigns an identity to the Scheduled Castes separate from other categories cannot be stretched to draw inferences about the existence or non-existence of internal differences among the Scheduled Castes. The only logical consequence is that each of the groups that is included in the list will receive the benefits that the Constitution provides to the Scheduled Castes as a class. The Supreme Court held that view taken in Chinnaiah that Schedudled Class is homogenous class is erroneous.

The Supreme Court overruled Chinnaiah Judgment and held that State in exercise of the power under Articles 15 (4) and 16 (4) can further classify the Scheduled Castes. Inter-se backwardness can, inter alia, be identified based on inadequacy of effective representation. However, it must be proved that inadequacy of effective representation of a Caste is because of its social backwardness. State must collect data on the inadequacy of representation in the "services of the State" because it is used as an indicator of backwardness.

The Supreme Court also held that Article 335 of the Constitution is not a limitation on the exercise of power under Articles 16 (1) and 16 (4). Rather it is restatement of the necessity of considering the claims of the Scheduled Tribes in Public Services. Efficiency of administration must be viewed in a manner which promotes inclusion and equality as required by Article 16 (1).

VISHAKA VS STATE OF RAJASTHAN

The Supreme Court in **Vishaka Vs. State of Rajasthan, (1997) Supp 3 SCR 404** held that sexual harassment of women at workplace violates Fundamental Right to "gender equality" and "right to life and liberty" under Articles 14, 15 and 21.

> Case Title : Vishaka Vs. State of Rajasthan
> Date of Judgment : 13.08.1997
> Bench : Chief Justice Sujata V. Manohar, Justice B. N. Kirpal

FACTS OF THE CASE

A social worker was brutally gang raped in a village of Rajasthan. The incident revealed the hazards to which a working woman may be exposed and the depravity to which sexual harassment can degenerate and the urgency for safeguards by an alternative mechanism in the absence of legislative measures.

Some social activists and NGO filed Writ Petition for enforcement of Fundamental Rights of working women under Article 14, 19 and 21.

THE FINDINGS OF THE SUPREME COURT

The Supreme Court observed that every such incident is violative of Fundamental Right to "gender equality" and Right of Life and Liberty under Article 14, 15 and 21 of the Constitution. One of the logical consequences of such an incident is also violation of victim's Fundamental Right under Article 19 (1) (g) to practice any profession or to carry out any occupation, trade and business.

The Supreme Court observed that gender equality includes protection from sexual harassment and right to work with dignity which is a universally recognized basic human right. In absence of domestic law occupying the field, the contents of International Conventions and norms are significant for the purposes of interpretation of the guarantee of gender equality.

The Supreme Court noted that Article 11 of Convention on the Elimination of All Forms of Discrimination against women provides that the right to work is an alienable right of all human beings. At the Fourth World Conference on women in Beijing, India has also made an official commitment, *inter alia*, to formulate and operationalize a national policy on women which will continuously guide and inform action at every level and in every sector, to set up a Commission of Women's Rights to act as a public defender of women's human rights, to institutionalize a national level mechanism to monitor the implementation of the Platform for Action.

The Supreme Court observed that the meaning and content of the Fundamental Rights guaranteed in the Constitution of India are of sufficient amplitude to encompass all the facets of gender equality including prevention of sexual harassment of abuse. The international conventions and norms are to be read into them in the absence of enacted domestic law occupying the field when there is no inconsistency them.

The Supreme Court laid down several guidelines for protection of women at workplaces. It includes the duty of the employer or other responsible person in work places or other institutions to prevent or deter the commission of acts of sexual harassment and to provide the procedures for the resolution, settlement or prosecution of acts of sexual harassment by taking all steps required.

SHAYARA BANO VS UNION OF INDIA (TRIPLE TALAQ JUDGMENT)

The Supreme Court with 3:2 majority held in **Shayara Bano Vs. Union of India, (2017) 797 SCR** that recognition and enforcement of Triple Talaq is constitutionally invalid.

Case Title : Shayara Bano Vs. Union of India
Date of Judgment : 22.08.2017
Bench : Chief Justice Jagdish Singh Khehar, Justice S. Abdul Nazeer, Justice Uday Umesh Lalit, Justice Rohinton Fali Nariman, Justice Kurian Joseph

FACTS OF THE CASE

Shayara Bano was divorced by her husband Rizwan Ahmad on 10.10.2015 by saying *"talaq, talaq, talaq, hence like this I divorce from you from my wife. From this date there is no relation of husband and wife. From today I am 'haram' and I have become 'naamharram'. In future you are free for using your life ..."*. The divorce was pronounced before two witnesses. The Petitioner sought declaration that the "talaq-e-biddat" pronounced by her husband on 10.10.2015 be declared *void ab initio*. It was also contended that such a divorce, which abruptly, unilaterally, and irrevocably severs ties of matrimony purportedly under Section 2 of the Muslim Personal Law (Shariat) Application Act, 1937, is unconstitutional.

Several other Writ Petitions were also under consideration of the Supreme Court questioning the constitutional validity of the Triple Talaq.

FINDINGS OF THE SUPREME COURT

Muslims in India are divided in mainly two sects – Shia and Sunni. The case pertains to only Sunni as Shia do not recognize Triple Talaq. Four sub-sects of Sunni are generally recognized – Hanafi School, Maliki School,

Shafi School and Hanbali School. Majority of Muslims in India follow Hanafi School. Hanafi School in India has supported Triple Talaq amongst the Sunni Muslims for centuries.

Marriage in Islam is a contract and it can be terminated in certain circumstances. Indeed, Prophet Mahomed had declared divorce to be the most disliked of lawful things in the sight of God.

The Supreme Court rejected the argument of Personal Law Board that 1937 Act was not meant to enforce personal law. The 1937 Act was only meant, as the non-obstante clause in Section 2 indicates, to do away with custom and usage which is contrary to Muslim Personal law. The Supreme Court observed that all forms of talaq are recognized and enforced by the 1937 Act. This would necessarily include Triple Talaq when it comes to the Muslim Personal Law applicable to Sunnis in India.

The Supreme Court observed that 1937 Act is a law made by the legislature before the Constitution came into force, as such it would fall squarely within the expression "laws in force" in Article 13 (3) (b) and would be hit by Article 13 (1) if found to be inconsistent with the provisions of Part III of the Constitution to the extent of such inconsistency.

The Supreme Court rejected the argument that Triple Talaq is an essential part of Islamic faith and would therefore be protected by Article 25 of the Constitution of India. The Supreme Court observed that Article 25 only protects essential religious practice. Triple Talaq is not essential religious practice of Islam.

The Supreme Court noticed the development of the doctrine of arbitrariness and its application to State action as a distinct doctrine on which State action may be struck down as being violative of the rule of law contained in Article 14.

The Supreme Court after surveying several judgments held that the test of manifest arbitrariness would apply to invalidate legislation as well as subordinate legislation under Article 14. Manifest arbitrariness must be something done by the legislature capriciously, irrationally and/or without adequate determining principle. Also, when something is done which is excessive and disproportionate, such legislation would be manifestly arbitrary.

The Supreme Court applied the test of manifest arbitrariness and observed that Triple Talaq is a form of Talaq which is itself considered to be something innovative, namely, that it is not in the Sunna, being an irregular or heretical form of Talaq. The Hanafi School of Shariat Law itself states that this form of Talaq though lawful is sinful in that it incurs the wrath of God.

The Supreme Court observed that the fact the Triple Talaq is instant and irrevocable, it is obvious that any attempt at reconciliation between the husband and wife which is essential to save the marital tie cannot take place. This form of Talaq is manifestly arbitrary in the sense that the marital tie can be broken capriciously and whimsically by a Muslim man without any attempt at reconciliation so as to save it. This form of Talaq must, therefore, be held to be violative of the Fundamental Right contained under Article 14 of the Constitution of India.

The Supreme Court struck down recognition and enforcement of Triple Talaq under the Muslim Personal Law (Shariat) Application Act, 1937.

JOSEPH SHINE VS UNION OF INDIA

The Supreme Court of India in **Joseph Shine Vs Union of India, (2018)11 S.C.R. 765** held that Section 497 IPC and Section 198 CrPC are violative of Article 14 and 21 of the Constitution. It was also held that adultery should not be treated as an offence.

Case Title : Joseph Shine Vs Union of India
Date of Judgment : 27.09.2018
Bench : Chief Justice Deepak Misra, Justice Rohinton Fali Nariman, Justice A.M. Khanwilkar, Justice D.Y. Chandrachud, Justice Indu Malhotra

---

FACTS OF THE CASE

The Writ Petition was field under Article 32 of the Constitution of India challenging the validity of Section 497 IPC. The matter was referred to the Constitution Bench for determination.

FINDINGS OF THE SUPREME COURT

Section 497 IPC provided that a man who takes or entices away a married woman with intent of having illicit intercourse is punishable with imprisonment up to two years or fine or both. Section 198 CrPC provided that only an aggrieved husband can file a complaint under Section 497 IPC.

In **Sowmithri Vishnu Vs Union of India AIR (1985) SC 1618** a Writ Petition under Article 32 had been filed under Article 32 wherein Section 497 IPC had been challenged on the ground that it confers right to husband to prosecute the adulterer but it does not confer right to wife to prosecute the woman with whom husband has committed adultery. Further, Section 497 does not confer right on the wife to prosecute her husband who has committed adultery. The Supreme court dismissed the petition on the ground that Section 497 treats wife as a victim and has been introduced to protect the sanctity of matrimonial home.

In **V. Revathi Vs. Union of India (1988) 2 SCC 72,** the Supreme Court held that Section 497 IPC is not discriminatory against wife. There is provision of punishment of outsider who violates the sanctity of matrimonial home with a rider that if such outsider is a woman she cannot be punished. Thus, there is reverse discrimination in favour of wife rather than against her.

Section 497 and Article 14

The Supreme Court noted that if adultery is committed with the consent of husband then there will be no offence under Section 497 IPC. This shows that Section 497 treats wife as property of husband and she is totally subservient to will of husband. Section 497 does not bring extramarital relationship with unmarried woman or widow under its preview.

Adultery means voluntary sexual relationship with any person other than wife or husband as the case may be. But Section 497 makes some of extramarital relations punishable while some of extramarital relations have not been made punishable. Section 497 does not treat wife of the adulterer as aggrieved person. The Court held that there is absence of rationality and logic in Section 497 as such it violates Article 14 of the Constitution being manifestly arbitrary.

Section 497 and Article 21

The Supreme Court noted that a woman has right to dignity. The Supreme Court in **State of Madhya Pradesh Vs Madanlal (2015) 7 SCC 681** held that dignity of women is part of her non-perishable and immortal self. The Supreme Court in **Pawan Kumar vs State of Himachal Pradesh 3 (2017) 7 SCC** held that the right to live with dignity as guaranteed under Article 21 of the Constitution cannot be violated by indulging in obnoxious act of eve-teasing. In **R Vs R (1991) 4 All ER 481** at P.484, Lord Denning observed that a wife is no longer her husband's chattel. She is beginning to be regarded by the laws as a partner in all affairs which are their common concern. The Supreme Court in **Voluntary Health Association of Punjab Vs Union of India (2013) 4 SCC 1** held that women have equal role to that of men in thinking, participating and leadership.

The Supreme Court was of view that there cannot be patriarchy monarchy over daughter or husband's monarchy over the wife.

The Supreme Court noted that in **K. S. Puttaswamy Vs Union of India 4 (2018) 5 SCC 1,** while laying immense stress on dignity, right to privacy has been held to be facet of Article 21. The Supreme Court noted that dignity of an individual has been emphasized in **National Legal Services Authority of India vs Union of India (2014) 5 SCC 438** and **Common Cause (A Registered Society) Vs Union of India 4 (2018) 5 SCC 1.**

The Court held that there cannot be any curtailment of right of dignity of a woman. Section 497 creates distinction based on gender stereotypes which creates dent in individual dignity of a woman as such Section 497 is violative of Article 21.

Is Adultery a crime ?

The Court was of view that adultery does not fit into concept of crime. It can be basis of divorce but it cannot fall in category of crime. Treating adultery as an offence will tantamount to State entering into private realm. The Court noted that in several jurisdictions i.e. People Republic of China, Japan, Australia, Brazil and Western European Countries, adultery is no longer a crime.

The Supreme Court held that Section 497 IPC is unconstitutional. It was also held that adultery should not be treated as an offence. Section 198 CrPC, which provides for procedure of filing of complaint, was also held unconstitutional. Judgments in Sowmithri Vishnu and V. Revathi were also overruled.

INDIAN YOUNG LAWYERS ASSOCIATION VS THE STATE OF KERALA (SABARIMALA JUDGMENT)

The Supreme Court in **Indian Young Lawyers Association Vs. The State of Kerala, (2018) 9 SCR 561** held that exclusion of entry of women of the age group of 10 to 50 years to Sabarimala Temple is a clear violation of the right of Hindu women to practice their religious beliefs under Article 25 of the Indian Constitution.

> Case Title : Indian Young Lawyers Association Vs. The State of Kerala
> Date of Judgment : 28.09.2018
> Bench: Chief Justice Deepak Misra, Justice Rohinton Fali Nariman, Justice A.M. Khanwilkar, Justice D.Y. Chandrachud, Justice Indu Malhotra

FACTS OF THE CASE

Writ Petition was filed under Article 32 of the Constitution of India seeking issuance of directions against the Government of Kerala, Devaswom Board of Travancore, Chief Thanthri of Sabarimala Temple and the District Magistrate of Pathanamthitta to ensure entry of female devotees between the age group of 10 to 50 years to the Lord Ayyappa Temple at Sabarimala which has been denied to them on the basis of certain custom and usage. The petition also sought declaration of Rule 3 (b) of the Kerala Hindu Places of Public Worship (Authorization of Entry) Rules, 1965 framed in exercise of the powers conferred by Section 4 of of the Kerala Hindu Places of Public Worship (Authorization of Entry) Act, 1965 as unconstitutional being violative of Articles 14, 15, 25 and 51 A (e) of the Constitution of India. Three judge bench of the Supreme Court referred the matter to Constitution Bench for determination of the issues.

FINDINGS OF THE SUPREME COURT

Followers of Lord Ayyappa whether Religious Denomination

The Supreme Court observed that Article 26 of the Constitution of India guarantees to every religious denomination the right - (i) to establish and maintain institutions for religious and charitable purposes, (ii) to manage its own affairs in matters of religion, (iii) to own and acquire movable and immovable property and (iv) to administer such property in accordance with law. For any religious mutt, sect, body, sub-sect or any section thereof to be designated as a religious denomination, it must be a collection of individuals having a collective common faith, a common organization which adheres to the said common faith, and last but not the least, the said collection of individuals must be labeled, branded and identified by a distinct name.

The Supreme Court observed that there is no identified group called ayyappans. Every Hindu can go to the temple. There is nothing on record to show that the devotees of Lord Ayyappa have any common religious tenets peculiar to themselves, which they regard as conducive to their spiritual well-being other than those which are common to the Hindu Religion. Thus, devotees of Lord Ayyappa are just Hindus and do not constitute a separate religious denomination.

Enforceability of Fundamental Rights under Article 25

Sabarimala Temple is a public temple. Travancore Devaswom Board having control and supervision of Sabarimala will be covered under definition of State under Article 12 of the Constitution.

The Supreme Court observed that Article 25 (1), by employing the expression "all persons" demonstrates that the freedom of conscience and the right to freely profess, practice and propagate religion is available, though subject to the restrictions delineated in Article 25 (1) itself, to every person including women. The right guaranteed under Article 25 (1) has nothing to do with gender or, for that matter, certain physiological factors, specifically attributable to women. Women of any age group have as much a right as men to visit and enter a temple in order to freely practice a religion as guaranteed under Article 25 (1).

The Supreme Court observed that the impugned Rule 3 (b) of the 1965 Rules, which stipulates exclusion of entry of women of the age group of 10 to 50 years, is clear violation of the right of such women to practice their religious beliefs, in consequence, make their fundamental right under Article 25 (1) a dead letter. As long as the devotees, irrespective of their gender and/or age group, seeking entry to temple of any caste are Hindus, it is their legal right to enter into a temple and offer prayers.

Neither public morality nor public health will be at peril by allowing entry of women devotees of the age group of 10 to 50 years into the Sabarimala temple for offering their prayers. The notions of public order, morality and health cannot be used as colorable device to restrict the freedom to freely practice religion and discriminate against women of the age group of 10 to 50 years by denying them their legal right to enter and offer their prayers at the Sabarimala temple for the simple reason that public morality must yield to constitutional morality.

Whether exclusion Essential Practice of Hindu Religion

The Supreme Court observed that the practice of exclusion of women of the age group of 10 to 50 years could not be regarded as an essential part of Hindu Religion. In the absence of any scriptural or textual evidence, exclusionary practice followed at the Sabarimala temple can not be given the status of an essential practice of Hindu Religion. By allowing women to enter into the Sabarimala temple for offering prayers, it cannot be imagined that the nature of Hindu religion would be fundamentally altered or changed in any manner.

Validity of Rule 3 (b) of the 1965 Rules

Section 3 of the Kerala Hindu Places of Public Worship (Authorization of Entry) Act, 1965 declares that every place of public worship which is open to Hindus generally or to any section or class thereof shall be open to all sections and classes of Hindus. Rule 3 (b) of Kerala Hindu Places of Public Worship (Authorization of Entry) Rules, 1965 put restrictions on women by custom or usage to enter a place of public worship. The law is well-settled on the point that when a rule-making power is conferred under any stature on an authority, the said power has to be exercised within the confines of the statute and no transgression of the same is permissible. A cursory reading of the Rule 3 (b) divulges that it is *ultra vires* the 1965 Act.

ROMESH THAPPAR VS. THE STATE OF MADRAS

The Supreme Court in **Romesh Thappar Vs. Union of India, (1950) SCR 594** held that freedom of expression includes freedom of propagation of ideas and such freedom is ensured by freedom of circulation.

> Case Title : Romesh Thappar Vs. Union of India
> Date of Judgment : 26.05.1950
> Bench : Chief Justice Hiralal J. Kania, Justice Mehr Chand Mahajan, Justice B.K. Mukherjea, Justice Saiyid Fazal Ali

FACTS OF THE CASE

The Petitioner was the printer, publisher and editor of recently started weekly journal in English called Cross Roads, which was printed and published in Bombay. The Government of Madras in exercise of their powers under Section 9 (1A) of the Madras Maintenance of Public Order Act, 1949 issued an order No. MS 1333 dated 1st March, 1950 whereby they imposed a ban upon entry and circulation of journal in Madras State for purposes of securing public safety and maintenance of public order.

The Petitioner challenged the ban before the Supreme Court under Article 32 of the Constitution of India.

FINDINGS OF THE SUPREME COURT

The Petitioner contended that the order passed by Government of Madras under Section 9 (1A) of Madras Maintenance of Public Order Act, 1949 contravenes his rights under Article 19 (1) (a) of the Constitution as such Section 9 (1A) of Madras Maintenance of Public Order Act, 1949 is void under Article 13 (1) of the Constitution.

A preliminary objection was raised by the Respondent that the Petitioner should have approached High Court under Article 226 before approaching the Supreme Court under Article 32 of the Constitution.

The Supreme Court rejected this contention. The Supreme Court observed that Article 32 does not merely confer power on the Supreme Court as Article 226 does on the High Courts, to issue certain writs for enforcement of rights conferred by Part III or for any other purpose, as part of its general jurisdiction. In that case it would have been more appropriately placed among Articles 131 to 139 which define that jurisdiction. Article 32 provides a "guaranteed" remedy for the enforcement of those rights and this remedial right is itself made a fundamental right by being included in Part III. This Court is protector and guarantor of Fundamental Rights and it cannot, consistently with the responsibility so laid upon it, refuse to entertain applications seeking protection against infringement of such rights.

The Supreme Court observed that freedom of expression includes freedom of propagation of ideas and such freedom is ensured by freedom of circulation. Liberty of circulation is as essential to that freedom as the liberty of publication.

The Supreme Court was of the opinion that unless a law restricting freedom of speech and expression is directed solely against the undermining of the security of state or the overthrow of it, such law cannot fall within the reservation under clause (2) of Article 19, although the restrictions which it seeks to impose may have been conceived generally in interest of public order. It follows that Section 9 (1A) which authorizes impositions of restriction for wider purpose of securing pubic safety or the maintenance of public order falls outside scope of authorized restrictions under clause (2) and is therefore void and unconstitutional.

The Petition was allowed and the order of the Respondents prohibiting the entry and circulation of the Petitioner's journal in the State of Madras was quashed.

UNION OF INDIA VS NAVEEN JINDAL

The Supreme Court in **Union of India Vs Naveen Jindal, (2004) 1 SCR 1038** held that right to fly the National Flag freely with respect and dignity is a Fundamental Right of a citizen within the meaning of Article 19 (1) (a) of the Constitution of India being an expression and manifestation of his allegiance and feeling and sentiments of pride for the nation.

Case Title : Union of India Vs Naveen Jindal
Date of Judgment : 23.01.2004
Bench : Chief Justice V. N. Khare, Justice Brijesh Kumar, Justice S. B. Sinha

FACTS OF THE CASE

Naveen Jindal, Managing Director of a Public Limited Company, was not allowed to fly the National Flag at the factory site at Raigarh in Madhya Pradesh by government officials on the ground that it was not permissible under Flag Code of India. This was challenged by Naveen Jindal before the High Court. High Court held that so long as a Citizen of India flies the National Flag in respectful manner, no restriction can be imposed on the basis of instructions contained in the Flag Code.

FINDINGS OF THE SUPREME COURT

The Supreme Court observed that National Flags are intended to project the identity of the country they represent and foster national spirit. Their distinctive designs and colours embody each nation's particular character and proclaim the country's separate existence. Thus, it is veritably common to all nations that a national flag has a great amount of significance. In order that the respect and dignity of the flag be fostered and maintained, several countries have laid down rules relating to use, display, etc of the flag, along with rules to provide against the burning, mutilation and destruction of the flag.

The Supreme Court observed that Flag Code contains the executive instructions of the Central Government. Ministry of Home Affairs has been allocated this function under Government of India (Allocation of Business) Rules, 1961 under Article 77 of the Constitution of India. Such provision will not come under definition of "law" under Article 13 of the Constitution.

The Supreme Court held that flying of National Flag being symbol of expression would come within the purview of Article 19 (1) (a) of the Constitution.

The Supreme Court observed that it is necessary to notice the distinction between the Constitution of India and that of United States of America. In USA, the first amendment gives an absolute right to a citizen of religion and free expression, but under Constitution of India Article 19 (1) (a) does not confer such an absolute right of free speech and expression. It only provides for a qualified right. Such a fundamental right of a citizen of speech and expression is subject to the regulatory measures contained in clause (2) thereof. So long as the expression is confined to nationalism, patriotism and love for motherland, the use of National Flag by way of expression of those sentiments would be a fundamental right. It cannot be used for commercial purpose or otherwise.

The Supreme Court observed that Flag Code is not a stature, thereby the Fundamental Right under Article 19 (1) is not regulated by it. But the guidelines as laid down under the Flag Code deserve to be followed to the extent it provides for preservation of dignity and respect for the National Flag. The right to fly the National Flag is not an absolute right. The freedom of expression for the purpose of giving a feeling of nationalism and for that purpose all that is required to be done is that duty to respect the flag must be strictly obeyed. The pride of a person involved in flying the National Flag is the pride to be an Indian and that, thus, in all respects to it must be shown. The State may not tolerate even the slightest disrespect.

The Supreme Court did not find merit in the appeal and dismissed the same.

SHREYA SINGHAL VS UNION OF INDIA

The Supreme Court in **Shreya Singhal Vs. Union of India AIR 2015 SC 1523** has declared 66A of Information Technology Act, 2000 invalid on the ground that it is in violation of Article 19 (1) (a) of the Constitution.

Case Title : Shreya Singhal Vs. Union of India
Date of Judgment : 24.03.2015
Bench : Justice R.F. Nariman, Justice J. Chelameswar

FACTS OF THE CASE

Section 66A of the Information Technology was introduced vide 2009 amendment to the Constitution. Section 66A provides for punishment of imprisonment upto three years and with fine to such persons who sends by computer resource or communication device any information that is grossly offensive or has menacing character, or any information which he knows to be false but for purpose to cause annoyance, inconvenience, danger, obstruction, insult, injury, criminal intimidation, enmity, hatred, ill will by making use of computer resource or communication device or any electronic mail or electronic mail message for purposes of causing annoyance or inconvenience or to deceive or mislead the addressee or recipient about origin of such messages.

Various Writ Petitions were found before the Supreme Court challenging Section 66A of Information Technology Act, 2000 on the ground that it violates freedom of speech and expression granted under Article 19 (1) (a) of the Constitution.

FINDINGS OF THE COURT

The Supreme Court noted that in Romesh Thapar Vs. State of Madras (1950) SCR 594 it was held that freedom of speech lay at the foundation of all democratic organizations. In S. Khusboo Vs Kannimal & Anr (2010)

5 SCC 600 the Supreme Court observed that right to freedom of speech and expression , although not absolute, is necessary for as we need to tolerate unpopular views. The Supreme Court noted that in Abrams Vs United States (250) US 616 (1919) and Whitney Vs California (71L.Ed 1095) the Supreme Court of USA has emphasized free trade or ideas.

The Supreme Court observed that there are three concepts have to be understood for comprehension of right to freedom of speech and expression-discussion, advocacy and incitement. Discussion and advocacy, however it may be unpopular, is covered under Article 19 (1) (a). Only at the stage of incitement reasonable restrictions can be imposed under Article 19 (2) in interest of pubic order, sovereignty and integrity of India, security of state, decency, morality etc.

The Supreme Court observed that expressions in Section 66A are completely open ended and undefined. The Supreme Court compared Section 66A with Section 268 IPC and Section 294 IPC and held that in comparison to other offences under IPC, Section 66A uses completely open ended, undefined and vague language. None of expression used in Section 66A is defined. Every expression used is nebulous in meaning. What may cause inconvenience or annoyance to one may not cause inconvenience or annoyance to another.

Information which are grossly offensive or which causes annoyance or inconvenience covers large amount of protected and innocent speech. A certain point of view expressed over internet pertaining to governmental, scientific, or literary matters may not be palatable to certain sections of society. Section 66A can be applicable to such view. Thus, Section 66A suffers from overbreadth and has a chilling effect

The Supreme Court held that expressions used in 66A are not only suffers from inexactitude but are also overboard and in violation of repeated injunctions of the Supreme Court that that restrictions on the freedom of speech and expression must be in narrowest terms.

The Supreme Court noted that in **the Superintendent, Central Prison, Fatehgarh Vs. Ram Manohar Lohia Case (1960) 2 SCR 821** Section 3 of UP Special Powers Act, was struck down on the ground that under the said section a wide net was cast to catch a variety of acts of instigation ranging from friendly advice to systematic propaganda. In **Kameshwar Prasad Vs The State of Bihar (1962) Supp. 3 SCR 369** Rule 4A of the Bihar Government Servants Conduct Rules, 1956 was invalidated on the ground it imposed blanket ban on all demonstration of whatever type- innocent as well as otherwise.

The Supreme Court relied on Ram Manohar Lohia (Supra) and Kameshwar Singh (Supra) and declared 66A unconstitutional on the ground of being in violation of Article 19 (1) (a) of the Constitution.

ASSOCIATION OF DEMOCRATIC REFORMS VS UNION OF INDIA (ELECTORAL BOND JUDGMENT)

The Supreme Court in its landmark judgment **Association of Democratic Reforms Vs. Union of India (2024) 2 S.C.R. 420** has held that Electoral Bond Scheme is violative of Article 19 (1) (a) of the Constitution. The supreme Court has also held that permitting unlimited contributions to political parties is arbitrary and violative of Article 14 of the Constitution.

Case Title : Association of Democratic Reforms Vs. Union of India
Date of Judgment : 15.02.2024
Bench : Chief Justice Dr Dhananjaya Y Chandrachud, Justice B R Gavai, Justice J B Pardiwala, Justice Manoj Misra, Justice Sanjiv Khanna

FACTS OF THE CASE

Parliament vide Finance Act, 2017 brought about various changes in framework of contribution to political parties by companies. Parliament amended Section 182 of the Companies Act, 2013 which dealt with corporate funding of elections. It omitted cap of 7.5% on corporate funding to political parties. Section 182 ((3) was also amended to require only disclosure of total amount contributed to a political party rather than contribution made by each political party. The Finance Act also amended Reserve Bank of India Act, 1934 by including Article 31 (3) which permitted State Bank of India to issue electoral bonds. The Finance Act also amended Section 13 A of the of Income Tax Act to the effect that Political Parties were not required to maintain record of contribution if such contribution was received through electoral bonds.

Ministry of Finance notified Electoral Bond Scheme in under Section 31 (3) of the RBI Act in 2018. Electoral Bond could have been purchased by a citizen of India or persons incorporated or established in India. Electoral

Bond could have been encashed by only a Political Party. The bonds were issued in denomination of Rs. 1000/-, 10,000/-, 1,00,000/-, 10,00,000/- and 1,00,00,000/-. Bonds were valid for 15 days. These bonds were not tradable.

Association of Democratic Reforms challenged these amendments before the Supreme Court under Article 32 of the Constitution of India.

FINDINGS OF THE SUPREME COURT

The Supreme Court held that the challenge to the Electoral Bond Scheme is within the scope of judicial review. The argument that the scheme is an economic policy was rejected and it was held that it was mainly concerned with electoral process. The Court also held that once it is prima facie proved that any policy has violated Fundamental Rights under Part III of the Constitution, onus shifts to the State to prove that the violation of fundamental rights are justified.

The Supreme Court noted the influence of money on electoral politics. The Court observed that challenge to electoral bond scheme can not be adjudicated in isolation without a reference to actual impact of money on electoral politics.

The Supreme Court noted that Political Party is a relevant political unit in the democratic set up in India. The Court held that information about funding of political parties is essential for exercising freedom to vote in an effective manner. The Electoral Bond Scheme is in violation of Article 19 (1) (a) of the Constitution.

The Supreme Court held that such violation is not justified as Electoral Bond Scheme does not fulfil least restrictive means test. There are other alternatives which impact the right to information minimally. The Supreme Court held that Union of India has failed to establish that Electoral Bond Scheme is the least restrictive means to balance the rights of informational privacy to political contributions and the right to information of political contributions.

The Court further held that treatment of individuals and companies and treatment of profit making and loss making companies and permitting unregulated influence of companies in governance and political processes are arbitrary and in violation of Article 14.

The Supreme Court declared Electoral Bond Scheme amendments done to Representation of People Act, Companies Act and Income Tax Act unconstitutional. The Supreme Court also inter alia directed SBI to stop issuance of electoral bonds and submit details of electoral bonds to Election Commission of India.

S RANGARAJAN VS P JAGJIVAN RAM

The Supreme Court in **S. Rangarajan Vs. P. Jagjivan Ram, 1989 SCR (2) 204** held that open criticisms of Government policies and operations is not a ground for restricting freedom of speech and expression under Article 19 (1) (a) of the Constitution.

Case Title : S. Rangarajan Vs. P. Jagjivan Ram
Date of Judgment : 30.03.1989
Bench : Justice K.J. Shetty, Justice K.N. Singh, Justice Kuldip Singh

FACTS OF THE CASE

The story of the movie titled "Ore Uru Gramathile" revolved around a Brahmin girl getting Adi Dravida caste certificate to get admission into college. She subsequently cleared IAS. In the movie , there were some references to caste system encouraged by political system and also reference to Dr. Ambedkar. The producer applied for "U" certificate for exhibition of the film. Examining committee refused to grant certificate. The Revising Committee agreed to issue "U" certificate subject to deletion of certain scenes. Granting of "U" certificate was challenged before the Single Bench of High Court which was dismissed but the Division Bench of High Court revoked "U" certificate granted to movie. The matter finally reached to the Supreme Court.

FINDINGS OF THE SURPEME COURT

The Supreme Court observed that motion pictures were originally considered as form of amusement to be allowed to titillate but not to arouse. They were treated as mere entertainment and not an art or a means of expression. But later decisions of American Supreme Court declared that expression by means of motion pictures are included within free speech and free press guarantee of the First Amendment.

The Supreme Court noted that framework of Indian Constitution differs from the First Amendment to the U.S. Constitution. Article 19 (1) (a) guarantees all citizens the right to freedom of speech and expression. The freedom of expression means the right to express one's opinion by words of mouth, writing, printing, picture or any other manner. It would thus include the freedom of communication or the right to propagate or publish opinion. But these rights are subject to reasonable restrictions in the interest of sovereignty and integrity of India, the security of state, friendly relations with foreign states, public order, decency or morality or in relation to contempt of court, defamation or incitement of offence. Framers of the Constitution intended to strike a balance between the liberty guaranteed and the social interest specified.

The Supreme Court observed that there is significant difference between the movie and other modes of communication. Movies have cumulative impact on the spectators. The movie has unique capacity to disturb and arouse feelings. It has as much potential for evil as it has for good. Censorship by prior consent is not only desirable but also necessary.

The Supreme Court did not agree with the view of the High Court. The Supreme Court observed that criticism of reservation policy or praising the colonial rule will not affect the security of the State and integrity of India. There is no utterance in the film threatening to overthrow the government by unlawful or unconstitutional means. There is no talk of secession.

The Supreme Court observed that in democracy it is not essential that everyone should sing the same song. Freedom of expression is the rule and taken for granted. Everyone has a fundamental right to form his own opinion on any issue of general concern. He can form and inform by any legitimate means.

The Supreme Court observed that movie is the legitimate and the most important medium in which issues of general concern can be treated. The producer may project his own messages which the others may not approve. The State cannot prevent open discussion and open expression, however hateful to its policies.

There does indeed have to be a compromise between the interest of freedom of expression and social interests. But the two interests simply cannot be balanced as if they are of equal weight. Our commitment to freedom of expression demands that it cannot be suppressed unless the situations created by allowing the freedom are pressing and the community interest is endangered. The anticipated danger should not be remote, conjectural or far-fetched. It should have proximate and direct nexus with the expression. The expression of thought should be intrinsically dangerous to the public interest. In other words, the expression should be inseparably locked up with the action contemplated like the equivalent of a "spark in the powder keg".

The Supreme Court concluded that Fundamental Freedom under Article 19 (1) (a) can be reasonably restricted only for the purposes mentioned in Articles 19 (2) and restriction may be justified on the anvil of necessity and not on the basis of convenience or expediency. Open criticisms of Government policies and operations are not a ground for restricting expression.

The Supreme Court allowed the appeals and reversed the judgment of the High Court.

KAUSHAL KISHOR VS STATE OF UTTAR PRADESH

The Supreme Court in **Kaushal Kishore Vs State of Uttar Pradesh (2023)4SCC1** held *inter alia* that reasonable restrictions provided under Article 19 (2) on right to freedom of speech and expression under Article 19 (1) (a) are exhaustive.

Case Title : Kaushal Kishore Vs State of Uttar Pradesh
Date of Judgment : 03.01.2023
Bench : Justice B.V. Nagarathna, Justice V. Ramasubramanian

FACTS OF THE CASE

The Supreme Court was dealing with two petitions in this matter. The case in Writ Petition (Criminal) No. 113 of 2016 was that Petitioner and his family members were travelling from NOIDA to Shahjahanpur to attend death ceremony of a relative. They were waylaid by a gang, their valuables snatched and wife and minor daughter were raped. Minister of Urban Development of UP described it as political conspiracy. The case in SLP (Diary) 34629/2017 was that Minister of Electricity in Kerala issued highly derogatory statement for women.

FINDINGS OF THE SUPREME COURT

(i) Are the grounds specified in Article 19(2) in relation to which reasonable restrictions on the right to free speech can be imposed by law, exhaustive or can restrictions on the right to free speech be imposed on grounds not found in Article 19 (2) by invoking other Fundamental Rights ?

Article 19 (2) provides for reasonable restriction on grounds of - (i) interests of sovereignty and integrity of India (ii) the security of the state (iii) friendly relations with foreign states (iv) public order (v) decency or morality (vi) contempt of court (vii) defamation and (viii) incitement to an offence.

The Supreme Court held that eight heads of restrictions under Article 19 (2) are exhaustive. Under the guise of invoking other Fundamental Rights, additional restrictions over and above those prescribed in Article 19 (2) cannot be imposed upon the exercise of one's fundamental rights.

(ii) Can a fundamental right under Article 19 or 21 of the Constitution of India be claimed other than against the "State" or its instrumentalities ?

The Supreme Court noted that there are some Articles in Part III where the mandate is directly to the State and there are other Articles where without injuncting the State, certain rights are recognized to be inherent, either in the citizens of the country or in persons. In fact, there are two sets of dichotomies that are apparent in the Articles contained in Part III. One set of dichotomy is between what is directed against the State and what is spelt out as inhering in every individual without reference to the State. The other dichotomies are between citizens and persons.

The rights conferred by Articles 15 (2) (a) and (b), 17, 20 (2), 21, 23, 24, 29(2) are obviously enforceable against non-state actors also.

The Supreme Court observed that its original thinking that these rights can be enforced only against state changed over a period of time. The transformation was from "State" to "Authorities" to "instrumentalities of state" to "agency of the Government" to 'impregnation with Governmental Character " to "enjoyment of monopoly status conferred by State" to "deep and pervasive control" to the "nature of the duties /functions performed".

The Supreme Court held that a fundamental right under Article 19/21 can be enforced even against persons other than the State or its instrumentalities.

(iii) Whether the State is under a duty to affirmatively protect the right of a citizen under Article 21 of the Constitution of India even against a threat to liberty of a citizen by the acts of omissions of another citizen or private agency ?

The Supreme Court observed that the understanding of this Court in **A. K. Gopalan Vs State of Madras (1950) SCR 88** that deprivation of personal liberty required a physical restraint underwent a change a **Kharak Singh Vs State of UP AIR 1963SC1295** and **Gobind Vs State of Madhya Pradesh (1975)2SCC148.** From there the law marched to the next stage in **Satwant Singh Sawhney Vs D. Ramarathnam AIR 1967SC1836,**

Assistant Passport Officer where a Constitution Bench held that the right to personal liberty included right of locomotion and right to travel abroad. It was held in the said decision that "liberty" in our Constitution bears the same comprehensive meaning as it given to the expression "liberty" by the 5th and 14th amendments to the US constitution and the expression "personal liberty" in Article 21 only excludes the ingredients of "liberty" enshrined in Article 19 of the Constitution. The court went on to hold that the expression "personal liberty" in Article 21 takes in the right of locomotion and to travel abroad but the right to move throughout the territories of India is not covered by it in as much as it is specially provided in Article 19.

The Supreme Court held that the State is under a duty to affirmatively protect the rights of a person under Article 21 whenever there is a threat to personal liberty even by a non-state actor.

(iv) Can a statement made by a Minister traceable to any affairs of State or protecting the Government be attributed vicariously to the Government itself, especially in view of the principle of the Collective responsibility ?

The Supreme Court observed that generally collective responsibility of the Council of Ministers either to the House or the People or the Legislative Assembly should be understood to corelate to the decisions and actions of the Council of Ministers and not to every statement made by every individual minister.

The Supreme Court held that – (i) the concept of collective responsibility is essentially a political concept. (ii) that the collective responsibility is that of the Council of Ministers (iii) such collective responsibility is to the House of the People/Legislative Assembly. It is not possible to extend this concept of collective responsibility to any and every statement orally made by a Minister outside the House of the People/Legislative Assembly.

(v) Whether a statement by a Minister, inconsistent with the rights of a citizen under Part three of the Constitution, constitutes a violation of such constitutional rights and is actionable as "Constitutional Tort" ?

The Supreme Court held that a mere statement made by a Minister inconsistent with the rights of a citizen under Part III of the Constitution may not constitute a violation of the constitutional rights and become actionable as Constitutional Tort. But if as a consequence of such statement, any act of omission or commission is done by officers resulting in harm or loss to a person/citizen then the same may be actionable as a constitutional tort.

EXCEL WEAR ETC VS UNION OF INDIA

The Supreme Court in **Excel Wear Etc Vs Union of India, (1979) 1 SCR 1009** held that the right to close business is an integral part of Fundamental Right to carry on a business.

> Case Title : Excel Wear Etc Vs Union of India
> Date of Judgment : 29.09.1978
> Bench : Justice Y.V. Chandrachud, Justice N.L. Untwalia, Justice Ranjit Singh Sarkaria, Justice A.D. Koshal, Justice A.P. Sen

FACTS OF THE CASE

Four Writ Petitions were filed challenging the constitutional validity of Section 25O and 25R of the Industrial Disputes Act, 1947.

In Writ Petition 644 of 1977, Excel Wear was a partnership firm and used to manufacture garments for exports. Around 400 workmen were employed in Petitioner's factory. Excel Wear was facing labour trouble and served notice on State Government for prior approval of closure under Section 25 -O (1), which was refused by State Government.

In Writ Petition 917 of 1977, Wadala Unit of Acme Manufacturing Co. Ltd. engaged in business of manufacturing and selling Diesel Oil Engines, Mechanical Lubricators, Engine Valves and Push Rods. The Petitioner decided to close down the undertaking due to huge loss, labour unrest, and industrial indiscipline. The Petitioner applied for prior leave under Section 25 (O) (1) of Industrial Disputes Act for closure which was refused.

In Writ Petition 959 and 960 of 1977, Apar Private Ltd. applied before the Government of Maharastra for prior approval for closure of factory under Section 25 (O) (1) which was refused.

FINDINGS OF THE SUPREME COURT

Section 25 O provided that an employer who intended to close down an undertaking of an industrial establishment to which the chapter applied had to serve for previous approval at ninety days before the date on which the intended closure is to become effective, a notice in prescribed manner, on the appropriate government stating clearly reasons for the intended closure of the undertaking.

Section 25 R provided for penal consequences for non-compliance of provisions of Section 25 O.

It was contended before the Supreme Court that a right to close down the business is an integral part of the right to carry on the business guaranteed under Article 19 (1) (g) of the Constitution of India. The impugned law imposed a restriction on the said Fundamental Right which is highly unreasonable, excessive and arbitrary. It is not a restriction but almost amounts to the destruction or negation of that right. The restrictions imposed is manifestly beyond permissible bounds of clauses (6) of Articles 19 of the Constitution.

The Supreme Court held that the right to close down a business cannot be equated with a right not to start or carry on a business at all. The extreme proposition urged on behalf of the employer by equating the two rights and placing them at par is not quite apposite and sound. If one does not start a business at all then perhaps under no circumstances, he can be compelled to start one. Such a negative aspect of a right to carry on a business may be equated with the negative aspect of the right embedded in the concept of right to freedom of speech, to form an association or to acquire or hold property. Perhaps under no circumstances, a person can be compelled to speak, to form an association or to acquire or hold a property. But by imposing reasonable restrictions, he too can be compelled not to speak, not to form an association or not to acquire or not to hold property. A total prohibition of business is possible by putting reasonable restrictions under Article 19 (6) on the right to carry on a business.

The Supreme Court further observed that the greater the restriction, the more the need for strict scrutiny by the Court. The contention put forward on behalf of the labour unions that the right to close down a business is not an integral part of the right to carry on a business or that it is not a Fundamental Right at all is also wrong. In one sense the right does appertain to property. But such a faith overlapping of the right to property engrafted in Article 19 (1) (f) or Article 31 must not be allowed to cast any shade or eclipse on the simple nature of the right. It can be certainly be restricted, regulated or controlled by law in the interest of general public.

The Supreme Court noted the difference between doctrinaire approach to problem of socialism and pragmatism. So long as the private ownership of an industry is recognized, it is not possible to say that principles of socialism and social justice can be pushed to such an extreme so as to ignore completely or to a very large extent the interests of another section of the public namely the private owners of the undertaking.

The Supreme Court observed that public interest and social justice do require the protection of labour. But it is not reasonable to give them protection against all unemployment after affecting the interests of so many persons interested including persons who have no connection with the management.

The Supreme Court found restrictions put under Section 25 (O) and 25 (R) unreasonable and declared Section 25 (O) invalid as a whole and Section 25 (R) so far it relates to the awarding of punishment for infringement of provisions of Section 25 (O).

DAMYANTI NARANGA VS. UNION OF INDIA

The Supreme Court held in **Damyanti Naranga Vs. Union of India, (1971) 3 SCR 840** that right to form an association includes the right to continue the association with the membership either chosen by the founders or regulated by rules made by the association.

Case Title : Damyanti Naranga Vs. Union of India
Date of Judgment : 23.02.1971
Bench : Chief Justice S.M. Sikri, Justice G.K. Mitter, Justice K.S. Hegde, Justice P. Jaganmohan Reddy, Justice V. Bhargava

FACTS OF THE CASE

Some eminent educationists assembled at Banaras and founded an association for the development of Hindi and its propagation throughout the country. The Association was named as Hindi Sahitya Sammelan. On 8th January, 1914, it was registered as Society under Society Registration Act, 1860 under the name Hindi Sahitya Sammelan. The Society owned landed properties at Allahabad and some other places.

In 1950, some differences arose between members of the society leading to passing of Hindi Sahitya Sammelan Act, 1956, by which the Society was converted in Statutory Body. This Act was declared void on the ground that it violated right to form association under Article 19 (1) (c) of original members.

Thereafter, the Parliament passed Hindi Sahitya Sammelan Act, 1963. It declared Hindi Sahitya Sammelan institute of national importance. The statutory Sammelan was constituted as body corporate. All rights and liabilities were transferred from society to the statutory body. The Act gave wide powers to governing body to make rules in respect of matters relating to membership including qualifications and disqualification of members. Provisions could be made under the new Act to include members whom original members may not have admitted. The number of new members could be so large that existing members might be left in minority.

The Act was challenged before High Court which held it valid. Finally the matter reached to the Supreme Court.

FINDINGS OF THE SUPREME COURT

It was contended that the right guaranteed under Article 19 (1) (c) is only to form an association and consequently any regulation of the affairs of the association, after it has been formed, would not amount to breach of a right.

The Supreme Court observed that the Act not only regulates the administration of the affairs of the society, but it alters composition of the society. The members who voluntarily formed the association, were now compelled to act with other members who had been imposed as members by the Act and in whose admission to membership, they had no say. It clearly interferes with the right to continue to function as members of the Association which was voluntarily formed by the original founders. The right to form an association necessarily implies that the persons forming the Association have also right to continue to be associated with only those whom they voluntarily admit in the Association. Any law, by which members are introduced in the voluntary Association without any opinion being given to the members to keep them out or any law which takes away membership of those who have voluntary joined it, will be a law violating the right to form an association. If it is accepted that the right guaranteed by Article 19 (1) (c) is confined to the initial stage of forming an Association and does not protect the right to continue the Association with the membership either chosen by the founders or regulated by rules made by the Association, the right would be meaningless because as soon as an Association is formed a law may be passed interfering with its composition, so that the Association formed may not be able to function at all. The right can be effective only if it is held to include within its right to continue the Association with its composition as voluntarily agreed upon by the persons forming the Association.

The Supreme Court held that the Act, in so far as it interferes with the composition of the Society , violates the right of the original members of the Society to form an association guaranteed under Article 19 (1) (c).

The Supreme Court observed that validity of the Act is not protected by Article 19 (4) as the same has not been passed in interest of sovereignty and integrity of India or in interest of public order or morality.

The Supreme Court declared the Act invalid.

KHARAK SINGH VS STATE OF U.P.

The Supreme Court held in **Kharak Singh Vs State of U.P. (1964) 1 SCR 332** that right to "move" denotes nothing more than a right of locomotion and that in the context the adverb "freely" would only connote that the freedom to move is without restriction and is absolute.

Case Title : Kharak Singh Vs State of U.P.
Date of Judgment : 18.12.1962
Bench : Chief Justice Bhuvneshwar P. Sinha, Justice N. Rajagopala Ayyangar, Justice Syed Jaffer Imam, Justice J.C. Shah, Justice J.R. Mudholkar, Justice K. Subbarao

---

FACTS OF THE CASE

The Petitioner was challaned in case of dacoity but was released as there was no evidence against him. Police used to maintain two types of history sheets – (i) Class A for dacoits, burglars, cattle thieves, and railway goods wagon thieves and (ii) Class B for those who are confirmed and professional criminals who commit crimes other than dacoity, burglary. History sheet of the Petitioner had been opened in the category of class A.

Frequently the chaukidar of the village and sometimes police constables entered his house, knocked and shouted at his door, woke him up during the night and thereby disturbed his sleep. When the Petitioner left his village he had to inform the same to the police station. Police station of his destination was contacted and there also he was kept under surveillance.

The Petitioner filed Petition under Article 32 of the Constitution of India before the Supreme Court.

FINDINGS OF THE SUPREME COURT

The issue before the Supreme Court was whether "surveillance" under the impugned chapter XX of UP Police Regulations constituted an infringement of Fundamental Rights of citizens.

It was contended by State that the impugned regulations did not constitute an infringement of any of the freedoms guaranteed by Part III of the Constitution. Even if they infringe, they were reasonable restrictions.

Regulation 236 provided for secret picketing of the house or approaching to the house of suspects; domiciliary visits at night; periodical inquires by an officer not below the rank of sub-inspector into repute, habits, associations, incomes, expenses and occupation; the reporting by constables and chauki-dars of movements and absence from home; the verification of movements and absences by means of inquiry slips; and the collection and record on history -sheet of all information bearing on conduct.

It was contended by the Petitioner that aforesaid regulation was in violation of Article 19 (1) (d) , which provides for right to move freely throughout territory of India and Article 21.

The Supreme Court observed that secret picketing of houses of the suspects is to ascertain the identity of the person or persons who visit the house of the suspect, so that the police might have a record of the nature of the activities in which the suspect is engaged. It does not infringe Article 19 (1) (d) or Article 21.

The Supreme Court held that intrusion into residence of a citizen and knocking at this door at night causing disturbance to his sleep and comfort does not violate right to move freely under Article 19 (1) (d). Right to "move" denotes nothing more than a right of locomotion and that in the context the adverb "freely" would only connote that the freedom to move is without restriction and is absolute i.e. to move wherever one likes, whenever one likes and however one likes subject to any valid law enacted or made under clause 5. By knock at the door or by the man being aroused from his sleep his locomotion is not impeded or prejudiced in any manner.

But Supreme Court held that knocking at the door violates right to life and personal liberty under Article 21 as unauthorized intrusion into a person's home and the disturbance caused to him is in violation of a common law right of a man – an ultimate essential of ordered liberty, if not very concept of civilization.

It was contended by the Petitioner that shadowing of a person obstructed his free movement or in any event was an impediment to his free movement within Article 19 (1) (d) of the Constitution. The argument that freedom postulated under Article 19 (1) (d) was not confined to a mere physical restraint hampering movement but that the term "freely" used in the Article connoted a wider freedom transcending mere physical restraints and included psychological inhibitions was rejected by the Supreme Court. The Supreme Court held that Article 19 (1) (d) is not infringed by a watch being kept over the movements of the suspect.

The Supreme Court also observed that right of privacy has not been guaranteed under the Constitution. Subsequently in **Justice K. S. Puttaswamy Vs. Union of India (2017) 10 SCC 1** the Supreme Court has held that right to privacy is implicit under Article 21.

The Supreme Court struck down domiciliary visits as constitutional.

SELVI VS STATE OF KARNATAKA

The Supreme Court in **Smt. Selvi Vs. State of Karnataka, 2010 (7) SCC 263** held that involuntary Polygraph Examination, Narcoanalysis and Brain Electrical Activation Profile (BEAP) during investigation of case violates Article 20 (3) of the Constitution.

> Case Title : Smt. Selvi Vs. State of Karnataka
> Date of Judgment : 05.05.2010
> Bench : Chief Justice K.G. Balakrishnan, Justice J.M. Panchal, Justice R.V. Raveendran

FACTS OF THE CASE

Several criminal appeals were filed before the Supreme Court challenging involuntary administration of certain scientific techniques, namely narco-analysis, polygraph examination and the Brain Electrical Activation Profile (BEAP) for improving investigation in criminal cases.

FINDINGS OF THE SUPREME COURT

Polygraph Examination is based on premise that a subject lying will produce physiological responses which will different from normal circumstances. Physiological responses are recorded through various instruments attached with the subject.

Narcoanalysis Test involves administration of intravenous drugs which impact the consciousness of the subject and he becomes less inhibited to answer any question put by administrators.

BEAP is a process for detecting whether subject is familiar with certain information by measuring activity in brain that is triggered by exposure of certain stimuli.

Whether administration of Polygraph Examination, Narcoanalysis and BEAP violates "right against self-incrimination" under Article 20 (3)?

Right against self-incrimination is Fundamental Right under Article 20 (3) of the Indian Constitution. Article 20 and Article 21 have been given exalted status under the Constitution and these Articles cannot even be suspended during emergency. Such rights are also available under USA jurisprudence under Fifth amendment. International Covenant on Civil and Political Rights also states that every one has right to not to be compelled to testify against himself or to confess guilt.

Section 161 (2) CrPC prescribes that when a person is being examined by a police officer, he is not bound to answer such questions which have tendency to expose him to criminal charge or a penalty or forfeiture. Section 313 (3) CrPC lays down that the accused will not make himself liable to punishment for not answering any question or giving false answers. Section 315 (1) CrPC mandates that if the accused does not tender evidence in his defense the same will not be subject of comment or any adverse inference.

The Court noted that right against self-incrimination is based on two premises – firstly, ensuring reliability of statement of the accused and secondly, such statement is made voluntarily. When a person is compelled to testify, there is higher chance of such testimony to be false.

It was contended before the Supreme Court that these techniques boost investigation and materials discovered after applying these techniques can be used as admissible evidence.

The Supreme Court concurred with the view taken in **M. P. Sharma Vs Satish Chandra (1954) SCR 1077** and **Nandini Satpathy Vs P. L. Dani (1978) 2 SCC 424** which held that right against self-incrimination is available at investigation stage. The Supreme Court noted that after **Miranda Vs Arizona 384 US 436 (1966)**, warning to the accused regarding right of silence has become ubiquitous feature in USA Criminal System. If no such warning is given, there is automatic presumption of compulsion. In India position is different as there is no automatic presumption of compulsion but if compulsion is proved statements given by accused is not admissible in evidence.

Rights against self-incrimination protects persons who have been formally accused as well as suspects of the crime. It also extends to witnesses who apprehend that their answers could expose them to criminal charges, witnesses cannot invoke protection of Article 20 (3) in administrative and quasi-criminal proceedings.

Whether results acquired through these techniques are barred under Article 20 (3) ?

Only such material is protected under Article 20 (3) which lead to incrimination by themselves or furnish a link in chain of evidence which could lead to the same result. Any testimony for purpose of identification or corroboration with the facts already known to the investigators are not barred.

The Supreme Court held that compulsory administration of Narcoanalysis Test amounts to "testimonial compulsion" and triggers the protection of Article 20 (3). The Court also dispelled the arguments that Polygraph Test and BEAP are covered material evidence such as bodily substances or physical objects and held that compulsory Polygraph Test and BEAP will also be covered under "Testimonial" acts and will be in violation of Article 20 (3).

Whether involuntary administration of Polygraph Examination, Narcoanalysis or BEAP are covered under reasonable restrictions under Article 21 ?

The Supreme Court held that subjecting a person to Polygraph Examination, Narcoanalysis or BEAP violates right of privacy of accused persons. These techniques are also against fair trial. Subjects have no control over revelation made during drug induced stage as such it frustrates object of legal consultation provided to the accused.

Further the questionable scientific reliability of these techniques is in conflict of principle of "beyond reasonable doubt" in criminal proceedings.

MANEKA GANDHI VS. UNION OF INDIA

Maneka Gandhi Vs. Union of India, (AIR 1978 SC 597) was one of the landmark judgments of the Supreme Court which expanded scope of Article 21 and held that procedure contemplated by Article 21 must be in conformity with Article 14. Such procedure must be right, just and fair.

Case Title : Maneka Gandhi Vs. Union of India
Date of Judgment : 25.01.1978
Bench : Chief Justice M. Hameedullah Beg, Justice Y.V. Chandrachud, Justice P.N. Bhagwati, Justice V.R. Krishna Iyer, Justice N.L. Untwalia, Justice Syed Murtaza Fazal Ali, Justice P.S. Kailasam

FACTS OF THE CASE

Smt. Maneka Gandhi was holder of passport issued under Passport Act, 1967. She received a letter dated 2nd July, 1977 from Regional Passport Officer informing her that her passport has been impounded under Section 10 (3) (c) of the Act in public interest. Smt. Maneka Gandhi requested for statement of reasons for making order for impounding of the passport. The Ministry of External Affairs informed her that it has decided not to furnish a statement of reasons "in interest of the general public".

Smt. Maneka Gandhi challenged the order before the Supreme Court under Article 32 of the Constitution.

FINDINGS OF THE COURT

Interpretation of Personal Liberty

One of the ground raised in the Petition was that right to go abroad is part of "personal liberty" enumerated under Article 21 and no body can be deprived of this right except procedure established by law. It was contended that there was no procedure provided under the Passport Act and if there was any such procedure was unreasonable and arbitrary as it does not provide opportunity to be heard.

The Supreme Court noted that a narrow interpretation of "personal liberty" has been done in **A. K. Gopalan Vs. State of Madras (1950 SCR 88)** so as to confine the protection of Article 21 to freedom against unlawful detention. In **Kharak Singh Vs. State of UP (1964) 1 SCR 332** the majority opinion took the view that "personal liberty" in Article 21 is a compendious term which includes variety of rights other than those dealt in various clauses of Article 19. While Article 19 deals with particular species or attributes, Article 21 deals with the residual rights. The minority opinion held that both are independent rights but there are overlapping. There is no question of one being carved out by another. The Supreme Court noted that the majority opinion held in Kharak Singh has been overruled by **R. C. Cooper Vs. Union of India (1973) 3 SCR 530** wherein it was held that Fundamental Rights granted under Part III are not distinct and mutually exclusive.

The Supreme Court observed that the attempt of the Court should be to expand the reach and ambit of Fundamental Rights. The Supreme Court held that the expression "personal liberty" is Article 21 is of the widest amplitude and it covers a variety of rights which go to constitute the personal liberty of man and some of them have been raised to the status of distinct Fundamental Rights and given additional protection under Article 19. The Supreme Court noted that in **Satwant Singh Sawhney vs D Ramarathnam (1967 3 SCR 525)** right to go abroad has been held to be right covered under Article 21.

The Passports Act, 1967 provides for procedure for issuance, refusal, cancellation and impounding of passport but issue is whether such procedure is sufficient compliance with Article 21 . Any such procedure cannot be arbitrary, unfair or unreasonable.

Inter-relationship between Article 14, 19 and Article 21

The Supreme Court observed that in light of **R. C. Cooper Vs. Union of India (1973) 3 SCR 530 , Shambhu Nath Sarkar Vs. State of West Bengal 1973 1 SCR 856** and **Haradhan Saha Vs State of West Bengal 1975 1 SCR 778**, if a law depriving a person of "personal liberty" and prescribing a procedure for that purpose within meaning of Article 21 has to stand the test of one or more of the Fundamental Rights conferred under Article 19 and Article 14. The Court also discussed scope of Article 14. The Court held that procedure contemplated by Article 21 must be in conformity with Article 14. Such procedure must be right, just and fair.

Article 14 strikes at arbitrariness in State action and ensures fairness and equality of treatment. The principle of reasonableness, which legally as well as philosophically an essential element of equality or non-arbitrariness, pervades Article 14 like a brooding omnipresence and the procedure contemplated by Article 21 must answer the test of reasonableness in order to be in conformity with Article 14. It must be "right, just and fair" and not arbitrary, fanciful or oppressive; otherwise, it would be no procedure at all and the requirement of Article 21 would not be satisfied. Thus due process was read by the Supreme Court in Procedure established by law.

Natural Justice and Procedure Established by Law

The Supreme Court noted that there are two main principles of Natural Justice – *Nemo Judex in Sua Causa* and *audo alteram partem*. Natural justice is a great humanizing principle ensuring fairness and has become pervasive in administrative actions. The court held that principle of natural justice is applicable to both quasi-judicial bodies and administrative bodies.

The Supreme Court observed that *audi alteram* rule is sufficiently flexible to permit modifications and variations to suit exigencies of myriad kinds of situations. It may be full- fledged hearing or minimal hearing. It may be a hearing prior to the decision or a post decisional remedial hearing. A fair opportunity of being heard upon the order impounding the passport would satisfy the mandate of natural justice.

The Court noted that in instant case no such opportunity has been given to Smt Maneka Gandhi as such procedure adopted was in violation of the Article 21.

Direct and Inevitable Effect Test

The Supreme Court also deliberated over the nature of test for determining constitutionality of a statute on the touchstone of Fundamental Rights. The Court noted that in A K Gopalan the test developed was of directness of leg-islation and not what will be the result of statute otherwise valid. The Court was of the view that direct object of order was preventive detention and not the infringement of the right of freedom of speech and expression, which was only consequential effect. In R. C. Cooper case the test of "direct consequence and effect" of state action on Fundamental Rights was propounded.

The Court held that right of freedom of speech and expression is available not only within the territory of India but also outside. The Court held that right to go abroad is not covered under Right to speech and expression under 19 (1)

(a) as such provisions of Passport Act imposing restrictions are not violative of Article 19 1 (a) or (g)

Smt. Maneka Gandhi was given opportunity of representation, which was to be disposed of by the Government expeditiously.

FRANCIS CORALIE MULLIN VS. THE ADMINISTRATOR, UNION TERRITORY OF DELHI

The Supreme Court in **Francis Coralie Mullin Vs. The Administrator, Union Territory, (1981) 2 SCR 516** held that right to live includes right to live with human dignity and all that goes along with it.

Case Title : Francis Coralie Mullin Vs. The Administrator, Union Territory
Date of Judgment : 13.01.1981
Bench : Justice P.N. Bhagwati, Justice Syed Murtaza Fazal Ali

FACTS OF THE CASE

The Petitioner was a British citizen. She was arrested and detained under COFEPOSA Act. While under detention, she faced difficulty in having interview with her lawyer and family members. Her daughter of five years and her sister were allowed to meet only once a month. She was facing difficulty in meeting with her lawyer as lawyer could only meet after getting permission from District Magistrate in presence of nominated custom officer. These conditions have been imposed by conditions of detention laid down by Delhi Administration issued under Section 5 of COFEPOSA Act. The Petitioner challenged the constitutional validity of these provisions.

FINDINGS OF THE SUPREME COURT

Petitioners challenged the aforesaid provisions on the ground that they were in violation of Article 14 and Article 21 of the constitution as undertrial prisoners were allowed meeting twice a week and convicted prisoner was allowed once a week.

The Supreme Court noted that there is a vital distinction between preventive detention and punitive detention. Punitive detention is intended to inflict punishment on a person who is found by judicial process to have committed an offence, while preventive detention is not by way of punishment at all, but it is intended to preempt a person from indulging in conduct injurious to society. The power of preventive detention has been recognized as necessary evil and is tolerated in a free society in the larger interest of security of State and maintenance of public order. It is drastic power to detain a person without trial and there are many countries where it is not allowed to be exercised except in times of war or aggression.

The Supreme Court noted that after Maneka Gandhi judgment, apart from Article 22, Article 21 also lays down restriction on the power of preventive detention. It is no longer enough to secure compliance with prescription of Article 21 that there should be a law prescribing some semblance of a procedure for depriving a person of his life or personal liberty, but the procedure established by law must be reasonable, fair and just and if it is not so, the law would be void.

The Supreme Court observed that the prisoner or detenu has all the fundamental rights and other legal rights available to a free person save those which are incapable of enjoyment by reasons of incarceration.

The Supreme Court observed that right to life is not limited to protection of limb and faculty but includes right to live with human dignity and all that goes along with it, namely, the bare necessities of life such as adequate nutrition, clothing, and shelter and facilities for reading, writing and expressing oneself in diverse forms, freely moving about and mixing and commingling with fellow human beings. Of course, the magnitude and content of the components of this right would depend upon the extent of the economic development of the country, but it must include the right to the basic necessities of life and also the right to carry on such functions and activities as constitute the bare minimum expression of the human self. Every act which offends against or impairs human dignity would constitute deprivation *pro tanto* of this right to live and it would have to be in accordance with reasonable, fair and just procedure established by law which stands the test of other Fundamental Rights. Any form of torture or cruel, inhuman or degrading treatment would be offensive to human dignity. The Supreme Court observed that a prisoner or detenu cannot move outside prison, but he would be entitled to have interview with family members and friends.

The Supreme Court observed that same result will follow if seen from perspective of right to personal liberty under Article 21. Right to personal liberty would include right to socialize with members of family and friends subject to valid prison regulations.

The Supreme Court declared provisions in question violative or Article 14 and Article 19.

SHANTISTAR BUILDERS VS NARAYAN KHIMALAL TOTAME

The Supreme Court in **Shantistar Builders Vs Narayan Khimalal Totame, (1990)1SCC520** held that right to reasonable residence is included in right to life under Article 21.

> Case Title : Shantistar Builders Vs Narayan Khimalal Totame
> Date of Judgment : 31.01.1990
> Bench : Justice Ranganath Misra, Justice P.B. Sawant, Justice K. Ramaswamy

FACTS OF THE CASE

Under Urban Land (Ceiling and Regulation) Act, 1979, urban agglomerations have been divided into four classes and a ceiling has been provided for each classification. Section 10 of the Act provided that the vacant land in excess of the ceiling vests in the State by way of acquisition and the vacant sites thus acquired by the State are intended to be utilized for purposes of housing. There was provision for treating land in excess of ceiling limit not as excess if such land was to be used for creating dwelling houses for weaker sections.

It was the case of the aggrieved persons that the builder had violated the conditions imposed in the order of exemption. The need of the weaker sections of society was not being attended to and a big racket had been formed by the real estate speculators to eliminate the economically weaker sections and persons genuinely in need of housing accommodation and to make unauthorized and illegal profit out of such transactions. Respondents also challenged the sanction of escalation of price following the demand of the builder and alleged that the legislative purpose of according exemption have been departed from. Respondents also claimed that applications from genuine persons belonging to the economically weaker sections have been overlooked and persons not entitled to the benefit have been registered by the builders.

FINDINGS OF THE SUPREME COURT

The Supreme Court observed that basic needs of man have traditionally been accepted to be three - food, clothing and shelter. The right to life is guaranteed in any civilized society. That would take within its sweep the right to food, the right to clothing, the right to decent environment and a reasonable accommodation to live in. The difference between the need of an animal and a human being for shelter has to be kept in view. For the animal, it is the bare protection of the body, for a human being it has to be a suitable accommodation which would allow him to grow in every aspect – physical, mental and intellectual. The Constitution aims at ensuring fuller development of every child. That would be possible only if the child is in a proper home. It is not necessary that every citizen must be ensured of living in a well-built comfortable but a reasonable home particularly for people in India it can even be mud-built thatched house or mud-built fire-proof accommodation.

The Supreme Court further observed that with the increase of population and the shift of the rural masses to urban areas over decades the ratio of poor people without houses in the urban areas has rapidly increased. This is a feature which has become more perceptible after independence. Apart from the fact that people in search of work move to urban agglomerations, availability of amenities and living conveniences also attract people to move from rural areas to cities. Industrialization is equally responsible for concentration of population around industries. These are features which are mainly responsible for increase in the homeless urban population. Millions of people today live on the pavements of different cities of India and a greater number lived animal like existence in jhuggis.

The Supreme Court held that since a reasonable residence is an indispensable necessity for fulfilling the Constitutional goal in the matter of development of man and should be taken as included in "life" in Article 21, greater social control is called for and exemption granted under Section 20 and 21 should have to be appropriately monitored to have the fullest benefit of the beneficial legislation.

The Supreme Court directed the Central Government to prescribe appropriate guidelines laying down true scope of the term "weaker sections of the society" so that everyone charged with administering the statute would find it convenient to implement the same. The Supreme Court also issued certain guidelines to State of Maharashtra.

NATIONAL LEGAL SERVICES AUTHORITY VS UNION OF INDIA

The Supreme Court in **National Legal Services Authority Vs Union of India, (2014) 5 SCR 119** inter alia issued directions for identifying Hijra and eunuchs as third gender for safeguarding their rights.

Case Title : National Legal Services Authority Vs Union of India
Date of Judgment : 15.04.2014
Bench : Justice A.K. Sikri, Justice K.S. Radhakrishnan

FACTS OF THE CASE

National Legal Services Authority has filed Writ Petition before the Supreme Court of India seeking declaration that non-recognition of Transgender Community is in violation of Article 14 and 21 of Indian Constitution. Third-gender status for transgenders was also sought.

FINDINGS OF THE SUPREME COURT

Historical Aspects

Transgenders comprise of Hijras, eunuchs, Kothis, Aravanis, Jogappas, Shiv Shakthis etc. The Supreme Court noted that in Hindu Mythology there are abundant references to transgenders. Transgenders are told to have accompanied Lord Rama when he was being exiled to Forest. There are references to transgenders in Mahabharat and Jain Texts also. Hijras also played important role in royal courts of Islamic and Mughal rulers. The Supreme Court noted that during British Rule a discriminatory approach was adopted towards transgenders and were prosecuted under Criminal Tribes Act, 1871.

Gender Identity and Sexual Orientation

The Supreme Court noted that Gender Identity refers to a person's intrinsic sense of being male, female or transgender or transsexual person. Small group of people are born with bodies which incorporate both or certain aspects of male or female physiology. The world grapples with the question of attribution of gender to persons who believe that they belong to opposite sex. Some persons even go through surgical procedure to alter their body which confirm their perception to gender. Gender identity thus is self-identification as man, woman, transgender or other-identified category. Sexual orientation refers to individual's enduring physical, romantic or emotional attraction to another person.

United Nations on Gender Identity and Sexual Orientation

Article 6 of Universal Declaration of Human Rights, 1948 and Article 16 of International Covenants on Civil and Political Rights, 1966 (ICCPR) recognize that every human being has inherent right to live and this right will be protected by law.

Yogyakarta Principles drafted by a distinguished group of Human Rights experts address a broad range of Human Rights standards and their application to sexual orientation and gender identity. Human beings of all sexual orientation and gender identity are entitled to the full enjoyment of all human rights. Yogyakarta Principles also recommended States to take steps against discrimination on ground of sexual orientation and gender identity.

The Supreme Court surveyed various judgments of different jurisdictions on treatment to persons who have gone through surgery to change their sex and noted that jurisprudence has evolved from judgment in **Corbett Vs Corbett (1970) 2 All ER 33** wherein Court in England was concerned with conversion from male to female transsexual. The Court in the said case had held that the gender will be decided on the basis of biological sex at the time of birth. European Court of Human Rights in **Christine Goodwin Vs United Kingdom (Application No 28957/95)** and **Van Kuck Vs Germany (Application No. 35968/97)** has recognized rights of transgender persons.

The Supreme Court held that rights of transsexual persons who have undergone SRS, the test to be applied is not the "Biological Test" but the "Psychological Test" because psychological factor and thinking of transsexual has to be given primacy than binary notion of gender of that person.

The Court also noted that many countries have passed legislations against discrimination on the ground of gender identity and sexual orientation.

Indian Scenario

The Supreme Court noted that several types of Hijras i.e. Hijras, Eunuchs, Aravanis and Thirunangi, Kothi, Jogtas and Jogappas, Shiv Shakthis exist in India. Transgender people face several discrimination in India. The Court noted that HIV and sexually transmitted diseases are increasing in transgender community.

The Supreme Court noted India lacks legislations in respect of persons belonging to transgender community. The Court noted that International Conventions including Yogyakarta principles are not inconsistent with the various Fundamental Rights guaranteed under the Indian Constitution, must be recognized and followed.

The Court held that Article 14 does not restrict "person" to male and female only. Hijra/Transgenders are also covered under expression "person" and has protection of Article 14. Prohibition of discrimination on ground of "sex" under Article 15 and 16 also includes prohibition of discrimination on the ground of gender identity. State is also liable to grant employment opportunities to transgender community under Article 16 (4).

The Supreme Court held that Article 19 (1) (a) includes one's right to expression of his self-identified gender. Self-identified gender can be expressed through dress, words, action or behavior or any other form. No restriction can be placed on one's personal appearance or choice of dressing.

The Supreme Court noted that right to dignity is inherent in Article 21. Legal identity is part of right to dignity and freedom guaranteed under Constitution of India. The Supreme Court held that self-determination of gender is an integral part of personal autonomy and self-expression and falls within the realm of personal liberty guaranteed under Article 21.

The Supreme Court issued various directions for safeguarding the interests of transgenders. The Court declared transgenders as third gender. Transgender persons' right to self-determine their gender was also recognized. Union and State Governments were also directed to treat them as socially and educationally backward class of citizens. The Supreme Court also directed for creation of medical facilities and welfare schemes of transgender persons.

SUPRIYO @ SUPRIYA CHAKRABORTY VS UNION OF INDIA

The Supreme Court in **Supriyo @ Supriyo Chakraborty Vs Union of India, (2023 SCC OnLine SC 1348)** held that right to marry is not a Fundamental Right recognized by Constitution of India.

Case Title : Supriyo @ Supriyo Chakraborty Vs Union of India
Date of Judgment : 17.10.2023
Bench : Chief Justice Dr Dhananjaya Y Chandrachud, Justice Sanjay Kishan Kaul, Justice S. Ravindra Bhat, Justice Hima Kohli, Justice P.S. Narasimha

FACTS OF THE CASE

Petitioners were members of LBGTQIA + (Queer) community. The petitioner claimed that they are aggrieved of the fact that State discriminates against the queer community by impliedly excluding them from institution of marriage. The Petitioners sought legal recognition of their relationship with partner in form of marriage.

It was contended by the Petitioners that Special Marriage Act and Foreign Marriage Act are violative of Article 14, 15, 19, 21 and 25 of the Constitution so far as they do not provide for the solemnization of marriage between same-sex, gender non-conforming or LGBTQ couples.

FINDINGS OF THE SUPREME COURT

The Supreme Court rejected the argument that it does not have power to decide the issue and such a decision can only be arrived at through a process that reflects electoral will. The Supreme Court rejected the argument and held that its power to do justice is not limited either by the manner in which Article 32 has been constructed or by any part of the Constitution. It is amply clear form both the plain meaning of Article 32 as well as the Constituent

Assembly debates it has the power to issue directions, orders, or writs for the enforcement of the rights incorporated in Part III of the Constitution.

The Supreme Court observed that queerness is a natural phenomenon which is known to India from ancient times. Queerness is not urban or elite.

The Supreme Court observed that there is no universal concept of marriage. Marriage is understood differently in law, religion and culture. The concept of marriage is not static and gone through sea change over time. The institution of marriage is built and re-built by societies, communities, and individuals. The only facet of marriage which is constant across religion, community, caste and region is that the couple is a legally binding relation-ship – one which recognizes an emotional bond of togetherness, loyalty and commitment – that is recognized by the law.

No Fundamental Right to marry

The Supreme Court observed that the Constitution does not expressly rec-ognize a Fundamental Right to marry. Yet it cannot be gainsaid that many of our constitutional value, including the right to life and liberty may com-prehend the values which a marital relationship entails. They may at the very least entail respect for the choice of a person whether and when to enter upon marriage and the right of chose a marital partner.

Constitutionality of Special Marriage Act, 1954

The Supreme Court held that it cannot strike down constitutional validity of Special Marriage Act, 1954 or read down words due to constitutional limitations. It cannot read words into the provisions of the Special Marriage Act, 1854 and provisions of other allied laws because that would amount to judicial legislations. The Court in the exercise of the power of judicial review must steer clear of matters, particularly those impinging on policy which fall in the legislative domain.

Rights of Queer Couples

The Supreme Court held that freedom of all persons including queer couples to enter into a union is protected by Part III of the Constitution. The failure of the State to recognize the bouquet of entitlements which flow from a union would result in a disparate impact on queer couples who cannot marry under the current legal regime. The state has an obligation to recognize such unions and grant them benefit under law.

The Supreme Court held that in Article 15 (1), the word "sex" must be read to include "sexual orientation" not only because of the causal relationship between homophobia and sexism but also because the word "sex" is used as a marker of identity which cannot be read independent of the social and historical context.

The Supreme Court held that the right to enter into union cannot be restricted based on sexual orientation. Such a restriction will be violative of Article 15. This freedom is available to all persons regardless of gender identity or sexual orientation.

Validity of Regulation 5 (3) of Adoption Regulations, 2022

The Supreme court held that unmarried couples (including queer couples) can jointly adopt a child. Regulation 5 (3) of the Adoption Regulations is ultra vires the Juvenile Justice (Care and Protection) Act, 2016, Article 14 and 15. Regulation 5 (3) is read down to exclude the word "marital". The reference to a "couple" is Regulation 5 includes both married and unmarried couples as well as queer couples.

The Supreme Court also directed Union Government, State Government and UT to take steps to ensure that queer community is not discriminated. The Supreme Court also issued several directions to police authorities to protect queer persons from harassment. The Supreme Court also directed the Committee to be formed under chairmanship of Cabinet Secretary to define entitlements of queer couples.

SUCHITA SRIVASTAVA VS CHANDIGARH ADMINISTRATION

The Supreme Court in **Suchita Srivastava Vs. Chandigarh Administration, (2009) 13 SCR 989** held that a woman's right to make reproductive choices is also a dimension of "personal liberty" as understood under Article 21 of the Constitution of India.

Case Title : **Suchita Srivastava Vs. Chandigarh Administration (2009) 13 SCR 989**

Date of Judgment : 28.08.2009

Bench : Chief Justice K.G. Balakrishnan, Justice B.S. Chauhan, Justice P. Sathasivam, Chief Justice K.G. Balakrishnan

FACTS OF THE CASE

The victim had become pregnant as a result of rape committed on her which she was inmate at a government run welfare institution located at Chandigarh. The Chandigarh administration approached High Court seeking approval for termination of pregnancy on the ground that she was mentally retarded as well as an orphan. High Court appointed an expert body for inquiry into the facts. On 17.07.2009, the High Court directed for termination of pregnancy in spite of Expert Body's findings that the victim had expressed her willingness to bear a child.

THE FINDINGS OF THE SUPREME COURT

The Supreme Court considered two aspects – Firstly, whether it was correct for the High Court to direct termination of pregnancy without consent of the woman ? and Secondly, whether a woman is unable to take an informed decision what is appropriate standard for *parens patriae* jurisdiction of a Court ?

The Supreme Court disagreed with the view of the High Court as the victim had clearly expressed her willingness to bear the child. Her reproductive choice should be respected in spite of other factors such as the lack of understanding of the sexual act as well as apprehensions about her capacity to carry the pregnancy to its full term and the assumption of maternal responsibilities thereafter. The supreme noted that Section 3 of the Medical Termination of Pregnancy Act, 1971 provides that consent has to be taken even from mentally retarded woman.

The Supreme Court observed that a woman's right to make reproductive choices is also a dimension of "personal liberty" as understood under Article 21 of the Constitution of India. It is important to recognize that reproductive choices can be exercised to procreate as well to abstain from procreating. The crucial consideration is that a woman's right to privacy, dignity and bodily integrity should be respected. This means that there should be no restriction whatsoever on the exercise of reproductive choices such as a woman's right to refuse participation in sexual activity or alternatively the insistence on use of contraceptive methods. Furthermore, women are also free to choose birth control methods such as undergoing sterilization procedures. Taken to their logical conclusion, reproductive rights include a woman's entitlement to carry a pregnancy to its full term, to give birth and to subsequently raise children.

The Supreme Court observed that however there is also compelling state interest in protecting life of the prospective child. Therefore, the termination of pregnancy is only permitted when the conditions specified in the applicable statute have been fulfilled. Hence provisions of MTP Act can also be said to be reasonable restrictions on exercise of reproductive choices.

The Supreme Court noted that the woman in question is a major. She is only mentally retarded not mentally ill.

The Supreme Court observed that High Court had acted in its *parens patriae* jurisdiction. Traditionally this jurisdiction has been invoked in cases of minors and persons who are unable to take informed choices. Courts in other jurisdictions have developed "best interest test " and "substituted judgment test" in making decision on behalf of mentally retarded persons.

The Court concluded that the victim's pregnancy cannot be terminated without her consent.

JUSTICE K. S. PUTTASWAMY VS UNION OF INDIA (PRIVACY JUDGMENT)

The Supreme Court in **Justice K. Puttaswamy Vs Union of India, (2017) 10 S.C.R. 569** held that Right to Privacy is a Fundamental Right under Article 21 of the Constitution of India.

Case Title : Justice K. Puttaswamy Vs Union of India
Date of Judgment : 24.08.2017
Bench : Chief Justice Jagdish Singh Khehar, Justice S Abdul Nazeer, Justice Sanjay Kishan Kaul, Justice D Y Chandrachud, Justice Abhay Manohar Sapre, Justice Rohinton Fali Nariman, Justice R K Agrawal, Justice S A Bobde, Justice J Chelameswar

FACTS OF THE CASE

In **M P Sharma Vs Satish Chandra 1954 AIR 300** and **Kharak Singh Vs State of U.P. 1963 AIR 1295** right to privacy has not been held to be a Fundamental Rights In **Gobind vs State of Madhya Pradesh 1975 AIR 1378** and **R. Rajagopal Vs. State of Tamilnadu 1994 SCC (6) 632** contrary views have been expressed. In light of conflicting judgments, Constitution Bench consisting of nine judges determined whether Right to Privacy is fundamental right.

FINDINGS OF THE SUPREME COURT

The Supreme Court in **A K Gopalan Vs State of Madras AIR (1950) SC 27** has taken a narrow view of Right to Life and Personal Liberty. The Supreme Court held in the said case that personal liberty meant absence of bodily restraint. If a person is detained as per procedure established by law such detention cannot be challenged. The Supreme Court also held in this case that Fundamental Rights vested in different articles are distinct.

The view was further corroborated in **Shivakant Shukla Vs ADM Jabalpur AIR 1976 SC 1207** wherein the Supreme Court held that detentions during proclamation of emergency was legal and cannot challenged.

In **R C Cooper Vs Union of India (1970) AIR 564,** the Supreme Court held that Fundamental Rights vested under different articles are not distinct. They are interdependent.

Maneka Gandhi Vs Union of India (1978) AIR 597 was a landmark judgment wherein the Supreme Court held that not only there should be procedure established by law but such procedure should also be just, fair and reasonable.

Evolution of Right to Privacy

Right to Privacy has not been explicitly mentioned under the Indian Constitution as is the case with the Constitution of the United States.

In **M P Sharma Vs Satish Chandra 1954 AIR 300,** the Supreme Court was concerned with whether search by police is in violation of Article 20 (3) of the Constitution. The Supreme Court observed that Right to Privacy has not been granted under Indian Constitution as is the case in the Constitution of USA.

In **Kharak Singh Vs State of U.P. 1963 AIR 1295,** extensive police surveillance including midnight knocks under UP Police regulations were challenged before the Supreme Court. The Supreme Court held that freedom to move through territory of India under Article 19 (1) (f) is not infringed by midnight knock as his locomotion is not impeded or prejudiced in any manner. The Supreme Court also observed that Right to Privacy is not guaranteed right under the Constitution of India.

In **Gobind vs State of Madhya Pradesh 1975 AIR 1378** the Supreme Court held that even if there is right of privacy the same will not be absolute and subject to regulations made by state.

In **R. Rajagopal Vs. State of Tamilnadu 1994 SCC (6) 632** the Supreme Court held that publication about one's life without consent is in violation of Right to Privacy.

In **State of Maharastra Vs Madhukar Narayan Mardikar AIR 1991 SC 207** the Supreme Court held that every woman has right to privacy.

The Supreme Court held that Right to Privacy is a constitutional protected right mainly under Article 21 of the Constitution. Privacy is constitutional core of Human Dignity. Privacy includes preservation of personal intimacies, sanctity of family life, marriage, procreation, the home and sexual orientation. Privacy also connotes right to be left alone. Privacy safeguards individual autonomy and choices. Privacy protects heterogeneity and recognizes the diversity and plurality of culture. Privacy is not lost when a person enters a public space.

Like other Fundamental Rights, Right to Privacy is not absolute right. Restrictions can be imposed by making law which stipulates a procedure which is just, fair and reasonable.

Right to Privacy has both negative and positive contents. The negative contents prohibit intrusion in Right to Privacy. The positive contents impose obligation to take measures to protect right to privacy.

The Supreme Court in **Navtej Johar Vs Union of India AIR 2018 SC4321** relied on Puttaswamy while decriminalizing consensual sex among adults including homosexual sex.

The Supreme Court in **Indian Young Lawyers Association Vs State of Kerala AIR 2018 SC 243** also relied on Puttaswamy while holding that exclusion of women from visiting temple is contrary to constitutional values.

JUSTICE K. S. PUTTASWAMY (RETD.) VS UNION OF INDIA (AADHAAR JUDGMENT)

The Supreme Court with 4: 1 majority in Justice **K. S. Puttaswamy (Retd.) Vs. Union of India, (2018) 8 SCR 1 (Aadhaar Judgment)** held that Aadhaar Act does not create a surveillance state or violate Right to Privacy.

Case Title : Justice K. S. Puttaswamy (Retd.) Vs. Union of India
Date of Judgment : 26.09.2018
Bench : Chief Justice Dipak Misra, Justice A.K. Sikri, Justice A.M. Khanwilkar, Justice D.Y. Chandrachud, Justice Ashok Bhushan

FACTS OF THE CASE

Aadhaar was conceptualized in 2006. By September, 2010 enrolment process for Aadhaar started with nationwide launch. UAIDI has been established initially vide administrative order primarily to lay down policy for implementation of Unique Identification Scheme. Subsequently, the Aadhaar (Targeted Delivery of Financial and other Subsidies, Benefits and Services) Act, 2016 was passed. Several Writ Petitions had been filed in the Supreme Court challenging the vires of the Aadhaar Act including that of Justice Puttaswamy (Retd).

FINDINGS OF THE SUPREME COURT

(i) Whether the Aadhaar Project creates or has tendency to create surveillance state and thus it is unconstitutional ?

The Supreme Court held that Aadhar project does not create a surveillance state. During enrollment minimum biometric data i.e. iris and fingerprint is captured. The authority does not collect purpose, location or detail of the transaction. The information collected remain in silos. There is no merging of silos. There are sufficient authentication security measures.

The Supreme Court directed that authentication records are not to be kept for more than six months. An individual whose data is to be released has to be afforded an opportunity of hearing. Section 33 (2) of the Act was struck down. Section 57 of the Aadhar Act which enabled body corporate and individual to seek authentication was also struck down.

(ii) Whether Aadhaar Act violates right to privacy and is unconstitutional on this ground ?

The Supreme Court held that all matters pertaining to individual do not form part of right to privacy. Only those matters over which there would be reasonable expectation of privacy are protected under Article 21.

Aadhaar Scheme is backed by statute. The objective of the Act is to ensure social benefit for deserving community. Aadhaar Act is aimed at offering subsidies and benefits to marginalized section of society. This is an aspect of social justice which is an obligation under Directive Principles of State Policy under Part IV of the Constitution.

The Court observed that Aadhaar Act also meets the test of proportionality. The Court was of the view that Aadhaar Act balances the right to privacy of individuals with that of social justice to marginalized sections of society.

The Court also gave directions to the effect that no deserving person will be denied the benefit of scheme on failure of authentication. Benefits and services under Section 7 are those which have colour of some kind of subsidies. CBSE, NEET, UGC, JEE etc can not make Aadhaar mandatory.

(iii) Whether Children can be brought within the sweep of Section 7 and 8 of the Aadhar Act ?

The Supreme Court held that children can be brought within the sweep of Section 7 and 8 with consent of Parents. On attaining majority children will have option to exit from Aadhar Project. In case of admissions to school Aadhaar will not be compulsory as it is neither a service not a subsidy.

(iv) Whether Aadhar Bill could have been passed as Money Bill ?

The Supreme Court held that Aadhaar Bill has been validly passed as Money Bill as it has several elements of money bill. It makes receipt of subsidy, benefit or service subject to establishing identity by the process of authentication under Aadhaar or furnish proof of Aadhaar etc. Such subsidy, benefit or service has to be paid from consolidated fund of India. Section 7 is core provision of Aadhar Act and it satisfies conditions of Article 110.

(v) Whether Section 139 AA of the Income Tax Act, 1961 is violative of Right to Privacy and therefore unconstitutional ?

The Supreme Court applying the tests (i) the existence of law (ii) a legitimate state interest and (iii) test of proportionality held that Section 139 AA is not unconstitutional.

(vi) Whether Rule 9 of the Prevention of Money Laundering (Maintenance of Records) Rules, 2005 and notifications issued thereunder for linking of Aadhaar with Bank Account is unconstitutional ?

The Supreme Court held that the provision in present form does not pass the proportionality test and is violative of Right to Privacy, which extends to banking details of a person. The provision stipulates that in case of non-linking of Aadhar with Bank Account, holder of the Bank Account will not be able to operate the Bank Account, which amounts to deprivation of property.

(vi) Whether circular dated March 23, 2017 issued by the Department of Telecommunications mandating linking of mobile with Aadhaar is illegal and unconstitutional ?

The Supreme Court held the circular unconstitutional as it was not backed by any law.

HUSSAINARA KHATOON VS HOME SECRETARY, STATE OF BIHAR

The Supreme Court in **Hussainara Khatoon Vs State of Bihar (1979) SCR 169** held that right to speedy trial is implicit under Article 21 of the Constitution.

Case Title : Hussainara Khatoon Vs State of Bihar
Date of Judgment : 09.03.1979
Bench : Justice P.N. Bhagwati, Justice O. Chinnappa Reddy

FACTS OF THE CASE

Kapila Hingorani, a public interest lawyer who is also known as "mother of Public Interest Litigation", filed a Petition under Article 32 of the Constitution before the Supreme Court in respect of precarious conditions of pre-trial prisoners in Bihar. Six prisoners had signed the Petition, one of them was Hussainara Khatoon.

FINDINGS OF THE SUPREME COURT

Supreme Court noticed that large number of children, men and women were in jail for years and years awaiting trial in courts of law. The offences with which some of them are charged were trivial, which even proved, would not warrant punishment for more than a few months, perhaps for a year or two and yet these unfortunate forgotten specimens of humanity were in jail, deprived of their freedom, for periods ranging from three to ten years without even as much as their trial having commenced. Law has become an instrument of injustice to these prisoners.

The Supreme Court noted that there can be little doubt after the dynamic interpretation placed by this Court on Article 21 in **Maneka Gandhi Vs Union of India (1978) AIR 597** that a procedure which keeps such a large number of people behind bars without trial so long cannot possibly be regarded as reasonable, just and fair so as to be in conformity with the requirement of that Article.

The Supreme Court noted that one of the reasons of pre-trail detention is unsatisfactory bail system which proceed on erroneous assumption that risk of monetary loss is only deterrent from fleeing from justice. Code of Criminal Procedure requires execution of personal bond having monetary implications. If this was not enough the courts mechanically and as a matter of course insist that the accused should produce sureties who will stand bail for him and these sureties must again establish their solvency to be able to pay the amount of the bail in case the accused fails to appear to answer the charge. It is here that the poor find our legal and judicial system oppressive and heavily weighted against them and a feeling of frustration and despair occurs upon them as they find that they are unequal in comparison to non-poor.

The Supreme Court observed that it is high time that Parliament should realise that risk of monetary loss is not the only deterrent against fleeing from justice. If the Court is of the opinion that the accused has deep roots in society, it should release the accused on bail.

The Supreme Court noted that other infirmity in the legal system is delay in disposal of cases. Trial does not even commence for many years.

Speedy trail is of the essence of criminal justice system. In the USA, speedy trial is a constitutionally guaranteed right. Sixth amendment of the USA Constitution provides that in criminal prosecutions, the accused shall enjoy the right to speedy and pubic trial. The Supreme Court observed that under our constitution speedy trial, although not specifically enumerated under Fundamental Right, is implicit under broad sweep and content of Article 21. No procedure which does not ensure a reasonable quick trial can be regarded as reasonable, fair or just and it would fall foul of Article 21. There can be no doubt that speedy trail is an integral and essential part of the Fundamental Right to life and liberty enshrined in Article 21.

M. H. HOSKOT VS STATE OF MAHARASHTRA

The Supreme Court in **M. H. Hoskot Vs. State of Maharashtra (1978)AIR 1548** held that indigent prisoners have to be provided free services of lawyers for filing appeal.

Case Title : M. H. Hoskot Vs. State of Maharashtra (1978)AIR 1548
Date of Decision : 17.08.1978
Bench : Justice V.R. Krishna Iyer, Justice D.A. Desai, Justice O. Chinnappa Reddy

FACTS OF THE CASE

Dr. Hoskot was a reader in Saurashtra University. Dr. Hoskot approached Dabholkar, a block maker of Bombay and placed an order to prepare an embossing seal in the name of Karnataka University, Dharwar and forged a letter of authority purporting to have been signed by the personal assistant to the Vice-chancellor of the said University authorizing him to get the seal made. Dabholkar had doubts and gave information to police. The Session Court convicted Dr. Hoskot under Section 417 R/w 511 IPC, Section 467 IPC, Section 468 IPC, and Section 471 R/w 467 IPC but awarded soft sentence of simple imprisonment till rising of the court and some fine. High Court enhanced the sentence to rigorous imprisonment of three years.

High Court judgment was pronounced in 1973 but the SLP before the Supreme Court was filed in 1978. Petitioner underwent full time of imprisonment during this period. As per the Petitioner delay was on account of non-service of copy of judgment of the High Court.

FINDINGS OF THE SURPEME COURT

The Supreme Court refused to entertain the Special Leave Petition on merit in light of concurrent finding of Sessions Court and the High Court, but the Supreme Court passed observation on two aspects.

The Supreme Court observed that the trial judge has confused between correctional approach to prison treatment and nominal punishment verging on decriminalization of serious social offences. The first is basic and the second is pathetic. Court which ignores the grave injury to society implicit in economic crimes by the upper-berth "mafia" ill serves social justice. Soft sentencing justice is gross injustice where many innocents are the potential victims. Coddling is not correctional any more than torture is deterrent.

The Supreme Court also dealt with legal aid to prisoners. The Supreme Court observed that most prisoners in this country belongs to the lower, illiterate bracket, suffer silent deprivation of liberty caused by unreasonableness, arbitrariness and unfair procedures behind the "stone walls" and "iron bars".

The Supreme Court observed the "procedure" mentioned in the Article 21 means fair not formal procedure. One component of fair procedure is natural justice. A first appeal from the Sessions Court to the High Court as provided in the Criminal Procedure Code, manifests this value upheld in Article 21. An effective right to appeal has two components – (i) service of a copy of the judgment to the prisoner in time to file an appeal and (ii) provision of free legal services to a prisoner who is indigent or otherwise disabled form securing legal assistance where the ends of justice call for such service.

The Supreme Court noted that free legal services to the needy is part of English criminal justice system. In USA, strengthened by the Powell, Gideon, and Hamlin cases, a counsel for the accused in the more serious class of classes which threaten a person with imprisonment is regarded as an essential component of the administration of criminal justice and as part of procedure fair-play.

The Supreme Court held that if a prisoner sentenced to imprisonment, is virtually unable to exercise his constitutional and statutory right of appeal, inclusive of special leave to appeal for want of legal assistance, there is implicit in the Court under Article 142, R/w Article 21 and 39A of the Constitution, power to assign counsel for such imprisoned individual for doing complete justice.

The Supreme Court directed that a free transcript of judgment while sentencing a person to prison term shall be delivered to the convict. If such order is delivered to jail authorities, order shall be delivered to the convict against written acknowledgement. Where prisoner wants to file appeal or revision, every facility for exercise of that right shall be made available by the Jail Administration. If prisoner is disabled to engage a counsel due to indigence or other reasons, Court shall assign competent counsel. State shall pay to the counsel tendering legal aid as fixed by the Court.

PREM SHANKAR SHUKLA VS DELHI ADMINISTRATION

The Supreme Court in **Prem Shankar Shukla Vs Delhi Administration, 1980 SCR (3) 855** held that handcuffing a prisoner during transit between the prison house and court house violates provisions of Article 14,19 and 21.

Case Title : Prem Shankar Shukla Vs Delhi Administration
Date of Judgment : 29.04.1980
Bench : Justice V.R. Krishna Iyer, Justice R.S. Pathak, Justice O. Chinnappa Reddy

FACTS OF THE CASE

Prem Shankar Shukla, a prisoner in Tihar jail, sent a telegram to a judge of the Supreme Court protesting against being handcuffed while being taken from prison to Delhi Courts, back and forth, for trial of their cases. The Supreme Court initiated *habeas corpus* proceedings on telegram of Prem Shankar Shukla.

He had approached earlier Delhi High Court for relief which had been dismissed. Finally, he approached the Supreme Court through telegram.

FINDINGS OF THE SUPREME COURT

The Supreme Court observed that to manacle a man is more than to mortify him. It is to dehumanize him and therefore to violate his very personhood, too often using the mask of "dangerous" and "security". It violates provisions of Article 14, 19 and 21.

The Supreme Court noted that even a prisoner is a person, not an animal and that an undertrial prisoner *a fortiori* so. Article 5 of the Universal Declaration of Human Rights, 1948 provides that no one shall be subjected to torture or to cruel, inhuman or degrading treatment or punishment. Article 10 of International Covenant on Civil and Political Rights provides that all persons deprived of their liberty shall be treated with humanity and with respect for the inherent dignity of the human person.

The Petitioner contended that his social status, family background and academic qualifications warrant his being treated as better class prisoner and he should not be handcuffed.

The Supreme Court observed that handcuff law must meet the demands of Article 14, 19 and 21. Handcuffing is prima-facie inhuman and 'therefore' unreasonable, is over harsh and at the first flush arbitrary. The competing claims of securing the prisoner from fleeing and protecting the personality from barbarity have to be harmonized.

The Supreme Court observed that social and economic importance cannot be basis for classifying prisoners for purposes of handcuffs. The Supreme Court held it arbitrary and irrational to classify prisoners for purposes of handcuffs into better class and ordinary class. No one can be fettered in any form based on superior class differentia as the law treats them equally.

The Supreme Court observed that the only circumstance which validates incapacitation by irons- an extreme measure- is that otherwise there is no other reasonable way of preventing escape, in the given circumstances.

The Supreme Court declared that the rule regarding a prisoner in transit between prison house and court house is freedom from handcuffs except the exceptional circumstances. The Supreme Court mandated the judicial officer before whom the prisoner is produced to interrogate the prisoner, as a rule, whether he has been subjected to handcuffs or other "iron" treatment and if has been, the official concerned shall be asked to explain the action forthwith in the light of this judgment.

RUDUL SAH VS STATE OF BIHAR

The Supreme Court in **Rudul Sah Vs State of Bihar** 983 SCR (3) 508 held that compensation can be granted to aggrieved persons under Article 32 against violation of Fundamental Rights.

Case Title : Rudul Sah Vs State of Bihar
Date of Judgment : 01.08.1983
Bench : Chief Justice Y.V. Chandrachud, Justice Amarendra Nath Sen, Justice Ranganath Misra

FACTS OF THE CASE

The Petitioner was acquitted by Court of Sessions, Muzaffarpur, Bihar on 3rd June, 1968, but he was released from jail after more than 14 years on October 16, 1982. The Petitioner filed *habeas corpus* petition before the Supreme Court wherein he prayed *inter alia* for his release and compensation.

FINDINGS OF THE SURPEME COURT

The Supreme Court sought explanation from Government of Bihar for keeping the petitioner in jail for more than 14 years after acquittal. The Government stated that the Petitioner was insane and on account of the same he was not released, but no proper evidence regarding the insanity was tendered.

The Supreme Court noted that Article 32 confers power on the Supreme Court to issue directions or orders or writs, including writs in nature of habeas corpus, mandamus, prohibition, quo warranto and certiorari, whichever may be appropriate, for the enforcement of any of the rights conferred by Part III. The right to move the Supreme Court by appropriate proceedings for the enforcement of the rights conferred by Part III is "guaranteed", that is to say, the right to move the Supreme Court under Article 32 for the enforcement of any of the rights conferred by Part III of the Constitution is itself a fundamental right.

The Supreme Court observed that Article 32 cannot be used as a substitute for the enforcement of rights and obligations which can be enforced efficaciously through civil and criminal courts. A money claim has to be agitated before a court of lowest grade competent to try it. The issue before the Supreme Court was whether it can award compensation under Article 32 of the Constitution consequential upon deprivation of Fundamental Rights.

The Supreme Court observed that Article 21 which guarantees the right to life and liberty will be denuded of its significant content if the power of this Court were limited to passing orders to release from illegal detention. One of the telling ways in which the violation of that right can reasonably be prevented and due compliance with the mandate of Article 21 secured, is to mulct its violators in the payment of monetary compensation. Administrative sclerosis leading to flagrant infringements of fundamental rights cannot be corrected by any other method open to the judiciary to adopt. The right to compensation is some palliative for the unlawful acts of instrumentalities which act in the name of public interest and which present for their protection the powers of the State as a shield. If civilization is not to perish in this country as it has perished in some others too well-known to suffer mention, it is necessary to educate ourselves into accepting that, respect for the rights of individuals is the true bastion of democracy. Therefore, the State must repair the damage done by its officers to the petitioner's rights.

The Supreme Court directed for payment of compensation of Rs. 30,000/- in addition of Rs. 5,000/- already paid.

SHEELA BARSE VS STATE OF MAHARASTRA

The Supreme Court in **Sheela Barse Vs. State of Maharashtra 1983 SCR (2) 337** has held that legal aid must be made available to prisoners in jail whether they are under-trial or convicted persons.

Case Title : Sheela Barse Vs. State of Maharashtra
Date of Judgment : 15.02.1983
Bench : Justice P.N. Bhagwati, Justice R.S. Pathak, Justice Amarendra Nath Sen

FACTS OF THE CASE

Sheela Barse, a journalist, sent a letter to the Supreme Court complaining about the custodial violence to women in police lock ups of Bombay. She had interviewed 15 women prisoners in the Bombay Central Jail and five out of fifteen women had said that they had been assaulted in the police lock up. The Supreme Court admitted the said letter as Writ Petition and issued notice to concerned parties. The Supreme Court also directed Dr. (Miss) A. R. Desai, Director of College of Social Work, Nirmala Niketan, Bombay to visit Bombay Central Jail and submit report to the Supreme Court.

FINDINGS OF THE SURPEME COURT

Supreme Court noted that legal assistance to a poor or indigent accused who is arrested and put in jeopardy of his life or personal liberty is a constitutional imperative mandated not only by Article 39A but also by Articles 14 and 21 of the Constitution. It is absolutely essential that legal assistance must be made available to prisoners in jails whether they be under-trail or convicted prisoners.

The Supreme Court observed that there were no adequate arrangements in Bombay Central Jail for legal assistance for women prisoners. The Supreme Court issued several directions for legal assistance to prisoners. The Supreme

Court directed *inter alia* for - (i) sending a list of all under- trial prisoners to Legal Aid Committee of the District showing separately male prisoners and female prisoners, (ii) to provide facilities to lawyers to enter the jail and interview prisoners, (iii) to furnish to the lawyers all relevant information (iv) to put up notices at prominent places of jail regarding visit of lawyers nominated by Legal Aid Committee

The Supreme Court also issued several directions for protection of women in police lock up in Maharashtra. The Supreme Court directed inter alia – (i) four or five lock up in good localities should be selected only for female suspects, (ii) Female suspects should not be detained where male suspects have also been detained, (iii) Interrogation of female suspects should be done in presence of female officers/constables, (iv) A person arrested should be informed about ground of arrest and right of such person to apply for bail (v) Police will give intimation of arrest of a person to nearest Legal Aid Committee. (vi) A lady judge to be appointed for periodic inspection of lock up (vii)Magistrate before whom such arrested person is produced shall inquire whether there has been any incidence of mal-treatment or torture in police custody.

D. K. BASU VS STATE OF WEST BENGAL

The Supreme Court in one of its landmark judgments **D. K. Basu Vs State of West Bengal, 1996 (Supp) 10 SCR284** issued guidelines to be followed by police officer while making an arrest. The Supreme court also held that State is vicariously liable to pay compensation in cases of wrongful arrest.

Case Title : D. K. Basu Vs State of West Bengal
Date of Judgment : 01.08.1997
Bench : Justice A. S. Anand, Justice Kuldip Singh

FACTS OF THE CASE

Legal Aid Services, an NGO registered under Society Registration Act, addressed a letter regarding custodial deaths in State of West Bengal. The same was treated as Writ Petition by the Supreme Court of India. Notices were issued to all the states and also Law Commission of India.

FINDINGS OF THE SUPREME COURT

The Supreme Court noted that growing cases of custodial violence is a matter of concern. It is committed by persons who are protectors of the citizens. It is committed within four walls of police station or lock up where the victim is totally helpless.

Torture has not been defined under the Constitution or under other penal laws. Torture is essentially and instrument to impose the will of the strong on the weak. Torture is a naked violation of human dignity and degradation which destroys individual personality

The Supreme Court noted that Custodial Violence is concern of global dimension. Article 5 of the Universal Declaration of Human Rights, 1948 states that no one will be subjected to torture or to cruel, inhuman or degrading treatment or punishment.

The Court noted that in England torture was resorted to get information regarding crime, the accomplices, case property and confessions. But with development of common law such inhuman practices have been done away with. Right to life and personal liberty under Article 21 has been held to include right to live with human dignity thus it will also include within itself a guarantee against torture. The Court noted that Article 20 and 22 also provide certain rights to arrested persons. The Court noted that Code of Criminal Procedures, 1973 also provides several safeguards in cases of arrest.

The Supreme Court observed that Police has right to arrest criminals and interrogate him during investigation but Police can not use third degree or torture in custody. Relevant para is as under :

The Court observed that freedom of individual has to yield to security of state. The right to interrogate detenus, arrestees or culprits in interest of the nation must take precedence over an individual's right to personal liberty. But actions of the State have to be just, fair and reasonable. Using any form of torture for extracting information would not be just, fair and reasonable and will offence Article 21. A crime suspect can not be tortured, or subjected to third degree methods or eliminated with a view to elicit information, extract information or derive knowledge about accomplices, weapons etc.

Directions in respect of Arrest

The Supreme Court issued following directions to be followed by police while making an arrest till legal provisions are made.

(1) Police personnel carrying out arrest or interrogation has to bear clear and visible identification and name tags with designation. The particulars of police personnel handling interrogation have to be recorded in register.

(2) Memo of arrest has to be made at the time of arrest. Such memo of arrest has to be attested by a family member of arrestee or a respectable person of locality. It has to be countersigned by arrestee and date and time of arrest has to be provided.

(3) Arrested person has right to inform about his arrest to one of his family members or a friend or any other person known to him

(4) Time, place of arrest and venue of custody has to be notified by the police where next friend or relative of arrestee resides outside the district or

town through legal aid organization and police station of the area concerned telegraphically

(5) The person arrested has to be informed about his right to inform someone about his arrest or detention as soon as he is arrested or detained.

(6) An entry has to be made in diary at the place of the detention regarding arrest and details of the person who has been informed have also to be entered into dairy. Particulars of police officials having custody have also to be entered into dairy.

(7) The Arrestee should be examined and any major or minor injury should be recorded. The Inspection Memo should be signed by arrestee as well as police officer.

(8) The arrestee should be subjected to medical examination every 48 hours during his detention in custody.

(9) Copies of all documents including Memo of Arrest has to be sent to Magistrate

(10) The arrestee may be permitted to meet his lawyer during interrogation

(11) Police Control room should be provided in every district and state headquarters and information regarding arrest and place of custody of arrestee has to be communicated to within 12 hours. Information regarding these have to be displayed at police control room.

Failure to follow these procedures will make liable the responsible personnel for departmental proceedings as well as contempt proceedings. Such contempt proceedings can be initiated before jurisdictional High Court.

Liability of State for compensation

The court noted that a mere declaration of invalidity of a wrongful arrest is not sufficient. Section 220 of IPC provides for punishment to an officer or authority who keeps a person in confinement with a corrupt or malicious motive. Section 330 and 331 of IPC provides for punishment for those who inflict injury or grievous hurt to extort confession or information in regard to commission of an offence. These statutory provisions are not sufficient.

The Supreme Court held that monetary and pecuniary compensation is an appropriate remedy for established infringement of Fundamental Rights to life by public servants and State is vicariously liable for the acts of the Public Servants. The claim of the citizen is based on principle of strict liability to which the defense of sovereign immunity is not available. In assessment of compensation, the emphasis has to be on compensatory and not on punitive element. The award of such compensation is without prejudice to other remedies under law.

MISS MOHINI JAIN VS STATE OF KARNATAKA

The Supreme Court held in **Miss Mohini Jain Vs. State of Karnataka, (1992) 3 SCR 658** that right to education flows directly from right to life under Article 21 of the Constitution. The right to life and the dignity of an individual cannot be assured unless it is accompanied by the right to education.

Case Title : Miss Mohini Jain Vs. State of Karnataka
Date of Judgment : 30.07.1992
Bench : Justice Kuldip Singh, Justice R. M. Sahai

FACTS OF THE CASE

Karnataka State Legislature enacted the Karnataka Educational Institutions (Prohibition of Capitation Fee) Act, 1984 with the object of eliminating the practice of collecting capitation fee for admitting students into educational institutions. The Karnataka Government issued notification under Section 5 (1) of the Act thereby fixing the tuition fee, other fees and deposits to be charged from the students by the Private Medical Colleges in the State.

Miss Mohini Jain was denied admission to Sri Siddhartha Medical College, Tumkur due to exorbitant tuition fee and capitation fee. Miss Mohini Jain filed Petition under Article 32 of the Constitution challenging the notification issued by Karnataka Government permitting the Private Medical Colleges in State of Karnataka to charge exorbitant tuition fee from students other than those admitted to government seats.

FINDINGS OF THE SUPREME COURT

The Supreme Court considered whether right to education is a Fundamental Right. The Supreme court observed that framers of the Constitution had made it obligatory for the State to provide education for its citizens. The preamble promises to secure justice "social, economic, and political" for citizens. A peculiar feature of the Indian Constitution is that it combines social and economic rights along with political and justiciable rights. The preamble embodies the goal which the State has to achieve in order to establish social justice and to make the masses free in the positive sense. The securing of social justice has been specifically enjoined an object of the State under Article 38 of the Constitution.

Can the objective which has been so prominently pronounced in the preamble and Article 38 of the Constitution be achieved without providing education to the large majority of citizens who are illiterate. The objectives flowing form the preamble cannot be achieved and shall remain on paper unless the people in this country are educated. The three- pronged justice promised by the preamble is only an illusion to the teaming-million who are illiterate. It is only the education which equips a citizen to participate in achieving the objectives enshrined in the preamble. The preamble further assures the dignity of the individual. The Constitution seeks to achieve this object by guaranteeing Fundamental Rights of each individual, which he can enforce through court of law if necessary. The Directive Principles in Part IV of the Constitution are also with the same objective. The dignity of man is inviolable. It is the duty of the State to respect and protect the same. It is primarily the education which brings-forth the dignity of a man.

The framers of the Constitution were aware that more than seventy percent of the people whom they were giving the Constitution of India were illiterate. They were also hopeful that within a period of ten years illiteracy would be wiped out from the country. It was with that hope that Articles 41 and 45 were brought in Chapter IV of the Constitution. An individual cannot be assured of human dignity unless his personality is developed and the only way to do that is to educate him. This is why the Universal Declaration of Human Rights, 1948 emphasizes " Education shall be directed to the full development of the human personality". Article 41 in Chapter IV of the Constitution recognizes an individual right "to education". It says that "the State shall, within the limits of its economic capacity and development, make effective provision for securing the right to education. Although a citizen cannot enforce the Directive Principles contained in Chapter IV of the Constitution but these were not intended to be mere pious declarations.

The Supreme Court observed that the Directive Principles which are fundamental in the governance of the country cannot be isolated from the Fundamental Rights guaranteed under Part III. These principles have to be read into the Fundamental Rights. Both are supplementary to each other. The State is under a constitutional mandate to create conditions in which the Fundamental Rights guaranteed to the individuals under Part III could be enjoyed by all. Without making "Right to Education" under Article 41 of the Constitution a reality the Fundamental Rights under Chapter III shall remain beyond the reach of large majority which is illiterate.

The Supreme Court observed that "Right to Life" is the compendious expression for all those rights which the Courts must enforce because they are basic to the dignified enjoyment of life. It extends to the full range of conduct which the individual is free to pursue. The right to education flows directly from right to life. The right to life under Article 21 and the dignity of an individual cannot be assured unless it is accompanied by the right to education. The State Government is under an obligation to make endeavour to provide educational facilities at all levels to its citizens. The Fundamental rights guaranteed under Part III of the Constitution of India including the right to freedom of speech and expression and other rights under Article 19 cannot be appreciated and fully enjoyed unless a citizen is educated and is conscious of his individualistic dignity.

The Supreme Court observed that opportunity to acquire education cannot be confined to the richer section of society. The Karnataka State has permitted opening of several new medical colleges under various private bodies and organizations. These institutions are charging capitation fee as a consideration for admission. Capitation fee is nothing but a price for selling education. The concept of "teaching shops" is contrary to the constitutional scheme and is wholly abhorrent to Indian Culture and heritage.

The Supreme Court held that charging capitation fee in consideration of admission to educational institutions, is a patent denial of citizen's right to education under the Constitution. To establish and administer educational institution is considered as religious and charitable object. Education in India has never been a commodity for sale. The State action in permitting capitation fee to be charged by state recognized educational institutions is wholly arbitrary and as such violative of Article 14 of the Constitution of India. The Capitation fee enables the rich to take admission where the poor, with better merit, can not take admission. Capitation fee is wholly arbitrary and violates Article 14.

The Supreme Court noted that tuition fee for government seats is only Rs. 2000 while other candidates had to pay Rs. 60,000/- under the notification. The Supreme Court held that Rs. 60,000/- per annum permitted to be charged from Indian Students from outside Karnataka is not tuition fee but a capitation fee and as such cannot be sustained and struck down the same.

COMMON CAUSE VS UNION OF INDIA

The Supreme Court in **Common Cause Vs Union of India, (2018) 6 SCR 1** held that right of live with dignity under Article 21 also includes the smoothening of process of dying in case of terminally ill patient or persons in Persistent Vegetative State with no hope for recovery.

Case Title : Common Cause Vs Union of India
Date of Judgment : 09.03.2018
Bench : Chief Justice Dipak Misra, Justice A.K. Sikri, Justice A.M. Khanwilkar, Justice D.Y. Chandrachud, Justice Ashok Bhushan

FACTS OF THE CASE

Common Cause, a registered society, filed a Writ Petition under Article 32 of the Constitution of India seeking to declare "right to die with dignity" as a Fundamental Right within the fold of "right to live with dignity" guaranteed under Article 21 of the Constitution. Directions were also sought to the effect that terminally ill patients should be able to execute living will, which can be presented to hospital for appropriate action in the event of the executant being admitted to hospital with serious illness which may threaten termination of life of the executant.

FINDINGS OF THE SUPREME COURT

In **P. Rathinam Vs Union of India (1994) 3 SCC 394,** it was held that the right to live would include the right not to live i.e. right to die or to terminate one's life. A person cannot be forced to enjoy the right to life to his detriment, disadvantage or disliking. Article 309 was declared *ultra vires* of the Constitution.

In **Gian Kaur Vs. State of Punjab (1996) 2 SCC 648** the Supreme Court overruled P. Rathinam and held that by no stretch of imagination, extinction of life can be read to be included in protection of life because Article 21 in its ambit and sweep cannot include within it the right to die as a part of Fundamental Rights guaranteed therein. The right to life including right to live with dignity would mean the existence of such a right up to end of natural life. In the context of a dying man who is terminally ill or in a persistent vegetative state, the Supreme Court observed that he may be permitted to terminate it by a premature extinction of his life in those circumstance. This category of cases may fall within the ambit of the "right to die" with dignity as a part of right to live with dignity, when death due to termination of natural life is certain and imminent and process of natural death has commenced.

In **Aruna Ramachandra Shanbaug Vs. Union of India (2011) 4 SCC 454**, the Supreme Court differentiated between active euthanasia and passive euthanasia and held that in cases of passive euthanasia High Court can grant approval for withdrawing life support of an incompetent person under Article 226 of the Constitution on the application filed by the near relatives or next friend or the doctors/hospital staff praying for permission to withdraw the life support of an incompetent person.

The Supreme Court observed that in Gian Kaur, euthanasia as a concept has not been decried. On the contrary it gives indication that in such situations, it is the acceleration of the process of dying which may constitute a part of right to life with dignity so that the period of suffering is reduced.

The Supreme Court observed that Gian Kaur has neither given any definite opinion with regard to euthanasia nor has it stated that the same can be conceived of only by legislation.

Active and Passive Euthanasia

The Supreme Court observed that euthanasia is basically an intentional premature termination of another person's life either by direct intervention (active euthanasia) or withholding life-prolonging measures and resources (passive euthanasia) either at the express or implied request of that persons (voluntary euthanasia) or in the absence of such approval/consent (non-voluntary euthanasia). Active euthanasia or positive euthanasia entails a positive act or affirmative action or act of commission entailing the use of lethal substances or forces to cause the intentional death of a person by direct intervention e.g. a lethal injection given to a person with terminal illness who is in terrible agony. Passive euthanasia, on the other hand, also called "negative euthanasia" or "non-aggressive euthanasia" entails withdrawing of life support measures or withholding of medical treatment for continuance of life, e.g. withholding of antibiotics in case of a patient where death is likely to occur as a result of not giving the said antibiotics or removal of the heart lung machine from a patient in coma. Further, voluntary euthanasia is where the consent is taken from the patient and non-voluntary euthanasia is where the consent is unavailable, for instances when the patient is in coma or is otherwise unable to given consent.

The Supreme Court observed that most of the countries have legalized passive euthanasia either by way of legislations or through judicial interpretation but there remains uncertainty whether active euthanasia should be granted legal status.

Passive Euthanasia and Article 21

The Supreme Court observed that the language employed in the Constitutional provision should be liberally construed, for such provision can never remain static. The Court has a duty to interpret Article 21 in a further dynamic manner and it has to be stated without any trace of doubt that the right to life with dignity has to include the smoothening of the process of dying when the person is in a vegetative state or is living exclusively by the administration of artificial aid that prolongs the life by arresting the dignified and inevitable process of dying. Such a right will come within the ambit of Article 21. Common law and statutory rights of terminally ill persons in other jurisdictions would indicate that all adults with the capacity to consent have the common law right to refuse medical treatment and the right of self-determination. Doctors would be bound by the choice of self-determination made by the patient who is terminally ill and undergoing a prolonged medical treatment or is surviving on life support, subject to being satisfied that the illness of the patient is incurable and there is no hope of his being cured. Any other consideration cannot pass off as being in the best interests of the patient.

Advance Directives

The Supreme Court observed that an inquiry into common law jurisdictions reveals that all adults with capacity to consent have the right of self-determination and autonomy. The said rights pave the way for the right to refuse medical treatment which has acclaimed universal recognition. A competent person who has come of age has the right to refuse specific treatment or all treatment or opt for an alternative treatment even if such decision entails a risk of death. The "emergency principle" or the "principle of necessity" has to be given effect to only when it is not practicable to obtain the patient's consent for treatment and his/her life is in danger. But where a patient has already made a valid advance directive which is free from reasonable doubt and specifying that he/she should not wish to be treated, then such directive has to be given effect to.

The Supreme Court observed that Advance Medical Directive would serve as a fruitful means to facilitate the fructification of the sacrosanct right to life with dignity. The said directive will dispel many a doubt at the relevant time of need during the course of treatment of the patient. That apart, it will strengthen the mind of the treating doctors as they will be in a position to ensure, after being satisfied, that they are acting in a lawful manner. But advance medical directive cannot operate in abstraction. There has to be safeguards. They need to be spelt out. The Supreme court also issued several guidelines for execution of advance directives.

SUBHASH KUMAR VS STATE OF BIHAR

The Supreme Court in **Subhash Kumar Vs. State of Bihar, (1991) AIR 420** held that right to live under Article 21 includes the right of enjoyment of pollution free water and air for full enjoyment of life.

Case Title : Subhash Kumar Vs. State of Bihar
Date of Judgment : 09.01.1991
Bench : Justice K.N. Singh, Justice N.D. Ojha

FACTS OF THE CASE

Subhash Kumar filed a Public Interest Litigation (PIL) under Article 32 of the Constitution seeking direction to West Bokaro Collieries and Tata Iron and Steel Company from discharging sludge and slurry in Bokaro river. The Petitioner contended that sludge/slurry discharged as an effluent from the washeries into the Bokaro river got deposited in the bed of the river and it also gets settled on land including the Petitioner's land bearing Plot No. 170. Such sludge/slurry adversely affects fertility of the land. River water no longer remains drinkable or irrigatable due to pollution of the water.

The Petitioner submitted that in spite of several representations, the State of Bihar and State Pollution Control Board have failed to take any action against the Company instead they have permitted the pollution of water and earning royalty.

FINDINGS OF THE SUPREME COURT

The Supreme Court observed that the Petition does not seem to have been filed in public interest. The Petitioner was buying slurry for the last several years. He wanted more and more slurry from the Respondents and for this purpose started harassing the company. He even removed company's slurry in unauthorized manner for which even criminal complaint was filed. He even filed Petition under Article 226 of the Constitution for permitting him to collect slurry from raiyati land.

The Supreme Court observed that Article 32 is designed for enforcement of Fundamental Rights of a citizen by the Supreme Court. It provides for an extraordinary procedure to safeguard the Fundamental Rights of a citizen. Right to live is a fundamental right under Article 21 of the Constitution. It includes the right of enjoyment of pollution free water and air for full enjoyment of life. If anything endangers or impairs the quality of life in derogation of laws, a citizen has right to have recourse to Article 32 of the Constitution for removing the pollution of water or air which may be detrimental to the quality of life.

But the Supreme Court observed that proceedings under Article 32 of the Constitution should be taken by a person genuinely interested in the protection of society on behalf of the community. Public Interest Litigation can not be invoked to satisfy personal grudge and enmity. If such petitions are entertained then it will be abuse of process of law.

The Supreme Court dismissed the petition and imposed cost of Rs. 5000/-.

VELLORE CITIZENS WELFARE FORUM VS UNION OF INDIA

The Supreme Court in **Vellore Citizens Welfare Forum Vs Union of India & Ors, (1996) 5 SCR 241** held that "precautionary principle" and "polluter pays principle" are part of environment law of the land.

Case Title : Vellore Citizens Welfare Forum Vs Union of India & Ors
Date of Judgment : 28.08.1996
Bench :Justice Kuldip Singh, Justice K. Venkataswami

FACTS OF THE CASE

Vellore Citizens Welfare Forum filed Writ Petition under Article 32 of the Constitution against pollution caused by various tanneries and other industries in Tamil Nadu. It was submitted before Court that untreated effluent was being drained on roadside, agricultural land and water ways causing degradation of soil. These effluents were also being discharged into river Palar causing water to be polluted and non-portable.

Various reports and affidavits were filed before the Supreme Court showing damage to soil and acute portable water shortage caused by these tanneries.

FINDINGS OF THE SUPREME COURT

The Supreme Court noted that leather industry has become major foreign exchange earner and employment generating industry but it does not give these industries right to degrade environment, destroy the ecology or pose as a health hazard.

The Supreme Court observed that development and ecology are not opposed to each other. Sustainable development is answer to this problem. The Court noted various international developments on aspect of sustainable development and noted that "Precautionary Principle" and "Polluter Pays" principles are essential features of sustainable development.

"Precautionary principles" mean environmental measures taken by Governments and Statutory authorities. Lack of scientific certainty should not be reason for postponing measures to prevent environmental degradation. The onus of proof is on the developer that his actions are environmentally benign.

The Supreme Court noted that Polluter Pays principle has been held to be sound principle in **Indian Council for Enviro- Legal Action Vs. Union of India 1996 AIR 1445.** Once activity carried on is proved to be hazardous or inherently dangerous, the person carrying on such activity is liable to make good the loss caused to affected persons. Polluting industries are absolutely liable to compensate for harm caused to villagers in the affected area, to the soil and to the ground water. Polluter pays principle means absolute liability to pay the victims of pollution as well as incur the cost of restoring the environmental degradation.

The Supreme Court in light of Article 21, Article 47, Article 48A and 51 A (g) held that precautionary principle and polluter pays principle are part of environmental law of the country.

The Supreme Court noted that even otherwise these principles being part of international customary law can be accepted as domestic law. It is almost accepted proposition of law that the rule of Customary International Law, which are not contrary to the municipal law, shall be deemed to have been incorporated in the domestic law and shall be followed by the Courts of Law.

The Supreme Court directed the Central Government to create an authority under Environment Protection Act, 1986 to deal with situation created by tanneries. It also directed that such authority will implement "precautionary principles" and "polluter pays" principles.

M C MEHTA VS UNION OF INDIA (OLEUM LEAK CASE)

The Supreme Court in **M C Mehta Vs Union of India, (1987) 1 SCR 819** held that where an enterprise is engaged in a hazardous or inherently dangerous activity and harm results to anyone on account of an accident in the operation of such hazardous or inherently dangerous activity , the enterprise shall be strictly and absolutely liable to compensate all those who are affected by the accident.

Case Title : M C Mehta Vs Union of India
Date of Judgment : 20.12.1986
Bench : Chief Justice P. N. Bhagwati, Justice C. J. Ranganath Misra, Justice G. L. Oza, Justice K. N. Singh

FACTS OF THE CASE

M C Mehta, an environmental activist, filed Writ Petition before the Supreme Court seeking closure and relocation of Shriram Caustic and Chlorine and Sulphuric Acid Plant from Kirti Nagar Delhi. During pendency of the petition, oleum gas leaked from the said plant and a lawyer practicing at Tis Hazari Courts died due to inhalation of oleum gas. Applications were filed by the Delhi Legal Aid & Advice Board and the Delhi Bar Association for award of compensation to the persons who had suffered harm on account of escape of oleum gas.

The case was referred to larger bench for determination of substantial issues related with Article 21 and Article 32.

FINDINGS OF THE SUPREME COURT

A preliminary objection was raised by the Shriram that there was no claim for compensation in the original petition as such Supreme Court should not decide constitutional issues arising out of these applications.

The Supreme Court rejected the preliminary objections. The Supreme Court observed that it is undoubtedly true that the Petitioner could have applied for amendment of the Writ Petition so as to include a claim for compensation but merely because he did not do so, the applications for compensation made by the Delhi Legal Aid & Advice Board and the Delhi Bar Association cannot be thrown out. These applications for compensation are for enforcement of Fundamental Rights to life enshrined in Article 21 of the Constitution and while dealing with such applications, a hyper technical approach cannot be adopted which would defeat the ends of justice. On numerous occasions it has been pointed out by the Supreme Court that where there is violation of Fundamental or other legal right of a person or class of persons who by reason of poverty or disability or socially or economically disadvantaged position cannot approach a Court of Law for justice, it would be open to any public spirited individual or social action group to bring an action for vindication of the fundamental or other legal right of such individual or class of individuals and this can be done not only by filing a regular writ petition but also by addressing a letter to the Court. If this Court is prepared to accept a letter complaining of violation of the Fundamental Right of an individual or a class of individuals who cannot approach the Court for justice, there is no reason why these applications for compensation which have been made for enforcement of the fundamental right of the persons affected by the oleum gas leak under Article 21 should not be entertained. The Court while dealing with an application for enforcement of Fundamental Right must look at the substance and not the form.

The Supreme Court observed that is well settled that Article 32 does not merely confer power on this Court to issue a direction, order or writ for enforcement of the Fundamental Rights but it also lays a constitutional obligation on this Court to protect the Fundamental Rights of the people and for that purpose it has all incidental and ancillary powers including the power to forge new remedies and fashion new strategies designed to enforce the Fundamental Rights.

The Supreme Court did not make any definite pronouncement on whether Shriram can be considered State under Article 12 of the Constitution.

The Supreme Court also considered the liability of an enterprise which are engaged in hazardous or inherently dangerous industry. The rule in **Ryland Vs. Fletcher** was evolved in 1866 which provided that who for his own purposes being on to his land and collects and keeps there anything likely to mischief if it escapes must keep it at his peril and if he fails to do so, is prima facie liable for the damage which is the natural consequence of tis escape. This is known as strict liability.

The Supreme Court moved beyond Ryland Vs. Fletcher and developed a new jurisprudence. The Supreme Court held that an enterprise which is engaged in a hazardous or inherently dangerous industry which poses a potential threat to health and safety of the persons working in the factory and residing in the surrounding areas owes an absolute non-delegable duty to the community to ensure that no harm results to anyone on account of hazardous or inherently dangerous nature of the activity which it has undertaken. The enterprise must be held to be under an obligation to provide that the hazardous or inherently dangerous activity in which it is engaged must be conducted with the highest standards of safety and if any harm results on account of such activity, the enterprise must be absolutely liable to compensate for such harm and it should be no answer to the enterprise to say that it had taken all reasonable care and that the harm occurred without any negligence on its part.

The Supreme Court directed Delhi Legal Aid and Advice Board to take up the cases of all those who claim to have suffered on account of oleum gas and to file actions on their behalf in the appropriate court for claiming compensation against Shriram.

M C MEHTA VS KAMAL NATH

The Supreme Court in **M C Mehta Vs Kamal Nath, (1996) Supp (10) SCR** 12 declared that public trust doctrine is a part of law of the land.

Case Title : M C Mehta Vs Kamal Nath
Date of Judgment : 13.12.1996
Bench : Justice Kuldip Singh, Justice S. Saghir Ahmad

FACTS OF THE CASE

The Supreme Court noticed an article in Indian Express dated 25th February, 1996 titled *" Kamal Nath dares the mighty Beas to keep his dreams afloat"*.

Span Motels Pvt. Ltd. , a company having links with Sh. Kamal Nath, owned "Span Resorts" in Kullu-Manali Valley. It floated another venture called "span club" and in the process encroached upon additional area of 22.2 bighas adjoining the motel and had built extensive stone, cemented and wire mesh created embankments along the river banks. Government of India subsequently approved leasing of additional 27 Bigha and 12 Biswa of forest land to the motel which included encroached land. Kamal Nath was minister in charge of Ministry of Environment at the relevant time.

There were serious acts of degradation of environment caused by the motel. The Supreme Court vide order dated May 6, 1996 directed the Central Pollution Control Board to inspect environment around the area in possession of the motel and file a report.

FINDINGS OF THE SUPREME COURT

The Supreme Court noted that the leasehold area in possession of motel is a part of the protected forest land owned by the State Government. The forest land of 27 Bigha 12 Biswa leased to the motel by the lease dated April 11, 1994 is situated on the right back of the river separated from the motel by a natural relief/spill channel. Leased land is connected with the motel by wooden bridge. 22.2 Bigha out of the leased land was encroached by the motel in 1988-89. Prior to 1995 several constructions were done. The mouth of natural spill had been blocked. The construction was done without any expert supervision. Due to the construction main course of river were divided into two.

It was contended by the Respondent that construction work has been done in the leased land and for purposes for safeguarding from flood.

The Supreme Court observed that forest land which has been given on lease to the Motel by the State Governments are situated at the bank of river Beas. The area, being ecologically fragile and full of scenic beauty, should not have been permitted to be converted into private ownership and for commercial gains.

The Supreme Court observed that that notion that the public has a right to expect certain land and natural areas to retain their natural characteristics is finding its way into law of the land.

The Supreme Court observed that ancient Roman Empire developed a legal theory known as the "Doctrine of the Public Trust". It was founded on the ideas that certain common properties such as rivers, sea-shore, forests and the air were held by Government in trusteeship for the free and unimpeded use of the general public. Our contemporary concern about the "environment" bear a very close conceptual relationship to this legal doctrine. Under the Roman Law these resources were either owned by no one (*Res Nullious*) or by every one in common (*Res Communious*). Under the English Common law, however, the Sovereign could own these resources but the ownership was limited in nature, the Crown could not grant these properties to private owners if the effect was to interfere with the public interests in navigation or fishing. Resources that were suitable for these uses were deemed to be held in trust by the Crown for the benefit of the public.

The Supreme Court further observed that the Public Trust Doctrine primarily rests on the principle that certain resources like air, sea, waters and the forests have such a great importance to the people as a whole that it would be wholly unjustified to make them a subject of private ownership, the said resources being a gift of nature. They should be made freely available to everyone irrespective of the status in life. The doctrine enjoins upon the Government to protect the resources for the enjoyment of the general public rather than to permit their use for private ownership or commercial purposes.

The Supreme Court further observed that our legal system-based on English Common Law- includes the public trust doctrine as part of its jurisprudence.

The State is the trustee of all natural resources which are by nature meant for public use and enjoyment. Public at large is beneficiary of the sea-shore, running waters, airs, forests and ecologically fragile lands. The State as a trustee is under a legal duty to protect the natural resources. These resources for public use cannot be converted into private ownership.

The Supreme Court held that large area of the bank of river Beas which is part of protected forest has been given on a lease purely for commercial purposes to the Motel. Himachal Pradesh Government committed patent breach of public trust by leasing the ecologically fragile land to the Motel Management. Both the lease transactions are in patent breach of the trust held by the State Government. The second lease granted in the year 1994 was virtually of the land which is part of river-bed.

The Supreme Court relied on **Vellore Citizens Welfare Forum Vs Union of India 1996 (5) SCC 647** and held that it is settled law that who pollutes the environment must pay to reverse the damage caused by his acts.

The Supreme Court declared that public trust doctrine is a part of law of the land. Lease granted to the motel was cancelled. Himachal Pradesh Government was directed to restore the original natural conditions. Motel was also directed to pay compensation.

IN RE : NOISE POLLUTION

The Supreme Court in **In Re : Noise Pollution (2005) Supp. (1) SCR 624** held that compulsorily exposing unwilling persons to hear a noise raised to unpleasant or obnoxious levels is in violation of the right of others to a peaceful, comfortable and pollution free life guaranteed by Article 21.

Case Title : In Re : Noise Pollution
Date of Judgment : 18.07.2005
Bench : Justice R.C. Lahoti, Justice Ashok Bhan

FACTS OF THE CASE

The Supreme Court heard two Writ Petitions in this matter. In first Petition, Sh. Anil K Mittal, an engineer by profession moved the Court pro bono publico. A 13 year girl was victim of rape and her cries could not be heard due to sound of loudspeaker. Later she set herself ablaze and died. The Petitioner claimed that loudspeakers are being used without any restriction in religious performances, bhajans and marriage ceremonies.

In the second petition, amendment dated 11.10. 2002 to Noise Pollution Control and Regulations Rules, 1999 was challenged. The amendment empowered the State Government to permit use of loudspeaker or public address system during night hours (between 10 P.M. to 12 P.M) mid-night on or during the cultural or religious occasions for a limited period not exceeding 15 days.

FINDINGS OF THE SUPREME COURT

The Supreme Court observed that Article 21 of the Constitution guarantees life and personal liberty to all persons. Right to life enshrined in Article 21 is not of mere survival or existence. It guarantees a right of person to live with human dignity. Therein are included all the aspects of life which go on to make a person's life meaningful, complete and worth living. The human life has its charm and there is no reason why the life should not be enjoyed along with all permissible pleasures. Anyone who wishes to live in peace, comfort and quiet within his house has a right to prevent the noise as pollutant reaching him. No one can claim a right to create noise even in his own premises which would travel beyond his precincts and cause nuisance to neighbors or others. Any noise which has the effect of materially interfering with the ordinary comforts of life judged by the standard of a reasonable man is nuisance. How and when a nuisance created by noise becomes actionable has to be answered by reference to its degree and the surrounding circumstances including the place and the time.

The Supreme Court observed that those who make noise often take shelter behind Article 19 (1) (a) pleading freedom of speech and expression. Undoubtedly, the freedom of speech and right to expression are Fundamental Rights but the rights are not absolute. Nobody can claim a fundamental right to create noise by amplifying the sound of his speech with the help of loudspeakers. While one has a right to speech, others have a right to listen or decline to listen. Nobody can be compelled to listen and nobody can claim that he has a right to make his voice trespass into ears or mind of others. Nobody can indulge into aural aggression. If anyone increases his volume of speech and that too with the assistance of artificial devices so as to compulsorily expose unwilling persons to hear a noise raised to unpleasant or obnoxious levels then the person speaking is violating the right of others to a peaceful, comfortable and pollution free life guaranteed by Article 21. Article 19 (1) (a) cannot be pressed into service for defeating the Fundamental Right guaranteed by Article 21.

After analyzing the word noise, the Supreme Court observed that the disturbance produced in our environment by the undesirable sound of various kind is called "noise pollution". Noise can disturb our work, rest, sleep and communication. It can damage our hearing and evoke other psychological and possibly pathological reactions.

The Supreme Court noted that sources of noise are road traffic, aircraft, railroads, construction, industry, noise in buildings and consumer products. Bursting of firecrackers is also a health hazard since it is responsible for both air pollution as well as noise pollution.

The Supreme Court observed that in India laws have been enacted for prevention of noise pollution, but the major issue lies in implementation of these laws. The Government has enacted Noise Pollution (Regulation and Control) Rules, 2000. Noise pollution can be dealt under Section 268, 290 and 291 of the Indian Penal Code. Under Section 133 of Cr.P.C the magistrate has power to deal with nuisance. Certain provisions of Motor

Vehicles Act also provide for reduction of noise. Noise has been included as pollutant under Air (Prevention and Control of Pollution) Act.

The Supreme Court held that by restricting the time of bursting the fire-crackers does not in any way violate the religious rights of any person as enshrined under Article 25 of the Constitution. The festival of Diwali is mainly associated with pooja performed on the auspicious day and not with firecrackers. In no religious text book it is written that Diwali has to be celebrated by bursting crackers.

The Supreme Court issued several directions including – (i) firecrackers have to evaluated on the basis of chemical composition. Firecrackers can be divided in sound emitting and light emitting. There will be complete ban on sound emitting fire crackers between 10 PM and 6 AM. Chemical contents of firecrackers should be displayed on the box. (ii) Noise level at the boundary of the public place shall not exceed 10 dB(A) above of ambient noise standard for the area or 75 dB (A) whichever is lower. No one will beat drum or use sound amplifier at night between 10PM to 6 AM except in public emergencies. (iii) No horn can be used during 10 PM to 6 AM in residential area. (iv) general awareness should be created towards hazardous effects of noise pollution.

BIJOE EMMANUEL VS. STATE OF KERALA

The Supreme Court in **Bijoe Emmanuel Vs. State of Kerala, (1986) 3 SCR 518** held expulsion of children of Jehovah faith from school for not singing national anthem was in violation of Fundamental Rights under Article 19 (1) (a) and Article 25 (1).

Case Title : Bijoe Emmanuel Vs. State of Kerala
Date of Judgment : 11.08.1986
Bench : Justice O. Chinnappa Reddy, Justice M.M. Dutt

FACTS OF THE CASE

Three children including of Bijoe Immanuel were faithful of Jehovah's witnesses. They used to attend school daily but when in the morning *"jana gana mana"* was being sung, they stood respectfully but did not sing. They did not sing as according to them it was against their religious faith. A member of Legislative Assembly questioned about the same in the Assembly and a commission was constituted. Commission reported that they were law abiding citizen and stood in respect in silence during singing of national anthem. But under the instructions of Deputy Inspector of Schools, the Head Mistress expelled the children on 26th July, 1985. Representation of the children before school authorities and writ petition before the High Court was dismissed. Finally Special Leave Petition was filed before the Supreme Court.

FINDINGS OF THE SUPREME COURT

The Supreme Court noted that children desisted from singing nation anthem because of their honest belief and conviction that their religion does not permit them to join any rituals except it be in their prayers to Jehovah their God. Jehovah's witnesses and their peculiar beliefs though little noticed in this country had been noticed in encyclopedia Britannica and have been subject of judicial pronouncements elsewhere.

The issue before the Supreme Court was whether expulsion of children from the school was consistent with the rights guaranteed by Article 19 (1) (a) and 25 (1) of the Constitution?

The Supreme Court observed that there is no law which obliges a person to sing national anthem. Article 51 A (a) imposed a duty on every citizen to abide by the Constitution and respect its ideals and institutions, national flag and national anthem. Proper respect had been shown in this case by standing. Not joining in singing is not a disrespect.

The Supreme Court observed that not singing national anthem does not violate provisions of Preventions of Insults to National Honor Act, 1971 as there has been no prevention from singing national anthem or disturbance to the assembly in singing national anthem.

The Supreme Court observed that Article 19 (1) (a) guarantees to citizens freedom of speech and expression. Article 19 (2) provides that nothing in Article 19 (1) (a) shall prevent a State from making any law in so far as such law impose reasonable restrictions on the exercise of the right conferred by Article 19 (1) (a) in the interests of the sovereignty and integrity of India, the security of the State, friendly relations with foreign States, public order, decency or morality or in relation to contempt of court, defamation or incitement to an offence. The law is well settled that any law made under Article 19 (2) to (6) must be "law" having statutory force. The two circulars issued by the department did not have any statutory force but were mere instructions.

The Supreme Court observed that Article 25 is an article of faith in the Constitution, incorporated in recognition of the principle that the real test of a true democracy is the ability of even an insignificant minority to find its identity under the country's constitution. This has to be borne in mind in interpreting Article 25.

The Supreme Court observed that Right to freedom of conscience and freely to profess, practice and propagate religion guaranteed by Article 25 is subject to (1) public order, morality and health; (2) other provisions of Part III of the Constitution; (3) any law regulating or restricting any economic, financial, political or other secular activity which may be associated with religious practice or providing for social welfare and reform or the throwing open of Hindu Religious institutions of a public character to all classes and sections of Hindus.

The Supreme Court observed that whenever the Fundamental right to freedom of conscience and to profess, practice and propagate religion is invoked, the act complained of as offending the Fundamental Rights must be examined to discover whether such act is to protect public order, morality and health, whether it is to give effect to other provisions of Part III of the Constitution or whether it is authorized by a law made to regulate or restrict any economic, financial, political or secular activity which may be associated with religious practice or to provide for social welfare and reform. Here again as mentioned in connection with Article 19 (2) to (6), it must be a law having the force of a Statute and not a mere executive or a departmental instruction.

The Supreme Court endorsed the view that a particular religious belief or practice appeals to our reasons or sentiment is not a relevant question but real question is whether the belief is genuinely and conscientiously held as part of the profession or practice of religion. If the belief is genuinely and conscientiously held it attracts the protection of Article 25 but subject to, of course, to the inhibitions contained therein.

The Supreme Court held that expulsion of children was in violation of Fundamental Rights enshrined under Article 19 (1) (a) and Article 25 (1).

S P MITTAL VS UNION OF INDIA

The Supreme Court in **S. P. Mittal Vs. Union of India, (1983)1SCR 729** held that Sri Aurobindo Society was not a religious denomination.

Case Title : S. P. Mittal Vs. Union of India
Date of Judgment : 08.11.1982
Bench : Chief Justice Y.V. Chandrachud, Justice P.N. Bhagwati, Justice O. Chinnappa Reddy, Justice V. Balakrishna Eradi, Justice R.B. Misra

FACTS OF THE CASE

Sri Aurobindo, a freedom fighter and philosopher set up his meditation and yoga Ashram at Pondicherry. Madam L. Alfassa, a french lady, became his disciple and was later known as mother. The disciples of Aurobindo formed a society known as Sri Aurobindo Society in 1960. The society is distinct from Aurobindo Ashram. Sri Aurobindo Society preaches and propagates the ideals and teaching of Ari Aurobindo through its numerous centres scattered throughout India. A cultural township known as Auroville was also set up. Sri Aurobindo society received large amount of funds from different organizations in India and abroad for development of township. After death of mother, there was mismanagement and irregularity in running of project. Keeping the international nature of project, the Union Government acquired the management and control of Auroville vide an ordinance which was replaced by Auroville (Emergency Provisions) Act, 1980. Constitutional validity of the Act was challenged, which reached finally to the Supreme Court.

FINDINGS OF THE SUPREME COURT

The Supreme Court determined following important issues in this case.

(i) Whether Parliament has legislative competence to enact the impugned statute ?

It was contended that Auroville (Emergency Provisions) Act, 1980 was a law related with State List and as such beyond legislative competence of Parliament. It was contended by the Petitioners that the Act falls under Entry 32 of List II of seventh schedule. The Supreme Court held that the Act does not even incidentally fall under Entry 32 of List II as it is no way related to constitution, regulation or winding up of society. Even if the subject matter of the impugned Act is not covered by any specific entry of List I or III of the Seventh Schedule of the Constitution it would in any case be covered by the residuary entry 97 of List I.

(ii) Whether impugned act infringes Articles 25, 26, 29 and 30 of the Constitution ?

The Supreme Court observed that the term "religion" has been considered in **The Commissioner, Hindu Religious Endowments Madras Vs. Sri Lakshmindra Thirtha Swamiar of Sri Shirur Math** wherein following proposition of law was held :

(a) Religious means a system of beliefs or doctrines which are regarded by those who profess that religion as conducive to their spiritual well being.

(b) A religion is not merely an opinion, doctrine or belief. It has its outward expression in acts as well.

(c) Religion need not be theistic.

(d) "Religious denomination" means a religious sect or body having a common faith and organization and designated by a distinctive name.

(e) A law which takes away the rights of administration from the hands of a religious denomination altogether and vests in another authority would amount to violation of the right guaranteed under clause (d) of Article 26.

"Religious denomination" takes color from word religion and it should satisfy three conditions-(a) It must be a collection of individuals who have a system of beliefs or doctrines which they regard as conducive or their spiritual well-being, that is, common faith;(b) Common organization and (c) Designation by distinct name

The Supreme Court held on the basis of Memorandum of Association of the Society, several application made by the Society claiming exemption under

Section 35 and Section 80 of the Income Tax Act, the repeated utterings of Sri Aurobindo and the Mother, that the Society and Auroville were not religious institution. There is no room of doubt that neither the society nor Auroville constitute a religious denomination and teaching of Sri Aurobindo only represented his philosophy and not a religion.

The Supreme Court held that even if it is assumed that society was a religious denomination, the impugned act has not violated Article 25 or 26. The impugned act does not curtail the freedom of conscience and right freely to profess, practice and propagate religion enshrined under Article 25. Article 26 confers right to religious denomination to establish, maintain institution for religious and charitable purpose and manage its own affairs. The impugned Act has not taken away the right of management in matters of religion of a religious denomination. The impugned had taken over only secular aspects of the society.

(iii) Whether impugned act is violative of Article 14 of the Constitution?

The Supreme Court held that on account of the uniqueness of the institution and on account of the involvement of the Government and stake being high one about public funds, Parliament could take a particular institution as a class in itself. Impugned Act has not violated Article 14 of the Constitution.

REV. STAINISLAUS VS STATE OF MADHYA PRADESH

The Supreme Court in **Rev. Stainislaus Vs. State of Madhya Pradesh, (1977)SCR (2) 611** held that there is no Fundamental Right under Article 25 to covert a person to one's own religion.

Case Title : **Rev. Stainislaus Vs. State of Madhya Pradesh**
Date of Judgment : 17.01.1977
Bench : Chief Justice A.N. Ray, Justice M. H. Beg, Justice Ranjit Singh Sarkaria, Justice P.N. Shinghal, Justice Jaswant Singh

---

FACTS OF THE CASE

Several appeals were filed before the Supreme Court challenging the vires of Madhya Pradesh Swatantrya Adhiniyam, 1968 and Orissa Freedom of Religion Act, 1967. These acts contained provisions for prohibition of forcible conversion of a person to one's own religion.

The Sub-divisional Magistrate of Baloda Bazaar sanctioned prosecution of Rev. Stainislaus for commission of offence under Section 3, 4 and 5 (2) of the Madhya Pradesh Act. Preliminary objections were taken by Rev. Stainilaus that State was not competent to pass the act and it was also contended that act was also violative of Article 25 of the Constitution. SDM as well as Sessions Court did not entertain the preliminary objection. The revision was filed before the High Court. The High Court held that these provisions did not violate Article 25 of the Constitution. It was also held that State Legislature was competent to pass this act under entry I of List II of Seventh Schedule.

On the other hand, Orissa High Court declared provisions of Orissa Freedom of Religion Act, 1967 ultra virus as it found that the State Legislature has no power to enact the impugned legislation which in pith and substance is a law relating to religion.

FINDINGS OF THE SUPREME COURT

It was contended by the Appellant that right to "propagate" religion under Article 25 includes right to "convert" a person to one's own religion.

The Supreme Court observed that the word "propagate" has been used in Article 25 (1) to transmit or spread one's religion by an exposition of its tenets. It has to be remembered that Article 25 (1) guarantees "freedom of conscience" to every citizen, and not merely to the followers of one particular religion, and that, postulates that there is no fundamental right to convert another person to one's own religion because if a person purposely undertakes the conversion of another person to his religion, as distinguished from his effort to transmit or spread the tenets of his religion, that would impinge on the "freedom of conscience" guaranteed to all the citizens of the country alike. What is freedom for one, is freedom for the other, in equal measure and there can be no such thing as a fundamental right to convert any person to one's own religion.

The Supreme Court observed that Article 25 and Article 26 have been made subject to public order, morality and health. It cannot predicated that freedom of religion can have no impact on public order. If communal passions are raised on the ground of forcible conversions, it will give rise to an apprehension of breach of public order affecting the community at large. Therefore, the impugned acts come within purview of Entry I of List II of Seventh Schedule. The aforesaid acts do not provide for regulation of religion but are related to maintenance of public order.

The Supreme Court allowed the appeal against judgment of Orissa High Court and set aside the same. On the other hand the Supreme Court dismissed the appeal against judgment of Madhya Pradesh High Court.

TMA PAI FOUNDATION VS STATE OF KARNATKA

The Supreme Court in its landmark judgment **TMA Foundation & Ors Vs. State of Karnataka & Ors, (2002) SUPP 4 SCR 587** reiterated that linguistic and religious minorities have to be identified at state level. The Supreme Court also held *inter alia* that unaided minority institutions can be autonomous except regulation for maintaining academic standards and atmosphere. State aided minority institutions have to admit students of other communities, ratio of which has to be determined based on type of institution, population, and educational needs of minorities.

Case Title : TMA Foundation & Ors Vs. State of Karnataka & Ors
Date of Judgment : 31.10.2002
Bench : Chief Justice B. N. Kirpal, Justice G. B. Pattanaik, Justice V. N. Khare, Justice Rajendra Babu, Justice S.S. M. Quadri, Justice Ruma Pal, Justice S. N. Variava, Justice K. G. Balakrishnan, Justice P. V. Reddi, Justice Ashok Bhan, Justice Arijit Pasayat

---

FACTS OF THE CASE

TMA Foundation challenged the provisions of Karnataka Educational Institutions Ordinance, 1984 which has been issued with the objective of preventing educational institutions from charging exorbitant fees. Several other Petitions were also under consideration before the Supreme Court. Writ Petition filed by the Islamic Academy of Educational and connected petitions were placed before a Bench of five judges. As the Bench was prima facie of the opinion that Article 30 did not clothe a minority educational institution with the power to adopt its own method of selection and the correctness of the decision of the Supreme Court in **St. Stephen's College Vs University of Delhi (1992) 1SCC 558** was doubted, it was directed that the questions that arose should be authoritatively answered by larger Bench. These cases were placed before seven judge Bench. Education was placed under Concurrent List vide forty-second amendment and thereafter the cases were referred to eleven judge Bench.

FINDINGS OF THE SUPREME COURT

Whether there is Fundamental Right to establish Educational Institutions?

The Court held that education is covered under "occupation" under Article 19 (1) (g) as such there is a fundamental right to establish educational institution under Article 19 (1) (g). Religious denomination has also fundamental right to establish educational institution under Article 26 (1). Religious and linguistic minority is also having fundamental right to establish educational institution under Article 30 (1).

Was educational scheme devised in Unni Krishnan correct in respect of private educational institutions ?

The Supreme Court in **Unni Krishnan J P and Ors Vs State of Andhra Pradesh (1993) 1 SCC 645** has held that commercialization of education was not permissible. The Supreme Court has devised scheme which has to followed while granting recognition/affiliation to private institutions. The Scheme inter alia provided for 50% frees seats which have to filled by nominee of University/Government on the basis of merit determined on common competitive examination and 50% payment seats by those candidates who are willing to pay based on inter se merit. The maximum fee has to prescribed by appropriate authority or competent court.

The Supreme Court observed that the scheme has resulted into higher expense than revenue to institutions. The restrictions imposed on the educational institutions by the scheme cannot be said to be reasonable. The Court noted that Unni Krishnan judgment has created some problems as payment seats candidates will be incurring cost of education of free seats candidates. More affluent students belonging to urban area are faring better in competitive examination and availing the free seats and students belonging to rural areas had to take admission in payment seats.

The Supreme Court held that any system of selection which deprive the private unaided educational institution right of rational selection are unreasonable. Surrendering the total process of selection to state will be unreasonable as was done in Uni Krishnan Case.

The Supreme Court overruled the decision in Unni Krishnan in respect of admission and fixation of fee in private unaided institutions.

Can private institutions be regulated by State ?

The Supreme Court held that the while state has right to prescribe qualifications for admission for private unaided colleges, such institutions have right to admit students of their choice, subject to objective and rational procedure of selection. Conditions can be made by Government for admission of small percentage of weaker sections granting them freeships and scholarships. The Court observed that profiteering is not permitted in Indian Conditions but such institutions have right to fix fee structure which lead to betterment of education facilities. Such institutions have also right to constitute its governing body for which qualifications may be prescribed by state. Any interference in appointment of persons on board or teachers by State will be unreasonable.

State can take regulate academic standards, atmosphere or infrastructure but State can not fix fee, or appoint teachers or control composition of governing board or nominating students for admission.

Authority granting recognition or affiliation to Private unaided educational institutions can lay down conditions in respect of academic and educational aspects but can not interfere in administration of such institutions.

Unaided professional institutions have to take recognition/affiliation from appropriate authority and follow the regulation required for ensuring academic standards, efficiency, uniformity and excellence. But state cannot interfere in administration and management.

In aided professional institutions State can make rules regarding merit based admission and apply reservation policy. State can also put fetters on administration and management of such institutions.

What will be unit of determining minority institution ?

The Supreme Court reiterated the view taken in **Re. Kerala Education Bill (1957–1959) SCR 995** that religious or linguistic minority has to determined at state level. Inclusion of education in Concurrent List vide 42nd amendment nowhere changes this position.

What will be extent of regulation of minority institutions ?

The Supreme Court held that unaided minority institutions can be autonomous except regulation for maintaining academic standards and atmosphere.

Minority Institutions established under Article 30 (1) availing state aid have to be read with Article 28 (3) and Article 29 (2). Article 30 (1) is not absolute and are subject to provisions of Article 28 (3) and Article 29 (2). Article 28 (3) provides that it will not be required for persons to take part in religious instruction in educations institutions receiving state aid or recognition. Article 29 (2) provides that there will not be any discrimination on ground of religion, race, caste or language in admission to educational institutions receiving state aid.

The Supreme Court held that receiving state aid does not alter the minority character of the minority institution covered under Article 30 (2).

The Supreme Court in Stephens College has held that minority institutions receiving state aid has to admit 50 % students from non-minority community. The rigid principle provided under **St. Stephens College Vs. University of Delhi (1992) 1SCC558** was overruled and minority institutions were given discretion to decide ratio depending on relevant factors. The minority institutions had to give preference in admission to minorities in the state.

ALIGARH MUSLIM UNIVERSITY VS. NARESH AGARWAL

The Supreme Court in **Aligarh Muslim University Vs. Naresh Agarwal, (2024) 11 SCR 1647** overruled **Azeez Basha Vs. Union of India 1968 SCR (1) 833** and formulated indicia for determining minority nature of an institution.

Case Title : Aligarh Muslim University Vs. Naresh Agrawal
Date of Judgment : 08.11.2024
Bench : Chief Justice Dr Dhananjaya Y Chandrachud, Justice Sanjiv Khanna, Justice Surya Kant, Justice J.B. Pardiwala, Justice Dipankar Datta, Justice Manoj Misra, Justice Satish Chandra Sharma

FACTS OF THE CASE

Muhammadan Anglo Oriental College was established in 1877 which was affiliated to Calcutta University and later Allahabad University. The Imperial Legislature passed the Aligarh University Act, 1920 which established and incorporated Aligarh Muslim University (AMU). AMU Act was amended in 1951 and 1965. These amendments were challenged before the Supreme Court in S Azeez Basha which was upheld on the ground that religious minorities do not have the right to administer educational institutions which were not established by them, even if they were administering them for some reason before the commencement of the Constitution.

Subsequently, the AMU framed policy reserving 50% seats for Muslims. Reservation Policy was challenged before the Allahabad High Court in Dr. Naresh Agrawal Vs Union of India wherein the single judge declared the policy unconstitutional relying on Azeez Basha. The decision of single bench was upheld by division bench.

The Supreme Court while hearing appeal found difference of opinion in **Azeez Basha** and **Anjuman-e- Rahmania Vs. District Inspector of Schools** and referred the matter to a seven-judge Bench.

FINDINGS OF THE SUPREME COURT

The Supreme Court observed that the purpose of Article 30 (1) is to ensure that the State does not discriminate against religious and linguistic minorities which seek to establish and administer educational institutions. The Purpose of Article 30 (1) is also to guarantee a "special right" to religious and linguistic minorities that have established educational institutions. This special right is the guarantee of limited state regulation in the administration of the institution. The State must grant the minority institution sufficient autonomy to enable it, to protect the essentials of its minority character. The regulation of the State must be relevant to the purpose of granting recognition or aid as the case may be. The special or additional protection is guaranteed to ensure the protection of the cultural fabric of religious and linguistic minorities.

The Supreme Court observed that it is settled law that right to "establish and administer" has to be read conjunctively. The special right that the provision guarantees to religious and linguistic minorities relates to the administration of educational institutions "of their choice". The expression "of their choice" is of an expansive nature indicating that the choice extends to the full range of educational institutions.

The Supreme Court observed that a distinction between educational institutions established before and after the commencement of the Constitution cannot be made for the purposes of Article 30 (1). Article 30 will stand diluted and weakened if it is only to apply prospectively to institutions established after the commencement of the Constitution. The protection and guarantee, if made applicable to only institutions after the commencement of the Constitution would debase and defile the object and purpose of the Act. Article 372 read with Article 13 (1) stipulates the laws which pre-date the Constitution are unconstitutional if they contravene the Fundamental Rights. The Provisions do not stipulate that laws which pre-date the Constitution cannot receive the additional protection which the Fundamental Rights offer. Right to administration in Article 30 (1) is one such protection.

The Supreme Court observed that teaching universities and colleges serve the common function of educating students. No distinction between the two can be drawn for the purposes of Article 30 (1) which guarantees minorities the right of greater autonomy in the administration of educational institutions to create a model of education which best serves the interests of the community. The word establishment and incorporation cannot be interchangeably used. They connote different meanings. The former refers to founding an institution, which in the case of teaching colleges that were converted to universities would refer to any person or community who undertook the efforts to establish the teaching college.

The Supreme Court observed that the incorporation of the University would not *ipso facto* lead to surrendering of the minority character of the institution. The circumstances surrounding the conversion of a teaching college to a teaching university must be viewed to identify if the minority character of the institution was surrendered upon the conversion. The Court may on a holistic reading of the Statutory provisions relating to the administrative set-up of the educational institution deduced if the minority character or the purpose of establishment was relinquished upon incorporation.

The Supreme Court rejected the argument that minority nature of an institution has to be tested a the time of establishment in pre-independent India. The status of the group/community had to be tested on the date of commencement of the constitution.

The Supreme Court overruled Azeez Basha wherein it has been held that an educational institution is not established by minority if it derives its legal character though a statute. The Supreme Court delineated following factors which have to be considered for determination of minority character of an institution –

(i) The indicia of ideation, purpose and implementation must be satisfied. First, the idea for establishing an educational institution must have stemmed from a person or group belonging to the minority community; second the educational institution must be established predominantly for the benefit of minority community; and third steps for implementation of idea must have been taken by the member(s) of the minority community;

(ii) The administrative-set up of the educational institution must elucidate and affirm the minority character of the educational institution and that it was established to protect and promote the interests of the minority community.

DR. ASHWANI KUMAR VS. UNION OF INDIA

The Supreme Court in **Dr. Ashwani Kumar Vs. Union of India** (2019) **12 SCR 30** has held that any direction to Parliament to enact legislative framework based upon the "Convention against Torture and Other Cruel, Inhuman, or Degrading Treatment or Punishment" adopted by United Nations General Assembly will be in violation of principle of separation of powers enshrined in the Constitution.

Case Title : Dr. Ashwani Kumar Vs. Union of India
Date of Decision : 05.09.2019
Bench : Justice Sanjiv Khanna, Justice Dinesh Maheshwari, Justice Ranjan Gogoi

---

FACTS OF THE CASE

Dr. Ashwani Kumar, former Law Minister and Member of Parliament, has filed Public Interest Litigation under Article 32 of the Constitution of India before the Supreme Court for issuing direction to the Parliament to enact legislative framework based upon the "Convention against Torture and Other Cruel, Inhuman, or Degrading Treatment or Punishment" adopted by United Nations General Assembly.

The aforesaid convention adopted by United National General Assembly was opened for signature, ratification and accession on 10th December, 1984. India has signed the convention on 14th October, 1997 but has not ratified the same.

The issue before the Supreme Court was whether the Supreme Court has power to give directions to the Parliament to enact legislative framework based on UN Convention.

FINDINGS OF THE SUPREME COURT

The Supreme Court noted that strict separation of powers as propounded by Montesquieu which is a feature of American constitution is not a feature of India or Great Britain. There are overlapping between Executive and Legislature in Parliamentary Democracy. But India has a written constitution which divides roles and functions of different organs of State. Adhering to Constitutional limits by every organ of state is a check against potential abuse of power.

The Constitution has specified roles for each organ of State. The Constitution empowers Parliament and State Legislatures to enact laws. The Executive has the primary responsibility for formulating policies and proposing legislations. Interpretation of laws and adjudication is function of judiciary. The Court noted that although the scope of judicial review has expanded, the Courts do not encroach upon field marked for Executive or Legislature.

The Supreme Court noted that it has in its various judgments ie. Kesavananda Bharti Vs State of Kerala, (1973) 4 SCC 225 , State of Rajasthan Vs Union of India, (1977) 3 SCC 592, I R Coelho Vs State of Tamil Nadu, (2007) 2 SCC 1, State of Tamil Nadu Vs State of Kerala, (2014)12 SCC 696   held that separation of powers is part of basic structure of the Indian Constitution. Constitution has made demarcation among three organs without drawing formal lines.

The Supreme Court noted that there is clear distinction between interpretation and adjudication by Courts and power of enact legislation. It is legitimate for a judge to make law within certain limits. Such law-making is in the process of elucidation and explanation. Such law-making is called "judge made law" and not legislation.

The Supreme Court observed that process and method of legislation and judicial adjudication are entirely different. Judicial adjudication involves applying rules of interpretation and law of precedents and notwithstanding deep understanding, knowledge and wisdom of an individual judge or the bench, it cannot be equated with law making in a democratic society by legislators given their wider and broader diverse polity.

The Supreme Court noted that judicial legislation will be against constitutional supremacy and subvert the legislative process.

The Supreme Court noted that Article 253 of the Constitution grants exclusive power on the Parliament to make laws for giving effect to any international agreement, treaty or convention. Further, treaty making is a political act which requires extensive consultation.

The Supreme Court observed that Supreme Court can always step in to protect Fundamental Rights. The Supreme Court noted that it has made interventions for protection of human rights in the Past. The Supreme Court in Sheela Barse Vs State of MaharasHtra (1983) 2 SCC 96 has issued guidelines for protection of rights of arrested persons including female prisoners. The Supreme Court has highlighted human rights aspects in Nilabati Behera Vs. State of Orissa, (1993) 2 SCR 581. The Supreme Court in D. K. Basu Vs. State of West Bengal (1997) 1 SCC 416 has issued directions for procedures followed during arrest.

The Supreme Court noted that Supreme Court will be within its powers to improve upon direction given in aforesaid cases but it can not give direction to Parliament to enact law and dismissed the Petition.

STATE OF UTTARANCHAL VS BALWANT SINGH CHAUFAL

The Supreme Court in **State of Uttaranchal Vs. Balwant Singh Chaufal, (2010) 1 SCR 678** issued several directions for curbing filing of Public Interest Litigation for extraneous considerations.

Case Title : State of Uttaranchal Vs. Balwant Singh Chaufal
Date of Judgment : 18.01.2010
Bench : Justice Mukundakam Sharma, Justice Dalveer Bhandari

FACTS OF THE CASE

Appointment of L. P. Nathani as Advocate General of Uttaranchal was challenged in a Public Interest Litigation before High Court. The High Court directed the State Government to take a decision on the same within fifteen days. The State of Uttaranchal preferred Special Leave Petition before the Supreme Court against the order of High Court. Despite service, Respondents did not appear before the Supreme Court.

FINDINGS OF THE SUPREME COURT

The Supreme Court observed that it is settled law that the Advocate General for the State can be appointed after attaining age of 62 years. Similarly, the Attorney General of India can be appointed after attaining age of 65 years. The Supreme Court held that it was a clear case of abuse of Public Interest Litigation.

Origin of PIL

The Supreme Court observed that PIL is product of realization of the constitutional obligation of the Court. A very large section of society because of extreme poverty, ignorance, discrimination and illiteracy had been denied justice for time immemorial and in fact they have no access to justice.

Pre-dominantly to provide access to justice to the poor, deprived, vulnerable, discriminated and marginalized sections of the society, this court had initiated, encouraged and propelled the public interest litigation. The rule of *locus standi* was diluted and the traditional meaning of "aggrieved person" was broadened to provide access to a very large section of the society which was otherwise not getting any benefit from the judicial system.

The Supreme Court noted that Public Interest Litigation has gone through three phases. The first phase dealt with cases of the Court where directions and orders were passed primarily to protect Fundamental Rights of the marginalized groups and sections of the society who because of extreme poverty, illiteracy and ignorance cannot approach this Court or the High Courts. The second phase dealt with cases relating to protection, preservation of ecology, environment forests, marine life, wildlife, mountain, rivers, historical monuments. The third phase dealt with the directions issued by Courts in maintaining the probity, transparency and integrity in governance.

PIL in other Countries

The Supreme Court noted that Australian Court has diluted the principle of aggrieved person for protection of environment. It was important that the Petitioner did not have any other motive than the stated one of protecting the environment. In USA also, the Supreme Court has diluted the stance and allowed organizations dedicated to protection of environment to fight cases even though such societies are not directly armed by the action in environment cases. In England the use of PIL has been comparably limited. The limited development in PIL has occurred through broadening the rules of standing. The South African Constitution has adopted with a commitment to "transform the society into one in which there will be human dignity, freedom and equality". Thus, improving access to justice falls squarely within the mandate of this constitution. In furtherance of this objective, the South African legal framework takes a favorable stance towards PIL by prescribing broad rules of standing and relaxing pleading requirements.

Abuse of Public Interest Litigation

The Supreme Court noted that such an important jurisdiction which has been carefully carved out, created and nurtured with great care and caution by the Courts is being blatantly abused by filing some petitions with oblique motives. The Supreme Court issued several directions to prevent the abuse of process of law and curbing PIL filed for extraneous considerations. The Supreme Court requested High Courts for framing uniform rules for handling of PIL. Credentials of the Petitioner should be checked before entertaining PIL. The Court should be satisfied that it involves substantial public interest.

MOHD AHAMAD KHAN VS SHAH BANO

The Supreme Court in **Mohd Ahmad Khan Vs Shah Bano, (1985) 3 SCR 844** emphasized the need of enactment of Uniform Civil Code under Article 44 of the Constitution.

> Case Title : Mohd Ahmad Khan Vs Shah Bano
> Date of Judgment : 23.04.1985
> Bench : Chief Justice Y.V. Chandrachud, Justice Ranganath Misra, Justice D.A. Desai, Justice O. Chinnappa Reddy, Justice E.S. Venkataramiah

FACTS OF THE CASE

The appeal involved an application filed by divorced muslim woman for maintenance under Section 125 of the Code of Criminal Procedure, 1973 (Cr.PC). The appellant, an advocate, was married to Shah Bano in 1932. They had three sons and two daughters. The Appellant drove Shah Bano from matrimonial home in 1975. The Respondent filed application for maintenance under Section 125 Cr.P.C. The appellant divorced Shah Bano on November 6, 1978 by irrevocable talaq. His defense was that he was not liable to pay maintenance as he had divorced his wife. The Magistrate ordered for payment of maintenance of Rs. 25 per month which was enhanced by the High Court to Rs. 179.20 per month. The Appellant filed Special Leave Petition before the Supreme Court.

FINDINGS OF THE SUPREME COURT

The Supreme Court observed that under Section 125 (1) (a), a person who has sufficient means neglects or refuses to maintain his wife, who is unable to maintain herself, can be asked by Court to pay a monthly maintenance. Section 125 (1) (b) provides that "wife" includes a divorced woman who had not married again. The religion practiced by spouse or spouses has no place in scheme of Section 125. Whether spouses are Hindus or Muslims, Christians or Parsis, Pagans or Heathens is wholly irrelevant in the application of these provisions. The reason being that Section 125 is part of criminal procedure and not civil laws. The liability imposed by Section 125 to maintain close relatives who are indigent is found upon the individual's obligation to the society to prevent vagrancy and destitution.

A divorced muslim woman, as long as she has not remarried, is a "wife" for the purposes of Section 125. The statutory right available to her under that section is unaffected by the provisions of the personal law applicable to her.

The Supreme Court observed that it would be wrong to hold that the Muslim husband, according to his personal law, is not under an obligation to provide maintenance, beyond the period of iddat to his divorced wife who is unable to maintain herself. There is no conflict between the provisions of Section 125 and those of Muslim Personal Law on the question of the Muslim husband's obligation to provide maintenance for a divorced wife who is unable to maintain herself. The Supreme Court noted that several aiyats in Quran imposes obligation on Muslim husband to make provision for or to provide maintenance to the divorced wife.

NEED FOR UNIFORM CIVIL CODE

The Supreme Court emphasized need of Uniform Civil Code. The Supreme Court observed that a common Civil Code will help the cause of national integration by removing disparate loyalties to laws which have conflicting ideologies. No community is likely to bell that cat by making gratuitous concessions on this issue. It is the State which is charged with the duty of securing a uniform civil code for the citizens of the country and unquestionably, it has the legislative competence to do so. Piecemeal attempts of courts to bridge the gap between personal laws cannot take the place of a Common Civil Code. Justice to all is a far more satisfactory way of dispensing justice than justice from case to case.

PROPERTY OWNER ASSOCIATION VS STATE OF MAHARASHTRA

The Supreme Court held in **Property Owner Association Vs. State of Maharashtra (2024) 16 SCC 1** has held that not every resource owned by an individual can be considered a 'material resource of the community' merely because it meets the qualifier of 'material needs'.

Case Title : Property Owner Association Vs. State of Maharashtra
Date of Decision : 05.11.2024
Bench : Chief Justice D. Y. Chandrachud, Justice Hrishikesh Roy, Justice B. V. Nagarathna, Justice Sudhanshu Dhulia, Justice J. B. Pardiwala, Justice Manoj Mishra, Justice Rajesh Bindal, Justice Satish Chandra Sharma, Justice A. G. Masih

FACTS OF THE CASE

The State Legislature of Maharashtra enacted the Maharashtra Housing and Areas Development Act, 1976 which received the assent of the President on 25th April 1977. The objective of the Act was to unify, consolidate and amend the laws relating to housing, repairing and reconstructing dangerous building and carrying out improvement in slum areas.

On 26th February, 1986 Government of Maharashtra inserted Chapter VIII A in the aforesaid Act vide an ordinance providing for acquisition of cessed properties for co-operative societies of occupiers. The provision of the Chapter envisaged acquisition of such properties by the state and their transfer to a cooperative society on payment of a hundred times the monthly rent of the premises if seventy per cent of the occupiers of the building make an application to this effect.

Property Owner Association challenged the provisions on the ground that compulsory acquisition of private property violated their constitutional rights.

FINDINGS OF THE SUPREME COURT

Article 39 (b) provides that the ownership and control of the material resources of the community are so distributed as best to subserve the common good. Article 31 C provides that laws giving effect to policy of state securing principles under Article 39 (b) and (c) shall be deemed to be void on the ground that it is inconsistent with or takes away or abridges any of the rights conferred by Article 14 or 19.

The Constitution Bench decided two important issues in this case :

(I) Whether Article 31C (as upheld in Kesavananda Bharati) survives in the Constitution after the amendment to the provision by the forty-second amendment was struck down by this court in Minerva Mills Case?

(ii) Whether the interpretation of Article 39 (b) adopted by Justice Krishna Iyer in Ranganatha Reddy and followed in Sanjeev Coke must be reconsidered. Whether the phrase "material resources of community" in Article 39 (b) can be interpreted to include resources that are owned privately and not by the state ?

The Supreme Court held that after Minerva Mills invalidated Section 4 of the Forty Second Amendment, the composite legal effect of Section 4 is nullified and the unamended text of Article 31 C stands revived.

Five judge Bench in Sanjiv Coke relied on minority opinion of the Justice Krishna Iyer in Ranganatha Reddy and concluded that material resources of the community are not confined to public-owned resources but include all resources, natural and man-made, public and private owned. The Supreme Court observed that it erred in relying on the observations in the opinion of Justice Krishna Iyer in Ranganath Reddy, when the binding opinion of the majority of judges expressly stated their ability to agree with those observations.

The Supreme Court observed that single-line observation in Mafatlal that the phrase "material resources of the community" used in Article 39(b) includes privately owned resources was *obiter dicta*.

The direct question referred to this bench is whether the phrase 'material resources of the community' used in Article 39(b) includes privately owned resources. Theoretically, the answer is yes, the phrase may include privately owned resources. However, this Court is unable to subscribe to the expansive view adopted in the minority judgement authored by Justice Krishna Iyer in Ranganatha Reddy and subsequently relied on by this Court in Sanjeev Coke.

Not every resource owned by an individual can be considered a 'material resource of the community' merely because it meets the qualifier of 'material needs'.

The inquiry about whether the resource in question falls within the ambit of Article 39(b) must be context-specific and subject to a non–exhaustive list of factors such as the nature of the resource and its characteristics; the impact of the resource on the well-being of the community; the scarcity of the resource; and the consequences of such a resource being concentrated in the hands of private players. The Public Trust Doctrine evolved by this Court may also help identify resources which fall within the ambit of the phrase "material resource of the community";

The term 'distribution' has a wide connotation. The various forms of distribution which can be adopted by the state cannot be exhaustively detailed. However, it may include the vesting of the concerned resources in the state or nationalisation. In the specific case, the Court must determine whether the distribution subserves the common good

AIIMS STUDENTS UNION VS AIIMS

The Supreme Court in **AIIMS Students Union Vs AIIMS, (2001) Supp 2 SCR 79** held that Fundamental Duties, though not enforceable by a writ of the court, yet provide a valuable guide and aid to interpretation of constitutional and legal issues.

Case Title : AIIMS Students Union Vs AIIMS
Date of Judgment : 24.08.2001
Bench : Chief Justice A. S. Anand, Justice R.C. Lahoti, Justice Shivaraj V. Patil

---

FACTS OF THE CASE

Three meritorious students challenged reservation granted in post graduate courses in AIIMS. The prospectus issued in 1995 declared that the selection shall be on merits. 15% seats were reserved for Scheduled Castes, 7.5% were reserved for Scheduled Tribes, 33% was reserved for those who served in Rural Area or belonged to Backward Area or had worked in Family Welfare Programmes, 33% reservation was for students from AIIMS. There was also 50% reservation discipline wise of AIIMS students subject to 33% in total.

Result of examination was declared on 08.01.1996. Writ Petitioners 1, 2 and 3 secured ranks 10, 12 and 89 respectively. Due to reservation policy in several disciplines, there were no seats available for open category candidates.

Reservation in favour of in-house candidates were challenged before Delhi High Court. Delhi High Court struck down reservation given to AIIMS at entry level and discipline wise.

FINDINGS OF THE SUPREME COURT

It was contended – firstly, that term reservation has been loosely employed here, what has been provided for is merely a source of entry or a channel for admission, the validity whereof is not required to be tested on the principles having relevance for Articles 15 and 16 of the Constitution. Secondly, reservation is justified on well accepted principle of institutional continuity.

The Supreme Court held that in house selection cannot be treated as a separate source of entry. Merit cannot be sacrificed to the extent of bidding almost a good-bye to merit resulting into candidates too low in merit being preferred to candidates too high in merit and margin of difference between the two being too wide. The division of seats between two classes coupled with two level reservation and unique percentile method is resulting in reservation which ensures to the extent of 100% of PG seats followed by guaranteed placement in the choicest of creamy disciplines to the candidates belonging to one category without regard to their competitive merit. This is not a reservation but a super-reservation and certainly not a source of entry.

The Supreme Court observed that as far back as in 1984, the Supreme Court had disapproved reservation in postgraduate courses on the ground of institutional preference though justified a reasonable institutional preference being allowed for the present having regard to broader considerations of equality of opportunity and institutional continuity in education.

The Supreme Court observed that preamble to the Constitution of India secures, as one of its objects, fraternity assuring the dignity of the individual and the unity and integrity of the nation to "we the people of India". Reservation unless protected by the Constitution itself, as given to us by the founding fathers and as adopted by the people of India, is sub-version of fraternity, unity and integrity and dignity of the individual. While dealing with Directive Principle of State Policy, Article 46 is taken note of often by overlooking Articles 41 and 47. Article 41 obliges the State inter alia to make effective provision for securing the right to work and right to education. Any reservation in favour of one is an inroad on the right of others to work and to learn. Article 47 recognizes the improvement of public health as one of the primary duties of the State. Public health can be improved by having the best of doctors, specialists and super specialists. Under-graduate level is a primary or basic level of education in medical sciences wherein reservation can be understood as the fulfilment of societal obligation of the State towards the weaker segments of the society. Beyond this, a reservation is a reversion or diversion from the performance of primary duty of the State. Permissible reservation at the lowest of primary rung is a step in the direction of assimilating the lesser fortunes in mainstream of society by bringing them to the level of others which they cannot achieve unless protectively pushed. Once that is done the protection needs to be withdrawn in the own interest of protectees so that they develop strength and feel confident of stepping on higher rungs on their own legs shedding the crutches. Pushing the protection of reservation beyond the primary level betrays "bigwigs'" desire to keep the crippled crippled forever. Rabindra Nath Tagore's vision of a free India cannot be complete unless "knowledge is free" and "tireless striving stretches its arms towards perfection".

The Supreme Court further observed that almost a quarter century after the people of India have given the Constitution unto themselves, a chapter on Fundamental Duties came to the incorporated in the Constitution. Fundamental Duties as defined in Article 51A are not made enforceable by a Writ Court just as the Fundamental Rights are, but it cannot be lost sight of that "duties" in Part IV A - Article 51A are prefixed by the same word "Fundamental" which was prefixed by the founding fathers of the Constitution to "rights" in Part III. Every citizen of India is fundamentally obligated to develop the scientific temper and humanism. He is fundamentally duty bound to strive towards excellence in all spheres of individual and collective activity so that the nation constantly rises to higher levels of endeavour and achievements. State is, all the citizens placed together, and hence though Article 51A does not expressly cast any Fundamental Duty on the State, the fact remains that the duty of every citizen of India is the collective duty of the State. Any reservation, apart from being sustainable on the constitutional anvil must also be reasonable to be permissible. In assessing the reasonability one of the factors to be taken into consideration would be whether the character and quantum of reservation would stall or accelerate achieving the ultimate goal of excellence enabling the nation constantly rising to the higher levels. In the era of globalization, where the nation as a whole has to compete with other nations of the world so as to survive, excellence cannot be given an unreasonable go by and certainly not compromised in its entirety. Fundamental Duties, though not enforceable by a writ of the court, yet provide a valuable guide and aid to interpretation of constitutional and legal issues. In case of doubt or choice, people's wish as manifested through Article 51 A can serve as a guide not only for resolving the issue but also for constructing or moulding the relief to be given by the Court. Constitutional enactment of Fundamental Duties, if it has to have any meaning, must be used by Courts as a tool to tab, even a taboo, on State action drifting away from constitutional values.

The Supreme Court declared the institutional reservation for AIIMS candidates ultra vires the Constitution.

RAI SAHIB RAM JAWAYA KAPUR VS STATE OF PUNJAB

The Supreme Court in **Rai Sahib Ram Jawaya Kapur Vs State of Punjab, (1955) 2 SCR 225** observed that the President has been made formal or constitutional head of the Government while real executive powers are vested in ministers or the Cabinet.

Case Title : Rai Sahib Ram Jawaya Kapur Vs State of Punjab
Date of Judgment : 12.04.1955
Bench : Chief Justice Mukherjea, Justice Vivian Bose, Justice Jagannadha Das, Justice Venkatarama Justice Ayyar, Justice Imam

---

FACTS OF THE CASE

In State of Punjab, all recognized schools had to follow the course of studies approved by Education Department of the Government. Prior to 1950, books on several subjects were published by publishers according to policies framed by the Government and submitted to Government for approvals. Government used to approve 3 to 10 books on each subject. Head Master of the School was given discretion to prescribe any book out of them.

State Government changed the policy from 1950 onwards. Books on some of subjects were being published by Government itself. On other subjects one book was being approved by the Government.

In 1952 "publishers" word was even omitted and invitation was given only to "authors" to submit books. In case of approval Government used to publish books.

Because of these policies business of several publishers were impacted. Some of them approached the Supreme Court under Article 32 of the Constitution of India.

FINDINGS OF THE SUPREME COURT

It was contended that Government has no power of printing textbooks without sanction of the legislature. The Supreme Court observed that it may not be possible to frame an exhaustive definition of what executive functions means and implies. Executive power connotes the residue of governmental functions that remain after legislative and judicial function have been taken away. The Constitution does not recognize separation of powers in strict rigidity but functions of different branches have been sufficiently differentiated. However, it does not follow that in order to enable the executive to function there must be a law already in existence and power of the executive are limited to merely carrying out the law.

The Supreme Court observed that Indian Constitution, though federal, has adopted British Parliamentary System where executive is deemed to have the primary responsibility for formulation of government policy and its transmission into law. The executive function includes both formulation of policy as well its execution.

Under Article 53 (1) of the Constitution vests executive powers with the President of India but Article 75 provides for Council of Ministers with the Prime Minister at its head to aid and advise the President in exercise of his functions. Thus, the President has been made formal and Constitutional head while real powers are vested in Council of Ministers. Similar situation exists in the State also. The Cabinet enjoying, as it does, a majority in the legislature concentrates in itself control of both executive and legislative functions.

If Government formulates policy for start of trade or business, a specific legislation is not necessary. It was also contended that the policy violates Fundamental Rights granted under Article 19 (1) (g) of the Constitution which guarantees to all persons right to carry on any trade or business. The Supreme Court observed that there is no Fundamental Right in publishers that any of the book published by them should be recognized by the Government as text book. The Court noted even before the impugned policy came into existence publishers had only a chance of their book prescribed as text book. Publishers can publish books of their choice but cannot claim that their books should be approved as text book. The decision of Government can be good or bad but cannot be said to be infraction of Fundamental Right enshrined under Article 19 (1) (g) of the Constitution.

MARU RAM VS UNION OF INDIA

The Supreme Court in **Maru Ram Vs Union of India, (1981) 1 SCR 1196** held that powers under Article 72 or Article 161 by the President or the Governor, as the case may be, have to be exercised on the aid and advice of Council of Ministers.

Case Title : **Maru Ram Vs Union of India**
Date of Judgment : **11.11.1980**
Bench : Chief Justice Y.V. Chandrachud, Justice V.R. Krishna Iyer, Justice P.N. Bhagwati, Justice Syed Murtaza Fazal Ali, Justice A.D. Koshal

---

FACTS OF THE CASE

Section 433 A of the Code of Criminal Procedure has been challenged before the Supreme Court in several Writ Petitions which provided that where a sentence of imprisonment of life is imposed on conviction of a person for an offence for which death is one of the punishments provided by law or where the sentence of death imposed on a person has been commuted under Section 433 into one of imprisonment for life, such person shall not be released from prison unless he had served at least fourteen years of imprisonment.

FINDINGS OF THE SURPEME COURT

It was contended by the appellants that Section 433 A violates Article 72 and 161 of the Constitution. Section 433 A is wholly arbitrary and irrational and violates Article 14. It was also contended that Section 433A Cr.P.C is violative of Article 20 (1).

The Supreme Court noted that before amendment many a murderer or other offender who could have been given death sentence by the court but has been actually awarded only life sentence might have been released the very next morning, or next year, after a decade or at any other time the appropriate Government was in mood to remit his sentence.

The Supreme Court observed that sentencing is a judicial function but execution of a sentence is ordinarily a matter of executive function. Once sentence has been imposed, the only way to terminate is before the stipulated term is by action under Section 432/433 Cr.P.C. or Article 72/161.

The Supreme Court observed that an order of remission does not wipe out the offence, it also does not wipe out the conviction. All that it does is to have an effect on the execution of the sentence.

The Supreme Court rejected that argument that Section 433 A violates Section 20 (1) of the Constitution as inflexible sentencing of 14 years retroactively enlarges the sentence. The Supreme Court observed that no greater punishment is inflicted by Section 433 A than the law annexed originally to the crime. Nor is any vested right to remission cancelled by compulsory 14 years in jail life once it is realized that a life sentence is a sentence for a whole life.

The Supreme Court also rejected the argument that Section 433 A violates Article 14 of the Constitution. The Supreme Court noted that the triple purposes of sentencing are retribution, deterrence, and rehabilitation. Deterrence has been accepted as valid punitive component. Incarceration for 14 years for gravest crimes like murder is not shocking. Further, even for correctional therapy, a long hospitalization in prison may be needed.

The Supreme Court held that Section 433 Cr. P. C. does not violate Article 72 or Article 161. Power under Article 72 and Article 161 cannot be equated with power granted under Section 433 A Cr.P.C. The source is different, the strength is different, although the stream may be flowing along the same bed. Two powers are far from being identical and obviously the constitutional power is "untouchable" and "unapproachable" and cannot suffer the vicissitudes of the simple legislative processes. Therefore Section 433 A cannot be invalidated as indirectly violative of Article 72 and Article 161.

The Supreme Court held that power under Article 72 and 161 of the Constitution can be exercised by the Central and State Governments, not by the President or Governor on their own. The advice of the appropriate Government binds the Governor or the President as the case may be.

The Supreme Court observed that considerations for exercise of power under Article 72/161 may be myriad and their occasions protean and are left to the appropriate government, but no consideration nor occasion can be wholly irrelevant, irrational, discriminatory or mala fide. Only in these rare cases will the court examine the exercise.

The Supreme Court held Section 433 Cr.P.C. constitutionally valid.

SHATRUGHAN CHAUHAN VS STATE OF UP

The Supreme Court in **Shatrughan Chauhan Vs. State of UP, (2014) 1 SCR 609** held that supervening events like delay in determination of mercy petitions, insanity of convict etc. can be grounds of commutation of death sentence.

Case Title : Shatrughan Chauhan Vs. State of UP
Date of Judgment : 21.01.2014
Bench : Chief Justice Sathasivam, Justice Ranjan Gogoi, Justice Shiva Kirti Singh

FACTS OF THE CASE

Several Writ Petitions were filed under Article 32 of the Constitution of India by either convicts, who were awarded death sentence or by their family members or by public spirited bodies like People's Union for Democratic Rights (PUDR) based on the rejection of mercy petitions by the Governor and the President of India.

It was contended by the Petitioners that the impugned executive orders of rejection of mercy petitions convicts were passed without considering the supervening events i.e. delay, insanity, solitary confinement, judgments declared per incuriam, procedural lapse etc which are crucial for deciding the same.

FINDINGS OF THE SUPREME COURT

Nature of Power under Article 72/161

The Supreme Court observed that both Articles 72 and 161 repose the power of the people in the highest dignitaries i.e. the President or the Governor of a State, as the case may be, and there are no words of limitation indicated in either of the two Articles. The President or the Governor, as the case may be, in exercise of power under Article 72/161 respectively, may examine the evidence afresh and this exercise of power is clearly independent of the judiciary. This Court, in numerous instances, clarified that the executive is not sitting as a court of appeal rather the power of President/Governor to grant remission of sentence is an act of grace and humanity in appropriate cases i.e. distinct, absolute and unfettered in its nature.

The Supreme Court observed that the power vested in the President under Article 72 and the Governor under Article 161 of the Constitution is a Constitutional duty. As a result, it is neither a matter of grace nor a matter of privilege but is an important constitutional responsibility reposed by the people in the highest authority. The power of pardon is essentially an executive action, which needs to be exercised in the aid of justice and not in defiance of it. Further, it is well settled that the power under Article 72/161 of the Constitution of India is to be exercised on the aid and advice of the Council of Ministers.

Limited Judicial Review

The Supreme Court relying on **Maru Ram Vs Union of India (1981) SCR (1) 1196** , **Epuru Sudhakar Vs. Govt. of A.P. (2006) 8 SCC 161** etc observed that it is clear that the President/Governor is not bound to hear a petition for mercy before taking a decision on the Petition. The manner of exercise of the power under the said articles is primarily a matter of discretion and ordinarily the courts would not interfere with the decision on merits. However, the Courts retain the limited power of judicial review to ensure that the Constitutional authorities consider all the relevant materials before arriving at a conclusion. Such grounds can be – (i) passing of order without application of mind, (ii) passing of order on extraneous or wholly irrelevant considerations (iii) relevant materials have been kept out of consideration (9) order suffering from arbitrariness.

Delay in determination of mercy petition

The Supreme Court was of view that undue, inordinate and unreasonable delay in execution of death sentence does certainly attribute to torture which indeed is in violation of Article 21 and thereby entails as the ground for commutation of sentence. However, the nature of delay i.e. whether it is undue or unreasonable must be appreciated based on facts of the individual cases and no exhaustive guidelines can be framed in this regard.

Insanity of the convict

The Supreme Court observed that if the death convict is insane and it is duly certified by the competent doctor, undoubtedly, Article 21 protects him and such person cannot be executed without further clarification from the competent authority about his mental problems. In view of the well established laws both at national as well as international sphere, insanity can be considered as one of the supervening circumstances that warrants for commutation of death sentence to life imprisonment.

The Supreme Court held that exercising of power under Article 72/161 by the President or the Governor is a constitutional obligation and not a mere prerogative. Considering the high status of office, the Constitutional framers did not stipulate any outer time limit for disposing the mercy petitions under the said articles, which means it should be decided within reasonable time. However, when the delay caused in disposing the mercy petitions is seen to be unreasonable, unexplained and exorbitant, it is duty of this Court to step in and consider this aspect. Right to seek for mercy under Article 72/161 of the Constitution is a constitutional right and not at the discretion or whims of the executive. Every constitutional duty must be fulfilled with due care and diligence otherwise judicial interference is the command of the Constitution for upholding its values.

The Supreme Court commuted the sentence of several convicts from death sentence into imprisonment of life.

JAYA BACHCHAN VS UNION OF INDIA

The Supreme Court in **Jaya Bachchan Vs Union of India, AIR (2006) SC 2119** held that for deciding the question as to whether one is holding an office of profit or not , what is relevant is whether the office is capable of yielding a profit or pecuniary gain and not whether the person actually obtained a monetary gain.

Case Title : Jaya Bachchan Vs Union of India
Date of Judgment : 08.05.2006
Bench : Chief Justice Y. K. Sabharwal, Justice C.K. Thakker, Justice R.V. Raveendran

FACTS OF THE CASE

The Government of Uttar Pradesh appointed Smt. Jaya Bachchan as Chairperson of Uttar Pradesh Film Development Council (UPFDC). Chairperson of UPFDC was conferred status of cabinet rank. She was entitled to honorarium of Rs. 5,000/- per month, daily allowance of Rs. 600/- per day within state and Rs. 750/- outside state, entertainment allowance of Rs. 10,000/-, staff car with driver, telephone, one P.S., One P.A., and two class IV employees, body guard and night escort, free accommodation, medical treatment, and free accommodation in government circuit houses.

Election Commission was of opinion that office of chairperson of UPFDC was "office of profit" under Article 102 (1) (a) of the Constitution of India. On the basis of opinion of the Election Commission, Smt. Jaya Bachchan was disqualified from being a member of Rajya Sabha. Smt. Jaya Bachchan filed Writ Petition under Article 32 against disqualification order.

FINDINGS OF THE SUPREME COURT

It was contended by Smt. Jaya Bachchan that conferment of cabinet post was only decorative. She did not receive any remuneration or monetary benefit from the State Government. She did not seek any residential accommodation nor used telephone or medical facilities. She has also not claimed any reimbursement. She claimed that as she has not received any monetary benefit as such her disqualification was invalid.

The Supreme Court observed that Clause (1) (a) of Article 102 provides that a person shall be disqualified for being chosen as, and for being, a member of either House of Parliament if he holds any office of profit under the Government of India or the Government of any State, other than an office declared by Parliament by law not to disqualify its holder. The term holds an office of profit though not defined has been the subject matter of interpretation in several decision of this Court. An office of profit is an office which is capable to yielding a profit or pecuniary gain. Holding an office under the Central or State Government to which some pay, salary, emolument, remuneration or non-compensatory allowance is attached, is holding an office of profit. The question whether a person holds an office of profit is required to be interpreted in a realistic manner. Nature of the payment must be considered as a matter of substance rather than of form. Nomenclature is not important. In fact, mere use of the word "honorarium" cannot take the payment out of the purview of profit, if there is pecuniary gain for the recipient. Payment of honorarium, in addition to daily allowances in the nature of compensatory allowances, rent free accommodation and chauffeur driven car at State expense are clearly in the nature of remuneration and a source of pecuniary gain and hence constitute profit. For deciding the question as to whether one is holding an office of profit or not , what is relevant is whether the office is capable of yielding a profit or pecuniary gain and not whether the person actually obtained a monetary gain. If the "Pecuniary gain" is "receivable" in connection with the office then it becomes an office of profit, irrespective of whether such pecuniary gain is actually received or not. If the office carries with it or entitles the holder to any pecuniary gain other than reimbursement of out of pocket/actual expenses, then the office will be an office of profit for the purposes of Article 102 (1) (a) . This position of law stands settled for over half a century commencing from the decisions of **Ravanna Subanna Vs. G. S. Kaggeerappa AIR (1954) SC 653; Shivamurthy Swami Inamdar Vs. Agadi Sanganna Andanappa (1971) 3 SCC 870; Satrucharla Chandrasekhar Raju Vs. Vvricheria Pradeep Kumar Dev (1992) 4 SCC 404** and **Shibu Soren Vs. Dayanand Sahay & Ors (2001) 7 SCC 425.**

The Supreme Concluded that in this case the office in question carried monthly honorarium, entertainment allowance, staff car with driver, telephone etc. These are pecuniary gains. The fact the Smt. Jaya Bachchan did not avail these benefits are not relevant to the issue. The Supreme Court dismissed the Writ Petition and upheld disqualification of Smt. Jaya Bachchan.

KIHOTO HOLLOHAN VS ZACHILLHU AND OTHERS

The Supreme Court in **Kihoto Hollohan Vs Zachillhu, 1992 1 SCR 686** upheld the Fifty-second Amendment of the Indian Constitution whereby Tenth Schedule has been introduced in respect of disqualification of members of Parliament or Legislative Assemblies in cases of political defections. The Supreme Court also held the decision of speaker regarding disqualification is amenable to judicial review on limited grounds of violation of constitutional mandate, mala fides, violation of principles of natural justice and perversity.

Case Title : Kihoto Hollohan Vs Zachillhu
Date of Judgment : 18.02.1992
Bench : Justice L. M. Sharma, Justice J. S. Verma, Justice S. C. Agarwal, Justice K. Jayachandra Reddy, Justice M. N. Venkatachaliah

---

FACTS OF THE CASE

Parliament vide Fifty-second amendment introduced Tenth Schedule in the Indian Constitution introducing anti defection measures. Tenth Schedule provided for disqualification of member of a House in case of voluntary giving up of membership of a Political Party or in case of voting contrary to direction of a Political Party or joining another Political Party. Tenth Schedule also empowered the Speaker or Chairman of a House, as the case may be, to determine question of disqualification. Para 7 of Tenth Schedule barred the jurisdiction of any Court in respect of disqualification of the member of a house. Fifty Second Amendment was challenged before the Supreme Court in this batch of Petitions.

FINDINGS OF THE SUPREME COURT

The Supreme Court determined following issues in this matter.

Whether Tenth Schedule violates freedom of speech ?

It was contended before the Supreme Court that Tenth Schedule violates freedom of speech, right to dissent and right to conscience which are essential democratic principles. The Supreme Court observed the freedom of speech of a member is not an absolute freedom. The provisions of Tenth Schedule do not intend to make a member liable to "Court" for anything said or vote given in house. Rights and Immunities granted under Article 105 (2) can not be elevated to status of Fundamental Rights and Tenth Schedule can not be struck down for being in violation of Article 19.

The Court noted that political party function on shared political belief. Voting contrary to view of the political party will embarrass its image and popularity. There may be circumstances where a member may vote or abstain from voting contrary to direction of political party, which has set up him as candidate and such circumstances have been accommodated. A member make take prior permission for such voting or his action may be condoned by Political Party.

The Supreme Court held that Tenth Schedule does not violate freedom to speech or freedom to vote or freedom of conscience. The Supreme Court also held that Tenth Schedule does not violate freedom under Article 105 and Article 194 of the Constitution.

Whether Tenth Schedule violates Article 368 (2) of the Constitution ?

It was contended that para 7 of the 10th Schedule is violative of Article 136, 226 and 227 of the constitution. The Court noted that Para 7 although directly does not impact these provisions it curtails operations of these articles in respect of matters falling under Tenth Schedule. As such, amendment would have required ratification by States in accordance with Article 368 (2) of the Constitution.

The Supreme Court also held that only Para 7 is invalid and severed from other provisions of the Tenth Schedule. Remaining provisions of Tenth Schedule is constitutionally valid.

Is decision of Speaker subject to judicial review ?

The Supreme Court observed the office of Speaker is tribunal under Para 6 (1) of the Tenth Schedule. The Court held that there is exercise of judicial power when dispute involves a decision on rights and obligations of the parties to it.

The Supreme Court held that finality clause under Para 6 does not exclude power of judicial review under Article 136, 226 and 227 but scope of such judicial review is limited. The scope of such judicial review are limited to infirmities based on violation of constitutional mandate, *mala fides*, violation of principles of natural justice and perversity.

Such judicial review cannot be available at a stage prior to the making of a decision by the Speaker/Chairman. *Qua timet* action will also not be permissible. Interference will also not be permissible at interlocutory stage of the proceedings.

Does office of Speaker pass the test of Independent and Impartial adjudicatory machinery ?

It was contended that determination of electoral disputes is essential feature of democracy. The Speaker does not have to resign to become speaker as such he can not be expected to be free from tugs and pulls of political polarizations.

The Supreme Court observed that office of Speaker is high and important in a democracy. The office of speaker can not be distrusted only because some of speakers have not maintained high standard.

KEISHAM MEGHACHANDRA SINGH VS THE HON'BLE SPEAKER MANIPUR LEGISLATIVE ASSEMBLY

The Supreme Court in **Keisham Meghachandra Singh Vs. Hon'ble Speaker Manipur Legislative Assembly (2020) 3 SCC 1** has held that if speaker refrains from taking a decision within reasonable time, it is within jurisdiction of the High Court or the Supreme Court to give direction to the Speaker for determination.

Case Title : Keisham Meghachandra Singh Vs. Hon'ble Speaker Manipur Legislative Assembly & Ors
Date of Decision : 21.01.2020
Bench : Justice V. Ramasubramanian, Justice Aniruddha Bose, Justice R.F. Nariman

FACTS OF THE CASE

None of the political parties had secured majority in 11th Manipur Legislative Assembly conducted in March, 2017. Congress emerged as largest party and secured 28 seats and BJP secured 28 seats. BJP staked claim for forming government and the same was permitted by the Governor. Respondent No. 3, who was set up as a candidate by congress, supported the government formed by BJP and was also appointed minister. Various applications were filed with the speaker for disqualification of Respondent No. 3. These applications were not being determined by the Speaker as such petitions were filed before the High Court. The High Court held that it has power to issue direction to the Speaker but refused to give any relief as similar issue was pending before the Constitution Bench of the Supreme Court.

FINDINGS OF THE SUPREME COURT

Appeals were filed before the Supreme Court. Additional Solicitor General appearing on behalf of the Speaker relying on reference to larger bench in **S.A. Sampath Kumar v. Kale Yadaiah and Ors. SLP(C) No. 33677/2015** has requested the Court to await the pronouncement by the larger bench. The supreme Court observed that there is no need to await the judgment in light of judgment of the Supreme Court in **Rajendra Singh Rana and Ors. Vrs-Swami Prasad Maurya and Ors. reported in (2007) 4 SCC 270,** which has also been delivered by five judge bench.

The Supreme Court noted that it has held in **Kihoto Hollohan v. Zachillhu & Ors. (1992) Supp. (2) SCC 65** that the power to resolve dispute under tenth schedule is a judicial power. Finality of decision under Para 6 (1) of the Tenth Schedule does not bar judicial review under Article 136, 226 or 227. But judicial review is limited to violations of constitutional mandates, mala fides, non-compliance with Rules of Natural Justice and perversity. Such judicial review is not available at a stage prior to making of a decision by the Speaker. No *quia timet* actions are permissible.

The Supreme Court observed that **Rajendra Singh Rana** has dealt with exactly the same issue and held that when a speaker refrains from deciding a petition within a reasonable time, there was clearly an error which attracted jurisdiction of the High Court in exercise of the power of judicial review.

The Supreme Court held that the same result would ensue even after reading **Kihoto Hollohan**. Relevant para is as under:

28. A reading of the aforesaid decisions, therefore, shows that what was meant to be outside the pale of judicial review in paragraph 110 of Kihoto Hollohan (supra) are quia timet actions in the sense of injunctions to prevent the Speaker from making a decision on the ground of imminent apprehended danger which will be irreparable in the sense that if the Speaker proceeds to decide that the person be disqualified, he would incur the penalty of forfeiting his membership of the House for a long period. Paragraphs 110 and 111 of Kihoto Hollohan (supra) do not, therefore, in any manner, interdict judicial review in aid of the Speaker arriving at a prompt decision as to disqualification under the provisions of the Tenth Schedule. Indeed, the Speaker, in acting as a Tribunal under the Tenth Schedule is bound to decide disqualification petitions within a reasonable period. What is reasonable will depend on the facts of each case, but absent exceptional circumstances for which there is good reason, a period of three months from the date on which the petition is filed is the outer limit within which disqualification petitions filed before the Speaker must be decided if the constitutional objective of disqualifying persons who have infracted the Tenth Schedule is to be adhered to. This period has been fixed keeping in mind the fact that ordinarily the life of the Lok Sabha and the Legislative Assembly of the States is 5 years and the fact that persons who have incurred such disqualification do not deserve to be MPs/MLAs even for a single day, as found in Rajendra Singh Rana (supra), if they have infracted the provisions of the Tenth Schedule.

The Supreme Court also made recommendations for constitution of permanent tribunal under a retired judge of the Supreme Court for adjudication of disputes on account of defection under 10th Schedule.

The Supreme Court refused to determine the disqualification petition as it was prerogative of the speaker but directed the speaker to determine the same within four weeks.

SUBHASH DESAI VS PRINCIPAL SECRETARY, GOVERNOR OF MAHARASTRA

The Supreme Court in **Subhash Desai Vs. Principal Secretary, Governor of Maharashtra, (2023) 8 SCR 857** held that (i) Speaker is empowered to determine disqualification under 10th Schedule in the first instance , (ii) Political Party has right to issue whip, (iii) Election Commission of India (ECI) and Speaker has concurrent power to determine award of symbol and disqualification respectively (iv) Governor has wrongly called upon Mr. Uddhav Thackeray to prove confidence in the Legislative Assembly and (v) referred **Nabam Rebia Vs. Deputy Speaker (2016) 8SCC 1** to larger Bench.

Case Title : Subhash Desai Vs. Principal Secretary, Governor of Maharashtra

Date of Judgment : 23.08.2022

Bench : Chief Justice D. Y. Chandrachud, Justice M. R. Shah, Justice Krishna Murari, Justice Hima Kohli, Justice P. S, Narasimha

FACTS OF THE CASE

14th Legislative Elections was conducted in October, 2019. Of 280 seats, BJP won 106 seats, Shiv Sena won 56 sears, NCP won 53 seats and INC 44 seats. Shiv Sena, NCP and INC formed a post-poll alliance which came to be known as Maha Vikas Aghadi. MVS successfully formed government with Mr. Uddhav Thackeray as Chief Minister. Mr Eknath Shinde was appointed as Leader of Shiv Sena Legislature Party (SSLP). Mr. Sunil Prabhu was appointed as Chief Whip.

SSLP fractured into factions. One led by Sh. Uddhav Thackeray and another led by Sh. Eknath Shinde. On 21st June, 2022 Meeting of MLA was called wherein Eknath Shinde was removed as Leader of SSLP. The decision was communicated to the Deputy Speaker, which was accepted by Deputy Speaker.

Concurrently, on the same date meeting of Shinde Group was conducted in Assam and Sh. Eknath Shinde was re-confirmed as Leader of SSLP and Sunil Prabhu was replaced with Bharat Gogawale. Shinde Group claimed that information regarding the same was shared with Deputy Speaker on 21st June, 2022 while Uddhava group claims that information was received on 22nd June, 2022.

On 23rd June, 2022 Sunil Prabhu filed Petition under 10th Schedule for disqualification of 15 MLA. On 27th June, Respondents filed Writ Petitions under Article 32 of the Constitution challenging the disqualification notices.

Sunil Prabhu again filed Petition for disqualification of two independent MLA, one MLA of Prahar Janshakti, and 22 MLA of Shiv Sena. On 28th June, 2022 Leader of Opposition wrote letter to the Governor claiming that Mr. Uddhava Thackrey did not enjoy confidence of majority requested for directing Mr. Uddhava Thackery to prove the same. The Governor directed Mr. Uddhava Thackrey to prove majority on 30th June, 2022.

On 29th June, 2022 , Sunil Prabhu filed Writ Petition before the Supreme Court for setting aside communication dated 28th June, 2022 by the Governor on the ground that disqualification petitions of 42 members were pending for determination. The Court declined to stay the trust vote. Sh. Uddhav Thackrey resigned.

On 30th June, 2022, Governor administered oath of office to Mr. Shinde and Mr. Fadnavis as Chief Minister and Deputy Chief Minister respectively. Suresh Prabhu issued two whips – one to vote against motion of confidence on 4th Juny, 2022 and another to vote for speaker candidate for Shiv Shena (Uddhava Group) Mr. Rajan Salvi scheduled on 3rd July, 2022. Mr. Rahul Narvekar of BJP emerged victorious for the post of speaker. 39 MLA of Shiv Sena voted in favour of Rahul Narvekar. Mr Suresh Prabhu initiated fresh disqualifications against these MLA. After assuming post of speaker, Mr. Rahul Narvekar appointed Eknath Shinde as leader of SSLP and recognized Bharat Gogawale as chief whip. On 4th July, Mr. Eknath Shinde won the confidence motion. Mr. Suresh Prabhu moved fresh disqualification again 39 MLA. Mr. Bharat Gogawale also moved petitions for disqualification of 14 MLA. On 19th July,, 2022, Mr. Eknath Shinde filed Petition before ECI for allotment of symbol of Shiv Sena (bow and arrow) , which was allowed by Election Commission.

The Supreme Court was considering six different writ petitions connected with this matter.

FINDINGS OF THE SUPREME COURT

Determination of Disqualification under Tenth Schedule

It was contended that the Supreme Court should decide the disqualification Petitions. The Supreme Court relying on **Kihoto Hollohan Vs Zachillhu (1992) Supp SCC 651** observed that the Speaker is expected to act fairly, independently and impartially while adjudicating the disqualification applications under the Tenth Schedule. Ultimately, the decision of the Speaker on the question of disqualification is subject to judicial review. The Supreme Court was of the opinion that the Speaker of Maharashtra Legislative Assembly is the appropriate authority to decide the question of disqualification under the Tenth Schedule.

The Supreme Court observed that Article 191 (2) provides that a person shall be disqualified for being a member of the Legislative Assembly if they are so disqualified under the Tenth Schedule. Article 190 (3) stipulates that if an MLA incurs a disqualification under the provisions of Article 191 (2) read with Tenth Schedule their seat shall thereupon become vacant. The term "thereupon" denotes that the seat becomes vacant only from such date when the Speaker decides the disqualification petition. An MLA has the right to participate in the proceedings of the House until they are disqualified.

The Supreme Court observed that Parliament undertakes innumerable functions on the floor of the House, including passing legislations and approving the annual budget. These actions of the legislators are irrevocable except in accordance with law. The constitutional sanctity of the proceedings in Parliament or the State Legislatures cannot be set in a state of uncertainty. To allow the validity of such proceedings to be subject to a future decision would lead to chaos. The action of the House in electing the Speaker, Mr. Rahul Narwekar is not invalid merely because some MLAs who participated in the election faced disqualification proceedings.

Appointment of Whip

The Supreme Court observed that political party and legislative party can not be conflated. A whip can only be appointed by the political party. The entire structure of the Tenth Schedule which is built on political parties would crumble if this requirement is not complied with.

The Supreme Court held that the decision of the speaker recognizing Mr. Gogawale as the chief whip of the Shiv Sena is illegal because the recognition was based on the resolution of the faction of the SSLP without undertaking an exercise to determine if it was the decision of the political party.

Concurrent Jurisdiction of Speaker and ECI

The Speaker and the ECI are empowered to concurrently adjudicate on the petitions before them under the Tenth Schedule and awarding of Symbols respectively

The Supreme Court observed that the purpose of the Symbols Order is to provide a uniform procedure for the recognition of Political Parties and to provide a uniform and just system for allotment of symbols for candidates to contest in elections. In order to reach a determination as to which group is entitled to the symbol, it becomes necessary for the ECI to adjudicate which group is the political party itself. In other words, the ECI determines who the "real" political party is and the symbol is allotted as a consequence of this decision.

The Supreme Court observed that subsequent to the decision in **Sadiq Ali Vs Election Commission of India (1972) 4 SCC 664** the Election Commission consistently applied test of majority in the legislature and organizational wings of the party to disputes. However, ECI may apply a test which is suitable to the facts of the particular dispute before it. It need not apply the same test to all disputes regardless of the suitability of the test to those facts and circumstances.

The Decision of the Governor

The Supreme Court held that Governor was not justified in calling upon Mr. Thackeray to prove his majority on the floor of the House because he did not have reasons based on objective material before him, to reach conclusion that Mr. Thackeray had lost the confidence of the House. However, the *status quo ante* cannot be restored because Mr. Thackeray did not face the floor test and tendered his resignation.

The Supreme Court also referred Nabam Rebia judgment to larger bench to seven judges wherein it has been held that it is permissible for a speaker to adjudicate upon disqualification petitions under Tenth Schedule after a notice of intention to move a resolution for their removal from the office of the Speaker is issued.

PANDIT M. S. M. SHARMA VS SRI KRISHAN SINHA

The Supreme Court in **Pandit M.S.M. Sharma Vs. Sri Krishan Sinha, 1959 SCR SUPL(1) 806** held that House of Commons has right to prohibit even true and faithful reporting of proceeding of house at the time of commencement of Indian Constitution and Indian Parliament and State Legislatures have also the similar power. The Supreme Court also held that freedom of speech referred under Article 194 (1) is different from freedom of speech guaranteed under Article 19 (1) (a) and cannot be cut down in any way by any law contemplated under Article 19 (2).

Case Title : Pandit M.S.M. Sharma Vs. Sri Krishan Sinha
Date of Judgment : 12.12.1958
Bench : Chief Justice S. R. Das, Justice N. H. Bhagwati, Justice B. P. Sinha, Justice K. Subba Rao, Justice K. N. Wanchoo

---

FACTS OF THE CASE

On May 30, 1957, there was a debate in the Bihar Legislative Assembly wherein one of the oldest members of the House made a speech critical of the administration of the government. Speaker held a part of the speech objectionable and directed it to be struck off and expunged. The Searchlight, a daily newspaper, published on 31st May, 1957 whatever has happened in the Legislative Assembly. Even the expunged part was also published. A Privilege Motion was moved and referred to Privilege Committee. On August 18, 1958, the Petitioner received notice to show cause why appropriate action should not be taken against him for breach of privilege. Writ Petition under Article 32 against the same was filed before the Supreme Court.

FINDINGS OF THE SUPREME COURT

The Supreme Court considered two issues in this case. Firstly, whether House of Legislature in India can prohibit entirely the publication of proceedings under Article 194 (3) or only expunged parts ? Secondly, whether Privilege under Article 194 (3) prevail over Fundamental Right under Article 19 (1) (a) ?

The Supreme Court noted that under Article 194 (3) the Legislative Assembly has all the privileges of House of Commons at the commencement of the Constitution.

It was contended that House of Commons had power and privilege to prohibit the publication in any newspaper of even a true and faithful report of tis proceedings and certainly the publication of any portion of speeches or proceedings directed to be expunged from the official record.

The Supreme Court noted that privileges of House of Commons can be grouped under two categories – those demanded from crown by the speaker of House of Commons at the commencement of each Parliament and grated as matter of course and those not so demanded. The first category included (i) freedom from arrest (ii) freedom of speech (iii) right to access to crown (iv) the right of having most favourable construction placed upon its proceedings. The second category included (i) the right to provide for the due composition of its own body (ii) the right to regulate its own body (iii) right to exclude strangers (iv) right to prohibit publication of its debates (v) right to enforce observation of its privileges by fine, imprisonment and expulsion.

Right to freedom of speech was of utmost importance for member of House of Commons. But sometimes it caused wrath of the Crown. One of the reasons for secrecy of proceedings of House of Commons was to protect themselves from Sovereign. This object could be achieved by prohibiting the publication of any debate and excluding the strangers. Thus, these privileges flow from right to freedom of speech of member of House of Commons.

The Supreme Court observed that House of Commons had, at the commencement of our constitution, the power or privilege of prohibiting the publication of even a true and faithful report of debates and proceedings that take place within the house. Article 194 (3) confers all such powers, privileges and immunities on the House of Legislature of States as Article 105 (3) does on the Houses of Parliament. The Supreme Court observed that our constitution clearly provided that until Parliament or the State Legislature, as the case may be, makes a law defining the powers, privileges and immunities of the House, its members and Committees, they shall have all the powers, privileges, and immunities and as yet to deny them powers, privileges and immunities after finding that the House of Commons had them at the relevant time, will be not to interpret the Constitution but to re-make it.

The Supreme Court held that provisions of freedom of speech referred under Article 194 (1) is different from freedom of speech guaranteed under Article

19 (1) (a) and cannot be cut down in any way by any law contemplated under Article 19 (2). The Supreme Court held that harmonious construction has to adopted and provisions of 19 (1) (a) which are general must yield to Article 194 (1) and latter part of clause (3) which are special.

The Supreme Court dismissed the Petition.

IN RE : KESHAV SINGH

The Supreme Court in **In Re: Keshav Singh, (1965) 1 SCR 413** held that the High Court has jurisdiction to entertain Petition under Article 226 against warrant issued by the Legislative Assembly.

Case Title : Re: Keshav Singh
Date of Judgment : 30.09.1964
Bench : Chief Justice P.B. Gajendragadkar, Justice A.K. Sarkar, Justice J.C. Shah, Justice K.N. Wanchoo, Justice M. Hidayatullah, Justice N. Rajagopala Ayyangar

FACTS OF THE CASE

A pamphlet was published by alleging corruption charges against one of the member of Legislative Assembly – Narsingh Narayan Pandey. A complaint was made in the Legislative Assembly that it amounted to breach of privilege of Narsingh Narayan Pandey and Legislative Assembly. The question was referred to Privilege Committee. Privilege Committee issued notice to four persons – Keshav Singh, Shyam Narayan Singh, Hub Lal Dubey and Mahatam Singh. It was alleged that the Keshav Singh, Shyam Narayan Singh and Hub Lal Dubey had printed and distributed the pamphlets. The Privilege Committee found Keshav Singh, Shyam Narayan Singh and Hub Lal Dubey guilty of contempt of Legislative Assembly. The Legislative Assembly passed a resolution that a reprimand be administered to the aforesaid persons. Shyam Narayan Singh and Hub Lal Dubey received the reprimand but Keshav Singh failed to appear. Warrant of arrest was issued against Keshav Singh. He was arrested and produced before Legislative Assembly. It was brought to notice of the Legislative Assembly that he has written a letter to Speaker stating that content of letter was correct and brutal attack has been made on democracy by issuing "Nadir Shahi Farman" . Legislative Assembly sentenced Keshav Singh for seven days imprisonment.

Detention of Keshav Singh was challenged before High Court. High Court issued notice and also granted bail to Keshav Singh.

The Legislative Assembly passed a Resolution on March 21, 1964 to the effect that two Judges, Petitioner and his Advocate has committed contempt of the House. Two Judges and Advocate of the Petitioner were directed to be brought to the Legislative Assembly in custody and Keshav Singh to be committed to prison for completing remaining term. The two Judges rushed to the High Court under Article 226 of the Constitution for setting aside resolution of the Legislative Assembly. Apprehending that serious problem had arisen, Full Bench consisting of 28 judges restrained the Speaker from issuing warrant.

The Legislative Assembly passed clarificatory resolution and withdrew the earlier resolution and directed the two Judges and the Advocate for the Petitioner to appear before House and offer explanation.

It appeared to the President that serious conflict between the State Legislature and High Court has arisen. The President referred the issue before the Supreme Court under Article 143 for its opinion.

FINDINGS OF THE SUPREME COURT

The Supreme Court observed that crux of matter lies in Article 194 (3). As per Article 194 (3) power, privileges and immunities of Legislative Assemblies were same as that of House of Commons at the commencement of the Constitution. This clause required that the powers, privileges, and immunities which are claimed by the House must be shown to have subsisted at the commencement of the Constitution i.e. on January 26, 1950.

The Supreme Court observed that although Legislatures have plenary powers they function within limits prescribed by the material and relevant provisions of the Constitution. The Supreme Court noted that all powers and privileges which were possessed by House of Commons at the relevant time cannot be claimed by the Legislatures.

The Supreme Court noted that Article 208 (1) empowers State Legislatures to make rules for regulating conduct of business of House but these rules are subject of provisions of the Constitution.

The Supreme Court also noted that Article 212 (1) lays down that the validity of any proceedings in the Legislature of a State shall not be called in question on the ground of any alleged irregularity of procedure. It can be inferred from this that a citizen can not challenge validity of proceedings on the ground of irregularity of procedure but can be challenged on ground of illegality.

Article 211 provides that no discussion shall take place in Legislature of a State with respect to conduct of any judge of Supreme Court or High Court in discharge of his duties. Conduct of a judge in relation to discharge of his duties cannot be legitimately discussed inside house. Such conduct cannot be made subject -matter of any proceedings under the latter part of Article 194(3).

The Supreme Court after surveying several authorities observed that right of House of Commons to issue general warrant arises out of being Superior Court of Record. Legislative history shows that Legislature in India are not superior courts of records. Legislative Assemblies in India have not discharged judicial functions and they can not be treated as Court of Record.

The Supreme Court observed that in the enforcement of Fundamental Rights guaranteed to the citizens, the right of the judicature to deal with matters brought before them under Article 226 or Article 32 cannot be subjected to the powers and privileges of the House under Article 194 (3).

The Supreme Court observed that if a citizen approaches the High Court on the ground that his fundamental rights have been infringed, the High Court will be entitled to examine his claim and that itself would introduce some limitations on the extent of powers claimed by the House in the present proceedings.

The Supreme Court held that in passing of order of interim bail, High Court cannot be said to have exceeded its jurisdiction.

RAJA RAM PAL VS HON'BLE SPEAKER , LOK SABHA

The Supreme Court in **Raja Ram Pal Vs. Hon'ble Speaker, Lok Sabha, (2007) 3 SCC 184** held that Parliament has power and privilege under Article 105 (3) to expel a member. The Supreme Court also held that it has power of judicial review of Parliamentary Actions in case of gross illegality and violation of constitutional provisions.

Case Title : Raja Ram Pal Vs. Hon'ble Speaker, Lok Sabha
Date of Judgment : 10.01.2007
Bench : Chief Justice Y. K, Sabharwal, Justice K. G. Balakrishnan, Justice C. K Thakker, Justice R. V. Raveendran, Justice D. K. Jain

---

FACTS OF THE CASE

Sting operation was conducted by online news site Cobrapost that was aired on private news channel on December 12, 2005. It showed ten MPs of Lok Sabha and one MP of Rajya Sabha accepting money for raising query in Parliament. Another private channel also telecasted a programme on December 19, 2005 alleging improper conduct of another MP of Rajya Sabha in respect of Member of Parliament Local Area Development Scheme (MPLAD).

The Presiding Officers of the Houses constituted committees for inquiry. Committee in its report found ten members of Lok Sabha guilty and unbecoming of a Member of Parliament and recommended for expulsion. Lok Sabha adopted a motion expelling ten members from Lok Sabha.

A similar process was adopted by Rajya Sabha. The Rajya Sabha referred the matter to Ethics Committee and on its recommendation expelled him.

Petitioner was also expelled on recommendation of Ethics Committee of Rajya Sabha for improper conduct in implementation of MPLAD Scheme.

FINDINGS OF THE SUPREME COURT

The Supreme Court noted that, conscious of high status of Parliament and State Legislatures, Constitution accorded certain powers, privileges and immunities to these bodies. Clause (1) of Article 105 and Article 194 confers freedom of speech in Parliament and State Legislatures though subject to provisions of the Constitution and subject to rules and orders regulating the procedure of Parliament or the Legislatures. Clause 2 of both the Articles grants inter alia absolute immunity to members of Legislatures from any proceedings in any Court in respect of anything said or any vote given by them in Legislatures or any Committee thereof. Clause (3) of both Articles declare that the powers, privileges and immunities of each House of Legislatures and the members and Committees thereof in other respects shall be such as may from time to time be defined by the Parliament or the State Legislature, as the case may be, by law and until so defined to be those as were enjoyed by the said Houses or members of the committees thereof immediately before coming into force of the Amendment in 1978.

The Supreme Court also noted that Article 122 restricts the jurisdiction of the Courts in relation to proceedings of the Parliament.

(i) Whether Supreme Court has jurisdiction to decide the content and scope of powers, privileges and immunities of the Legislatures?

The Supreme Court held that in view of clear enunciation of law by Constitutional Benches there ought not be any doubt left that whenever Parliament, or for that matter any State Legislature, claims any power of privilege in terms of the provisions contained in Article 105 (3) or Article 194 (3) as the case may be, it is the court which has the authority and the jurisdiction to examine, on grievance being brought before it , to find out if the particular power or privilege that has been claimed or asserted by the legislature is one that was contemplated by the said constitutional provisions.

(ii) Whether power and privileges of Legislatures include power to expel a member?

The Supreme Court has held in UP Assembly that a broad claim that all the powers enjoyed by the House of Commons at the commencement of the Constitution of India vest in an Indian Legislature cannot be accepted in its entirety because there are some powers which cannot obviously be so claimed.

The Supreme Court noted that Dr. Ambedkar reiterated that cataloguing of all the powers and privileges would have added to the volume of the Constitution and that the course of adopting the powers and privileges of the existing legislature under the Government of India Act, 1935 was inadvisable as that body had hardly any rights available. The draft Article was adopted after the abovementioned explanation and made part of the Constitution.

The Supreme Court rejected the argument that the termination of membership can be effected only in the manner laid down in Articles 101 and 102. The Supreme Court observed that disqualification and expulsion are two different concepts altogether and recognizing the Parliament's power to expel under Article 105(3) does by no means amount to adding a new ground for disqualification.

The Supreme Court observed that duration of house of five years cannot be interpreted to mean that it guarantees members term of five years. Expulsion is only an additional cause for shortening the term of a member. As far as salaries are concerned, salaries are dependent on membership and continuation of membership is altogether a different matter.

The Supreme Court also held that the power of expulsion does not violate the right of the constituency or any other democratic principles.

The Supreme Court also held that Article 19 (1) (g) cannot restrict the power of expulsion under Article 105(3). There have been numerous instances when power of expulsion has been applied by House of Commons. It was contended by the Petitioners that House of Commons derive its power of expulsion from its privilege of regulating its composition. Since the Parliament does not have power of its constitution, power of expulsion cannot be found under Article 105.

The Supreme Court observed that Legislative organs in India is regulated by Constitution in respect of composition and regulation of membership thereof. It must be held beyond the pale of all doubts that neither Parliament nor State Legislatures in India can assert power to provide for or regulate their own constitution in the matter claimed by the House of Commons in United Kingdom.

The Supreme Court made a detail survey of several authorities and rejected the contention that the source of power of expulsion in England was the privilege of the House of Commons to regulate its own constitution or that the source of power is single and indivisible and cannot be traced to some other source like independent or inherent penal power.

The Supreme Court observed that the right to enforce its privilege either by imposition of fine or by commitment to prison or by expulsion is not a part of any other privilege but is by itself a separate and independent power or privilege.

As far as contempt powers are concerned, the Supreme Court held that the power to punish for contempt in its totality has not been struck down by decision in UP Assembly. The different elements of this broad contempt power will have to be decided on an independent scrutiny of validity in appropriate case. Having found, however, that there is no bar on reading the power to punish for contempt in Article 105 (3), it is possible to source the power of expulsion through the same provision.

(iii) Whether Supreme Court has powers to interfere in exercise of powers by Legislatures, their members or committees ?

As far Judicial Review of Parliamentary action is concerned, the Supreme Court observed that the manner of exercise of the power or privilege by Parliament is immune from judicial scrutiny only to the extent indicated in Article 122 (1), that is to say the Court will decline to interfere if the grievance brought before it is restricted to allegations of irregularity or procedure. But in case of gross illegality or violation of constitutional provisions is shown, the judicial review will not be inhibited in any manner by Article 122 or for that matter by Article 105.

The Supreme Court did not find merit in the case and dismissed the same.

THE STATE OF KERALA VS. K. AJITH

The Supreme Court in **the State of Kerala Vs. K. Ajith 2021 6 SCR 774** held that privileges and immunities are not gateways to claim exemptions from the general law of land. particularly the criminal law, which governs the action of every citizen.

> Case Title : State of Kerala Vs. K. Ajith
> Date of Judgment : 28.07.2021
> Bench : Justice D.Y. Chandrachud, Justice M R Shah

FACTS OF THE CASE

The Finance Minister was presenting budget for Financial Year 2015-16 in Kerala Legislative Assembly. Respondents, who were members of opposition party, disrupted the presentation of budget, climbed over to the speaker dais and damaged furniture and articles including the speaker's chair, computer, mike, emergency lamp, and electronic panel causing loss of Rs. 2,20,093/-. FIR was registered under Section 447 and 427 R/w Section 34 IPC and Section 3 (1) of the Prevention of Damage to Public Property Act, 1984. On the completion of investigation, the final report under Section 173 of the Cr.P.C. was submitted and cognizance was taken by the Additional CJM. Assistant Public Prosecutor filed Application for withdrawal of case under Section 321 CrPC on several grounds including privileges of members of Legislative Assembly under Article 194 (3). The CJM declined to give consent for withdrawal. Criminal Revision Petition filed before the High Court was also dismissed. The matters reached to the Supreme Court.

FINDINGS OF THE SUPREME COURT

The Supreme Court observed that under Section 321 CrPC consent of the Court is required. The public prosecutor may withdraw from a prosecution not merely on the ground of paucity of evidence but also to further the broad ends of public justice. The Public Prosecutor has to formulate independent opinion. Merely the fact that proposal has come from the Government will not vitiate the application.

The Supreme Court noted that Article 105 and 194 provide in similar terms for the privileges and immunities of Members of Parliament respectively.

The Supreme Court observed that Clause (1) of Article 194 recognized the freedom of speech in legislature of every State. The freedom recognized by clause (1) is subject to provisions of the Constitution and standing orders regulating the procedure of State Legislatures. Clause 2 grants immunity which protects a member of the legislature from a proceeding in any court "in respect of anything said or vote given" in the legislature or in any committee of legislature. As far as clause (3) is concerned the Supreme Court observed that the ultimate source of the powers, privileges and immunities of a State Legislature and of the members and committees would be determined by way of a legislation. Until such legislation is enacted, the position as it stood immediately before the coming into force of Section 26 of the Forty-Fourth Amendment Act 1978 would govern.

The Supreme Court observed that Parliament is as yet to enact the law on the subject of parliamentary privileges. According to Article 194 (3) of the Constitution, the MLAs possess privileges that the members of the House of Commons possessed at the time of enactment of the Constitution. The Supreme Court after surveying several authorities of United Kingdom concluded that person committing criminal offence within the precincts of the House does not hold an absolute privilege. He would possess a qualified privilege and would receive immunity only if action bears nexus to the effective participation of the member of the House.

The Supreme Court observed that privileges and immunities are not gateways to claim exemptions from the general law of land. particularly the criminal law which governs the action of every citizen. To claim an exemption from the application of criminal law would be to betray the trust which is impressed on the character of elected representatives as the makers and enactors of the law.

The Supreme Court reiterated law laid down in Lokayukta, Justice Ripusudan Dayal (retired) Vs. State of Madhya Pradesh (2014) 4 SCC 473 that the members shall possess such privileges that are essential for undertaking their legislative functions. Alleged act of destruction of public property to lodge protest against presentation of budget cannot be regarded as essential for exercising their legislative functions.

The Supreme Court also rejected the contention that the prosecution against the respondents is vitiated for want of sanction of speaker.

The Supreme Court also observed that the video recording that was procured from the Electronic Control Room of the Assembly is not a copy of the broadcast of the incident in the local or national television but was a part of the internal records of the Assembly. Thus, the stored video footage of the incident was not broadcast, or in other words, published, for dissemination to the public. Since it was not a publication of house, it does not enjoy the protection of immunity under Article 194 (2) of the Constitution.

The Supreme Court did not find merit in appeal and dismissed the same.

SITA SOREN VS UNION OF INDIA

The Supreme Court in **Sita Soren Vs Union of India (2024) 3 SCR 462 overruled P. V. Narasimha Rao Vs. State 1998 4 SCC 626** and held that bribery is not immune under Article 105 (2) and the corresponding provision of Article 194.

Case Title : Sita Soren Vs Union of India
Date of Judgment : 04.03.2024
Bench : Chief Justice Dhananjaya Y Chandrachud, Justice A. S. Bopanna, Justice M. M. Sundresh, Justice P. S. Narasimha, Justice J. B. Pardiwala, Justice Sanjay Kumar, Justice Manoj Misra

---

FACTS OF THE CASE

An election for two seats of Rajya Sabha was held in Jharkhand on March 30, 2012. Smt. Sita Soren was member of Legislative Assembly of Jharkhand. An allegation was made against her that she has accepted bribe to vote in favour of an independent candidate. But at the time of voting she has voted in favour of candidate set up by her party. Criminal proceedings were initiated against her. She filed petition before the High Court for quashing of criminal proceedings seeking protection under Article 194 (2) of the Constitution relying on judgment of the Supreme Court in **P V Narasimha Rao.** The High Court refused to quash the proceedings citing that Smt. Soren has not voted in favour of the independent candidate as such the case is not covered under P V Narasimha Rao judgment.

Two judge bench of the Supreme Court referred the matter to the three judge bench. Three judge bench referred the matter to five judge bench. Five judge bench referred the matter to seven judge bench. Finally matter was heard by seven judge bench.

FINDINGS OF THE SUPREME COURT

The issue before the Supreme Court was whether a legislator who receives a bribe to cast a vote in a certain direction or speak about certain issues are protected by parliamentary privilege.

The Supreme Court surveyed the historical development of parliamentary privileges in India. The Supreme Court noted that prior to enactment of the Constitution, members of Legislatures in India did not enjoy such Parliamentary privileges as enjoyed by House of Commons in UK. Members of Parliament did not enjoy any immunity from criminal proceedings.

The Court noted that Article 105 has four clauses. Clause (1) grants freedom of speech in Parliament. The freedom of speech granted under clause (1) is distinct from freedom of speech and expression granted under Article 19 (1) (a). Clause (2) has two limbs. The first limb states that a member of Parliament shall not liable before any court in respect of anything said or any vote given. The second limb states that no person shall be liable before any court in respect of the publication by or under the authority or either House of Parliament of any report, paper, vote or proceedings. Clause (3) states that in respect of privileges not falling under clause (1) and (2), power, privileges and immunities will be such as defined by law made by Parliament. Till such law is made, they are those enjoyed by Parliament before coming into effect of Section 15 of 44th Amendment Act. Clause (4) extents privileges to all persons who have right to speak in Parliament. Before coming into force of Section 15 of 44th Amendment the power, privileges and immunities were such as enjoyed the House of Commons, its members and committees.

The Supreme Court observed that the privileges enshrined under Article 105 and Article 194 of the Constitution are of the widest amplitude but to the extent that they serve the aims for which they have been granted. The Framers of the Constitution would not have intended to grant to the legislature those rights which may not serve any purpose for the proper functioning of the House.

The Supreme Court propounded two fold test for determination of privilege of a member of Parliament. Firstly, the privilege claimed has to be tethered to functioning of the House and Secondly, its necessity must bear a functional relationship to the discharge of the essential duties of a legislator.

Applying the two fold test the Supreme Court held that bribery is not protected under Parliamentary privileges. The Court also noted that Constitution envisions probity in public life. Corruption and bribery of members of legislature erode the foundation of Parliamentary Democracy.

The Supreme Court held that prosecution for bribery is not excluded from the jurisdiction of the criminal court merely because it may also be treated by the House as contempt or a breach of its privilege.

The Supreme Court noted that P. V. Narasimha Rao judgment results in paradoxical outcome. When a legislator accepts a bribe and votes in agreed direction he is conferred with immunity. On the other hand when a legislator accepts a bribe and votes independently, he will prosecuted. The Supreme Court overruled majority view in P. V. Narsimha Rao judgment.

DR D. C. WADHWA VS. STATE OF BIHAR

The Supreme Court in **Dr. D. C. Wadhwa Vs. State of Bihar 1987 SCR (1) 798** held that Governor cannot promulgate ordinance under Article 213 successively without submitting the same to Legislature.

Case Title : Dr. D. C. Wadhwa Vs. State of Bihar
Date of Judgment : 20.12.1986
Bench : Chief Justice P. N. Bhagwati, Justice Ranganath Misra, Justice G. L. Oza, Justice K. N. Singh, Justice M. M. Dutt

FACTS OF THE CASE

The Governor of Bihar was promulgating and re-promulgating ordinances on massive scale. The Governor promulgated 256 ordinances between 1967 to 1981 and all these ordinances were kept alive for periods ranging between 1 to 14 years by re-promulgation from time to time. Out of 256 ordinances 69 were re-promulgated several times and kept alive with prior permission of President. Several ordinances were surviving for more than 10 years.

Power to promulgate ordinances was being used by Government of Bihar on large scale and after session of the State Legislature was prorogued, the same ordinances which had ceased to operate used to re-promulgated containing substantially the same provisions almost in a routine manner.

Re-promulgation of ordinances were done on a massive scale in a routine manner without even caring to get the ordinance replaced by Acts of the Legislature or considering whether circumstances existed which rendered it necessary for the Governor to take immediate action by way of re-promulgation of ordinance.

Three of these ordinances were challenged before the Supreme Court under Article 32 of the Constitution of India.

FINDINGS OF THE SUPREME COURT

The issue before the Supreme Court was whether this practice of the Government of Bihar was legitimate exercise of power under Article 213 of the Constitution.

The Supreme Court observed that the power conferred on Governor to issue ordinances is in nature of an emergency power which is vested in Governor for taking immediate action where such action may become necessary at a time when the Legislature is not in session. The primary law making authority under the Constitution is Legislature and not the Executive. When legislature is not in session circumstances may arise which render it necessary to take immediate action and in such a case in order that Public Interest may not suffer by reason of inability of the legislature to make law to deal with emergent situation, the Governor is vested with the power to promulgate ordinance. Every ordinance has to be placed before the Legislature and it ceases to have effect after expiration of six weeks from re-assembly of Legislature or before expiration of that period if assembly disapproves it by a resolution.

The object of Article 213 is that since the power to issue ordinance conferred on Governor is an emergent power exercisable when Legislature is not in session, such ordinance should have limited life.

The Supreme Court observed that since Article 174 provides that the Legislature shall meet at least twice in a year but six months shall not intervene between its last sitting in one session and the date appointed for its first meeting in the next session and an ordinance made by the Governor must cease to operate at the expiration of six weeks from the re-assembly of the Legislature, it is obvious that the maximum life of an Ordinance cannot exceed seven and half months unless it is replaced by an Act of the Legislature or disapproved by the resolution of the Legislature before the expiry of that period. The power to promulgate an Ordinance is essentially a power to be used to meet an extra-ordinary situation and it cannot be allowed to be perverted to serve political ends.

The Executive cannot continue the provisions of the ordinance in force without going to the Legislature. The law making function has been entrusted to Legislature. If the executive is permitted to continue the provisions of an ordinance in force by re-promulgation without submitting to the Legislature, it would be nothing sort of usurpation by executive of law making functions.

There may be a situation when where it may not be possible for the Government to introduce and push through in the Legislature a bill containing the same provisions as in the Ordinance, because the Legislature may have too much legislative business in a particular session or the time at the disposal of the Legislature in a particular Session may be short, and in that event the Governor may legitimately find that it is necessary to re-promulgate the ordinance. But otherwise it would be colorable exercise of power to continue an ordinance beyond the period specified by Constitution by adopting methodology of re-promulgation.

The Supreme Court observed that it is a settled law that Constitutional Authority cannot do indirectly what it is not permitted to do directly. If there is a constitutional provision inhibiting the constitutional authority from doing an Act, such provision cannot be allowed to be defeated by adoption of any subterfuge. That will be clearly a fraud on the Constitutional provision.

The Supreme Court observed that when the Constitutional provision stipulates that an ordinance promulgated by the Governor to meet an emergent situation shall cease to be in operation at the expiration of six weeks from the re-assembly of the Legislature and if the Government wishes the provisions of the Ordinance to be continued in force beyond the period of six weeks, it has to go before the Legislature which is the constitutional authority entrusted with the law making function. It would most certainly be a colorable exercise of power for the Government to ignore the Legislature and to re-promulgate the ordinance and thus to continue to regulate the life and liberty of the citizens through ordinance made by the Executive. Such a stratagem would be repugnant to the constitutional scheme as it would enable the Executive to transgress its constitutional limitation in the matter of law making in an emergent situation and to covertly and indirectly arrogate to itself the lawmaking function of Legislature.

The Supreme Court struck the Bihar Intermediate Education Council Ordinance, 1983 which was as yet in force.

SUPREME COURT ADVOCATE-ON-RECORED ASSOCIATION VS UNION OF INDIA (FOURTH JUDGES CASE)

The Supreme Court with 4:1 majority in **Supreme Court Advocate-on-Record Association Vs. Union of India, (2015) 13 SCR 1** declared Ninety Ninth Amendment and National Judicial Appointment Commission (NJAC) Act unconstitutional.

> Case Title : Supreme Court Advocate-on-Record Association Vs. Union of India
> Date of Judgment : 16.10.2015
> Bench : Justice Jagdish Singh Khehar, Justice J. Chelameswar, Justice Madan B. Lokur, Justice Kurian Joseph, Justice Adarsh Kumar Goel

FACTS OF THE CASE

The Constitution (One Hundred and Twenty -first Amendment) Bill, 2014 was passed by the Lok Sabha on 13th August, 2014 and by Rajya Sabha on 14th August, 2014. It received the ratification of more than one half of the States as required by Article 368 (2) of the Constitution and received the assent of the President on 31st December, 2014 when it became the Constitution (Ninety ninth Amendment) Act, 2014.

Simultaneous with the passage of the Constitution (One Hundred and Twenty-First Amendment) Bill, Parliament also passed the National Judicial Appointment Commission Bill, 2014 which received assent of the President on 31st December, 2014 and it was brought into force by a gazette notification issued on 13th April, 2015.

The Ninety Ninth Amendment provided for National Judicial Appointment Commission consisting of – (a) the Chief Justice of India, Chairperson, ex officio; (b) two other senior judges of the Supreme Court next to Chief Justice of India – Members , ex officio; (c) the Union Minister in charge of Law and Justice – Member, ex officio; (d) two eminent persons to be nominated by the committee consisting of the Prime Minister, the Chief Justice of India and the Leader of Opposition in the House of the People or where there is no such leader of Opposition, then the Leader of single largest Opposition Party in the House of the People.   One of the eminent person was to be nominated from amongst the persons belonging to the Scheduled Castes, the Scheduled Tribes, Other Backward Classes, Minorities or Women. An eminent person was to be nominated for a period of three years and was not eligible for re-nomination.

The Constitutional Validity of Ninety-ninth Amendment as well as National Judicial Appointments Commission were challenged before the Supreme Court.

FINDINGS OF THE SUPREME COURT

Article 124(2) provides that every Judge of the Supreme Court shall be appointed by the President by warrant under his hand and seal after consultation with such of the judges of the Supreme Court and of the High Courts in the States as the President may deem necessary for that purpose.

In **S. P. Gupta Vs. President of India AIR 1982SC149 (First Judges Case,)** the Supreme Court held that independence of judiciary is basic feature of the Constitution. In the appointment of a judge of the Supreme Court or the High Court, the word 'consultation' occurring in Article 124 (2) and in Article 217 (1) of the Constitution does not mean 'concurrence'. The ultimate power to appoint judges rests with the Union. The Supreme Court did not find the extant system of appointment of judges ideal and idea of collegium was floated as a replacement.

The majority view in the First Judges case was overruled in the **Supreme Court Advocate-on-Record Association Vs. Union of India AIR 1994 SC 268 (Second Judges Case)** and it was held that "consultation" in Article 217 and Article 124 of the Constitution meant that "primacy" in the appointment of judges must rest with the Chief Justice of India.

Special Reference No. 1 of 1998 (Third Judges Case) was a presidential reference, wherein the Supreme Court opined that the expression "consultation with the Chief Justice of India" in Articles 217 (1) and 222 (1) of the Constitution requires consultation with a plurality of Judges in the formation of the opinion of the Chief Justice of India. The sole individual opinion of the

Chief Justice of India does not constitute 'consultation' within the meaning of the said Articles.

The Supreme Court observed that earlier decisions in Second and Third Judges' case had to taken as binding precedents. Once it is so, it has to be held that primacy of the judiciary in appointment of judges is part of the basic structure. Appointment of judges is part of independence of judiciary.

The Supreme Court observed that in appointing two eminent members, although CJI is also a member, the fact remains that the PM and Leader of the Opposition have significant roles in appointing such members, who will have power not only equal to the CJI and two senior most judges of the Supreme Court in making appointment of judges of the Supreme Court and appointment/transfer of judges of the High Courts but also right to reject the unanimous proposal of the CJI and the two senior mots judges. Such composition of the Commission cannot be held to be conducive to the independence of judiciary. Appointment of judges of the Supreme Court and appointment/transfer of judges of High Court can certainly be influenced to a great extent by the Law Minister and two nominated members, thereby affecting the independence of judiciary.

The primacy of judiciary is integral to the independence of judiciary, separation of powers, federalism and democracy, rule of law and supremacy of the Constitution. The amendment does away with the primacy of even unanimous opinion of the judicial members.

The Supreme Court held that Ninety Ninth Amendment and NJAC Act damages the basic structure of the Constitution and are unconstitutional. The Supreme Court revived that pre-existing system was revived.

B. P. SINGHAL VS UNION OF INDIA

The Supreme Court in **B. P. Singhal Vs Union of India, 2010 (6) SCC 331**
held that Governor holds office at pleasure of the President as such President
has power to remove Governor without assigning any reason and without
any opportunity to show cause but such power can be exercised only for
valid and compelling reasons. The Supreme Court also held that the decision
to remove governor can be reviewed although on limited grounds.

Case Title : B. P. Singhal Vs Union of India
Date of Judgment : 07.05.2010
Bench : Chief Justice K. G. Balakrishnan, Justice P. Sathasivam, Justice
B. Sudershan Reddy, Justice R. V. Raveendran, Justice S. H. Kapadia

FACTS OF THE CASE

Governors of Uttar Pradesh, Gujarat, Haryana and Goa were removed by the
President on 02.07.2004. A Public Interest Litigation was filed against the
same under Article 32 of the Constitution.

FINDINGS OF THE SUPREME COURT

Locus of the Petitioner

The Supreme Court held that Petitioners had no locus in regard to the prayers
claiming relief for Individual Governors. But Petitioners have necessary locus
touching upon scope of Article 156 (1).

Doctrine of Pleasure

The Supreme Court noted that Article 156 (1) provides that Governor shall
hold office during pleasure of the President.

The Supreme Court noted that the pleasure doctrine has its origin in English Law with reference to the tenure of public servants under the Crown. There is a distinction between the doctrine of pleasure as it existed in a feudal set-up and the doctrine of pleasure in a democracy governed by rule of law.

The Supreme Court noted that Articles in the Constitution which refer to holding of office during pleasure of the President without any restrictions or limitations are Article 75 (2) relating to ministers, Article 76 (2) relating to Attorney General, and Article 156 (1) relating to Governor, Article 164 (1) relating to ministers in State and Article 165 (3) relating to Attorney General of State. Article 310 R/w Article 311 provide example of application of Doctrine of Pleasure with restrictions.

The Supreme Court observed that doctrine of pleasure as originally envisaged in England was a prerogative power which was unfettered. It meant that the holder of an office under pleasure could be removed at any time, without notice, without assigning cause and without there being a need of any cause.

Where rule of law prevails, there is nothing like unfettered discretion or unaccountable action. The degree of need for reason may vary. The degree of scrutiny during judicial review may vary. But the need for reason exists. As a result, when the Constitution of India provides that some offices will be held during the pleasure of President, without any express limitations or restrictions, it should however necessarily be read as being subject to the "fundamental of constitutionalism.

Therefore, in a constitutional set up, when an office is held during the pleasure of any Authority and if no limitations or restrictions are placed on the "at pleasure" doctrine, it means that the holder of the office can be removed by the authority at whose pleasure he holds office, at any time, without notice and without assigning any cause. The doctrine of pleasure, however, is not license to act with unfettered discretion to act arbitrarily, whimsically or capriciously. It does not dispense with the need for a cause for withdrawal of the pleasure. In other words, "at pleasure" doctrine enables the removal of a person holding office at pleasure of an Authority, summarily, without any obligation to give any notice or hearing to the person removed and without any obligation to assign any reasons or disclose any cause for the removal or withdrawal of pleasure. The withdrawal of pleasure cannot be at the sweet will, whim and fancy of the Authority, but can only be for valid reasons.

Limitation under Article 156 (1)

The Supreme Court noted that Governor has dual role – Governor acts as the head of State and also function as vital link between Union and

State. Governor is not an agent or employee of Union Government. Like the President, Governors are expected to be apolitical, discharging purely constitutional functions, irrespective of their political background, if any.

It was contended by Petitioners that provision of Article 156 (1) should be read in consonance with Article 156 (3) which provides for tenure of five years. The Supreme Court rejected this contention and held that Article 156 (1) has not been subjected to any exception. Clause (3) has been made subject to clause (1) of the Article 156.

The Supreme Court noted that recommendations of Sarkaria Commission in respect of removal of Governor remains recommendations and cannot override express provisions of Constitution.

The Court observed that when a Governor holds office during the pleasure of the Government and the power to remove at the pleasure of the President is not circumscribed by any conditions or restrictions, it follows that the power is exercisable at any time, without assigning any cause. However, there is a distinction between the need for a cause for the removal and the need to disclose the cause for removal. While the President need not disclose or inform the cause for his removal to the Governor it is imperative that the cause must exist.

The Supreme Court held that a Governor cannot be removed on the ground that he is out of sync with the policies and ideologies of the Union Government or the party in power at the Centre. Nor can he be removed on the ground that the Union Government has lost confidence in him. Change in government at Centre can not be a ground for removal of Governors holding office to make way for others favoured by the new government.

Scope of Judicial Review

The Supreme Court held that the decision to remove governor under Article 156 (3) is amenable to judicial review. What Article 156 (1) dispenses with is the need to assign reasons or the need to give notice but the need to act fairly and reasonably cannot be dispensed with. In the event of challenge of withdrawal of the pleasure, the court will necessarily assume that it is for compelling reasons. Where a *prima facie* case of arbitrariness or *mala fides* is made out, the Court can require the Union Government to produce records/materials to satisfy itself that the withdrawal of pleasure was for good and compelling reasons. What will constitute good and compelling reasons would depend upon the facts of the case. Having regard to the nature of functions of the Governor in maintaining centre-state relations, and the flexibility available to the Government in such matters, it is needless to say that there will be no interference unless a very strong case is made out. The Position, therefore, is that the decision is open to judicial review but in a very limited extent.

STATE OF PUNJAB VS. PRINCIPAL SECRETARY TO GOVERNOR OF PUNJAB

The Supreme Court in **State of Punjab Vs. Principal Secretary to Governor of Punjab,** (2023)15 **S.C.R.** 777 held that if the Governor withholds the assent to the Bill under Article 200, the Governor must mandatorily send the bill back for reconsideration to the State Legislature "as soon as possible".

Case Title : State of Punjab Vs. Principal Secretary to Governor of Punjab
Date of Judgment : 10.11.2023
Bench : Chief Justice K G Balakrishnan, Justice P Sathasivam, Justice B Sudershan Reddy, Justice R V Raveendran, Justice S H Kapadia

FACTS OF THE CASE

Sixteenth Vidhan Sabha was summoned on 3rd March, 2023. The Speaker adjourned the session sine die on 22nd March, 2023. The Speaker reconvened the session on 19th and 23rd June, 2023. During Course of the session, the Vidhan Sabha passed four bills namely The Sikh Gurudwara Amendment Bill, 2023, Punjab Affiliated Colleges (Security of Service) (Amendment) Bill, 2023, Punjab Universities Law (Amendment) Bill, 2023, and Punjab Police (Amendment) Bill, 2023. No Action was taken by the Governor on these bills. Sessions of Vidhan Sabha were sought to be reconvened since three money bills were to be introduced. The recommendation of the Governor was required in terms of the Provision of Article 207 (1) of the Constitution for the introduction of the Bill in Vidhan Sabha.

The Governor stated that he would take action according to law after the legality of the Vidhan Sabha session which was held on 19th and 20th June, 2023 is examined. He was considering whether to receive legal opinion from Attorney General or reserve the bill for consideration of the President. By another communication Governor communicated that the calling of session was patently illegal. The Governor advised to call fresh Monsoon/Winter Session.

Aggrieved by inaction of Governor, the State of Punjab approached the Supreme Court under Article 32 of the Constitution.

FINDINGS OF THE SUPREME COURT

The Supreme Court observed that in a Parliamentary Form of Democracy real power vests in elective representatives of people. The Governor as an appointee of the President is titular head of State. The fundamental principle of the Constitutional Law which has been consistently followed since the Constitution was adopted is that the Governor acts on the "aid and advise" of the Council of Ministers, save and except in those areas where the Constitution has entrusted the exercise of discretionary power to the Governor.

The Supreme Court noted that when a bill is presented under Article 200 to the Governor, three options are available before Governor – (i) either he assents the bill, (ii) he withholds the bill and (iii) he reserves the bill for consideration of the President. The proviso to Article 200 envisages that, as soon as possible, after the presentation to the Governor of the Bill for assent he may return a Bill, which is not a Money Bill, together with a message requesting that the House or Houses would reconsider the Bill or any specific provisions of the Bill and in particular consider the desirability of introducing such amendments which he may recommend. When a Bill is returned by the Governor, the legislature of the State is duty bound to reconsider the Bill. After the Bill is again passed by the legislature either with or without amendment and is presented to the Governor for assent, the Governor shall not withhold assent therefrom.

The Supreme Court observed that a proviso may fulfil the purpose of being an exception. Sometimes, a proviso may be in the form of an explanation or in addition to the substantive provision of a statute. The first proviso allows an ordinary bill to be returned to the legislature for reconsideration. But the concluding part of the First proviso stipulates that if a bill is again passed by Legislature either with or without amendments and sent back to the Governor, the Governor shall not withhold assent. The concluding phrase "shall not withhold assent therefrom" is a clear indicator that the exercise of power under the first proviso is relatable to the withholding of the assent by Governor to the Bill in first instance. The role ascribed by the First Proviso is recommendatory is nature.

The Supreme Court held that if the Governor withholds the assent to the Bill under the substantive part of Article 200, the Governor must mandatorily follow the course of action which is indicated in the first proviso of communicating to the State Legislature "as soon as possible" a message warranting the reconsideration of the Bill.

The Supreme Court observed that the expression "as soon as possible" is significant. It conveys a constitutional imperative of expedition. Failure to take a call and keeping a Bill for indeterminate periods is a course of action inconsistent with that expression, Constitutional language is not a surplusage.

The Supreme Court held that the Governor of Punjab was not empowered to withhold action on the Bills passed by the State Legislature.

The Supreme Court also held that the Constitution and established practice distinguish between adjournment *sine die* and prorogation of the session of the House. In this case, Vidhan Sabha was adjourned on 22nd March, 2023 without prorogation. Therefore, the Speaker was empowered to reconvene the sitting of the House within the same session.

The Supreme Court held that there is no valid constitutional basis to cast doubt on the validity of the session of the Vidhan Sabha which was held on 19th June, 2023, 20th June, 2023, and 20th October, 2023. Governor of Punjab must now proceed to take a decision on the Bills which have been submitted for assent.

K C GAJAPATI NARAYAN DEO VS STATE OF ORISSA

The Supreme Court in **K C Gajapati Narayan Deo Vs. State of Orissa, (1954) 1 SCR** 1 held that the idea conveyed by "colorable legislation" is that although apparently a legislature in passing a statute purported to act within the limits of its powers, yet in substance and in reality, it transgressed these powers, the transgression being veiled by what appears on proper examination, to be a mere pretence or disguise.

> Case Title : K C Gajapati Narayan Deo Vs. State of Orissa
> Date of Judgment : 29.05.1953
> Bench : Chief Justice Patanjali Sastri, Justice Mukherjea, Justice S. R. Das, Justice Ghulam Hasan, Justice Bhagwati

FACTS OF THE CASE

Orissa Legislature passed Orissa Estates Abolition Act, 1952, with objective to abolish all zamindari and other proprietary estates and interests in the State of Orissa and after eliminating all the intermediaries, to bring the ryots or the actual occupants of the lands in direct contact with the State Government.

It had provision that any sum payable for agricultural income tax for the previous year should be deducted from the gross asset of an estate for the purpose of arriving at its net income on the basis on which compensation was payable to the estate owners. Orissa Agricultural Income Tax Act, 1947 was amended twice to enhance the rate and reduce the highest slab. Amendment to Agricultural Income -Tax Act was challenged on the ground that the same is colourable exercise of power. The real objective is to reduce the income of intermediaries so that compensation paid to them are kept at minimum

FINDINGS OF THE SUPREME COURT

The Supreme Court observed that it may be made clear at the outset that the doctrine of colourable legislation does not involve any question of bona fides or mala fides on the part of legislature. The whole doctrine resolved itself into the question of competency of a particular legislature to enact a particular law. If the legislature is competent to pass a particular law, the motives which impelled it to act are really irrelevant. On the other hand, if the legislature lacks competency, the question of motive does not arise at all. Whether a statute is constitutional or not is thus always a question of power. A distinction, however exists between a legislature which is legally omnipotent like the British Parliament, the laws promulgated by which could not be challenged on the ground of incompetency, and a legislature which enjoys only a limited or a qualified jurisdiction.

If the Constitution of a State distributes the legislative powers amongst different bodies, which have to act within their respective spheres marked out by specific legislative entries, or if there are limitations on the legislative authority in the shape of Fundamental Rights, questions do arise as to whether the legislature in a particular case has or has not , in respect to the subject – matter of the statute or in the method of enacting it , transgressed the limits of its constitutional powers. Such transgression may be patent, manifest or direct, but it may also be disguised, covert and indirect and it is to this latter class of cases that the expression "colourable legislation" has been applied in certain judicial pronouncements. The idea conveyed by the expression is that although apparently a legislature in passing a statute purported to act within the limits of its powers, yet in substance and in reality, it transgressed these powers, the transgression being veiled by what appears on proper examination, to be a mere pretence or disguise.

The Supreme Court further observed that in other words, it is the substance of the Act that is material and not merely the form or outward appearance, and if the subject-matter in substance is something which is beyond the powers of that legislature to legislate upon, the form in which the law is clothed would not save it from condemnation. The Legislature cannot violate the constitutional prohibitions by employing an indirect method. In cases like these, the enquiry must always be as to the true nature and character of the challenged legislation and it is the result of such investigation and not the form alone that will determine whether or not it relates to the a subject which is within the power of the legislative authority. For the purpose of this investigation the Court could certainly examine the effect of the legislation and take into consideration its object, purpose or design. But these are only relevant for the purpose of ascertaining the true character and substance of enactment and the class of subjects of legislation to which it really belongs and not for finding out the motives which induced the legislature to exercise its powers.

The Supreme Court noted that the Orissa Agricultural Income Tax (Amendment) Act, 1950 is certainly a legislation on taxing agricultural income as described in Entry 46 of the List II of Seventh Schedule. The State Legislature had undoubted competency to legislate on agricultural income tax and the substance of the amended legislation of 1950 is that it purports to increase the existing rates of agricultural income tax. This may be unjust or inequitable, but that does not affect the competency of the legislature. If a legislature is competent to do a thing directly, then the mere fact that it attempted to do it in an indirect manner, cannot make the Act invalid.

The Supreme Court held that the Orissa Agricultural Income Tax (Amendment) Act, 1950 is not a colourable legislation.

INNOVENTIVE INDUSTRIES VS ICICI BANK

The Supreme Court in **Innoventive Industries Vs ICICI Bank, (2018) 1 SCC 407** held that provisions of Maharashtra Relief Undertaking (Special Provisions) Act, 1958 are repugnant to IBC under Article 254 of the Constitution as such void to that extent. The Supreme Court also held that non-obstante clause under Section 238 IBC will override limited non-obstante clause in Maharashtra Act.

Case TItle : Innoventive Industries Vs ICICI Bank
Date of Judgment : 31.08.2017
Bench: Justice Sanjay Kishan Kaul, Justice R. F. Nariman

FACTS OF THE CASE

The Appellant was a multiproduct company. The Appellant began to suffer losses due to labour problems. As the Appellant was not able to service financial assistance given to it, the appellant proposed corporate debt restructuring. Joint Lender Forum approved the restructuring plan. Section 7 Application was filed by ICICI Bank seeking initiation of CIRP against the appellant. In the reply the Appellant contended that there is no debt legally due as liabilities and enforcement thereof has been temporarily suspended for a period of one year vide notification dated 22nd July, 2015 and another year vide notification dated 18th July, 2016 under Maharashtra Relief Undertakings (Special Provisions) Act, 1958.

By order dated 17th January, 2017, NCLT held that the IBC would prevail against Maharashtra Act in view of non-obstante clause in Section 238 of the Code. Parliamentary Statute will prevail over State statute. Application was admitted by the NCLT. The appeal filed by the Appellant before the NCLAT was also dismissed.

FINDINGS OF THE SUPREME COURT

The Supreme Court noted that one of the objective of the IBC is to bring the insolvency law in India within a single umbrella with the object of speeding up the insolvency process. The Supreme Court made a detailed survey of several provisions of the Code.

Article 254 of the Constitution provides for inconsistency between laws made by Parliament and laws made by legislature of states.

The Supreme Court observed that repugnancy under Article 254 arises only if both Parliamentary and the State law is referable to List III in 7th Schedule of the Constitution of India. Doctrine of Pith and Substance has to be applied in order to test that both statutes fall under concurrent list. The Language of Article 254 speaks of repugnancy of not only merely a stature but also "any provision" thereof. The onus of showing that a statute is repugnant has to be on party attacking its validity. Inconsistency must be clear and direct and be of such nature as to bring two acts or parts into direct collision between each other. Repugnant statute of state is void to the extent of repugnancy. Only that portion of the State's statute which is found to be repugnant is to be declared void.

The Supreme Court held that Maharashtra Act is repugnant to IBC, which has been enacted by Parliament" as under the Maharashtra Act the State Government may take over management of the relief undertaking after which a temporary moratorium takes place under Section 4 of Maharashtra Act. Moratorium under Section 4 of Maharashtra Act directly clashes with moratorium under Section 14 IBC. Thus Central enactment being repugnant to the earlier state enactment by virtue of Article 254 (1) would operate to render Maharashtra Act void vis-à-vis action taken under later Central enactment.

The Supreme Court also relied on Section 238 of IBC and observed that later non-obstante clause of Parliamentary enactment will prevail over the limited non-obstante clause contained in Section 4 of Maharashtra Act.

The Supreme Court observed that Maharashtra Act cannot stand in way of the Corporate Insolvency Resolution Process under the Code.

The Supreme Court was of the view that NCLT and NCLAT has rightly admitted the application for initiation of CIRP and dismissed the appeal filed by the Appellant.

JINDAL STAINLESS LTD VS. STATE OF HARYANA

The Supreme Court held in **Jindal Stainless Ltd. Vs. State of Haryana, (2016) 10 SCR 1** that non-discriminatory tax does not *per se* constitute a restriction on the right to free trade, commerce and intercourse guaranteed under Article 301. The compensatory tax theory evolved in **Automobile Transport (Rajasthan) Ltd. Vs. the State of Rajasthan (1963) 1 SCR 491** has no juristic basis.

Case Title : Jindal Stainless Ltd. Vs. State of Haryana
Date of Judgment : 11.11.2016
Bench : Chief Justice T. S. Thakur, Justice A. K. Sikri, Justice S. A. Bobde, Justice Shiva Kirti Singh, Justice N. V. Ramana, Justice R. Banumathi, Justice A. M. Khanwilkar, Justice D. Y. Chandrachud, Justice Ashok Bhushan

FACTS OF THE CASE

Several States enacted laws which provide for levy of tax on the "entry of goods in local areas comprising the states" under Entry 52 of List II. The constitution validity of all these laws were challenged before Several High Courts on the ground that same were violative of the constitutionally recognized right to free trade, commerce and intercourse guaranteed under Article 301 of the Constitution of India. They were also assailed on the ground that the same were discriminatory and therefore violative of Article 304 (a) of the Constitution of India. These matters finally landed before the Constitution Bench for determination.

FINDINGS OF THE SUPREME COURT

The Supreme Court noted that the power to tax is an essential attribute of sovereignty. But such power is subject to constitutional limitations. Any such limitation must be express.

In **Atiabari Tea Company Ltd Vs. the State of Assam (1961) 1 SCR 809,** levy of taxes on certain goods carried by road and inland waterways in State of Assam under the Assam Taxation (on Goods Carried by Roads or Inland Waterways) Act has been challenged before the Supreme Court. The Supreme Court struck down the constitutional validity of the enactment holding that the impugned levy operated directly and immediately as a restriction on free trade, commerce and intercourse guaranteed under Article 301 of the Constitution of India.

The Supreme Court in **Automobile Transport (Rajasthan) Ltd. Vs. the State of Rajasthan (1963) 1 SCR 491** added a new dimension to the legal exposition in Atiabari case by declaring that taxes that were compensatory in nature fell outside Part XIII and could never be treated as restrictions offensive to Article 301 of the Constitution.

The Supreme Court in **Jindal Stainless Steel Ltd Vs. State of Haryana** overruled decisions in **Bhagatram Rajeev Kumar Vs Commissioner of Sales Tax, M.P. 1994 (6) Suppl. SCR 91** and **State of Bihar Vs. Bihar Chamber of Commerce 1996 (2) SCR 184** and declared that it is not just a remote benefit to the tax payer but only a direct and substantial benefit that would justify levy of compensatory taxes without offending Article 301 of the Constitution of India.

The Supreme Court noted that there is no constitutional basis for the Compensatory Tax Theory propounded by the majority judgment in Automobile Transport. If taxes are eventually meant to serve larger public good and for running the governmental machinery and providing to the people the facilities essential for civilized living, there is no question of a tax being non-compensatory in character in the broader sense.

The concept of compensatory tax obliterates the distinction between a tax and a fee. The essential difference between a tax and a fee is that while a tax has no element of *quid pro quo*, a fee without that element cannot be validly levied. The Concept of compensatory taxes being outside Part XIII is difficult to apply in actual practice.

The Supreme Court observed that Freedom of trade, commerce and intercourse is by no means absolute, the same being subject of the other provisions of Part XIII of the Constitution. Articles 301 and 302 show that the freedom of trade, commerce and intercourse is subject to restrictions which Parliament may by law impose in public interest. Article 303 restricts Parliament from making any law giving or authorizing the making of any discrimination between one State and another.

Article 304 (a) far from treating taxes as restriction per se, specifically recognizes the State Legislature's power to impose the same on goods imported from other States and Union Territories. Article 304 (a) recognizes the availability of the power to impose taxes on goods imported from other States, the legislative power to do so being found in Articles 245 and 246 of the Constitution. Such power to levy taxes is however subject to conditions that similar goods manufactured or produced in the State levying the tax are also subjected to tax and there is no discrimination on that account between goods so imported and goods so manufactured or produced. The limitation on the power to levy taxes is entirely covered by Clause (a) of Article 304 which exhausts the universe in so far as the State Legislature's power to levy of taxes is concerned. Resultantly a discriminatory tax on the import of goods from other states alone will work as impediment on free trade, commerce and intercourse within the meaning of Article 301. Reasonable restrictions in public interest referred to in Clause (b) of Article 304 do not comprehend levy of taxes as a restriction especially when taxes are presumed to be both reasonable and in public interest.

The Supreme Court held that non–discriminatory tax does not *per se* constitute a restriction on the right to free trade, commerce and intercourse guaranteed under Article 301.

ROJER MATHEW VS SOUTH INDIAN BANK LTD

The Supreme Court in **Rojer Mathew Vs Indian Bank Ltd and Ors, (2020) 6 SCC 1** struck down the Tribunal, Appellate Tribunal and other Authorities (Qualifications, Experience, and other Conditions of Service of Members) Rules, 2017. The Supreme Court referred the issue ,whether Part -XIV of Finance Act, 2017 could have been passed as money bill, to larger bench.

Case Title : Rojer Mathew Vs Indian Bank Ltd
Date of Judgment : 13.11.2019
Bench : Chief Justice Ranjan Gogoi, Justice N. V. Ramana, Justice D. Y. Chandrachud, Justice Deepak Gupta, Justice Sanjiv Khanna

---

FACTS OF THE CASE

Several Petitions were filed before the Supreme Court seeking intervention in several aspects of constitution and management of tribunals. Roger Mathew has claimed the Constitution of Debt Recovery Tribunals was not in consonance with spirit of judicial independence. Madras Bar Association had prayed for shifting the administration of Tribunals to Ministry of Law and Justice and judicial impact assessment of Tribunals. Kudrat Sandhu has filed Writ Petition challenging the Part XIV of Finance Act, 2017 whereby provisions of twenty five different enactments were amended in respect of qualifications, methods of appointment, terms of office etc.

FINDINGS OF THE COURT

The Supreme Court noted rise of Tribunals because judicial delays in regular courts and increasing number of specialized and commercial matters. Tribunals, although not strictly courts, they perform judicial functions. Technical members are included to comprehend and decide issues involving specialized aspects.

The Supreme Court noted that Tribunalisation is an international phenomena. Tribunals have present in several jurisdictions including UK, Canada and France. In India the genesis of tribunalisation can be traced back to formation of ITAT. Article 323A and 323 B were introduced vide 42nd Amendment Act which paved way for establishment of tribunals in different fields. Subsequently Administrative Tribunal Act, 1985, National Environment Tribunal Act, 1995, National Environment Appellate Authority Act, 1997 etc.

The Supreme Court in **Jaswant Paper Mills Ltd., Meerut Vs Lakhichand AIR 1963 SC 677** held that any adjudicatory body vested with power of taking evidence, summoning of witnesses must be categorized as Tribunal.

The Supreme Court in **R. K. Jain Vs Union of India (1993) 4 SCC 119** observed that members of tribunals exercise quasi-judicial functions as such it is imperative that they possess requisite legal expertise, judicial experience and an iota of legal training.

The Supreme Court in **L. Chandra Kumar Vs Union of India (1997) 3 SCC 261** observed that all tribunals be brought to administration of single nodal ministry most appropriately Ministry of Law of Justice.

The Supreme Court in **Union of India Vs R Gandhi, President, Madras Bar Association (2010) 11 SCC 1** observed that Tribunals must possess independence, security and capacity. It would be imperative to include member of judiciary as presiding officer of the Tribunal. Technical member can only be in addition to judicial member when specialized knowledge or know how is required.

The Supreme Court in **Madras Bar Association Vs Union of India (2014) 10 SCC 1** observed that procedure of appointment and conditions of service of members must be akin to judges of the Courts which were sought to be substituted by the Tribunals.

The Supreme Court in **Madras Bar Association Vs. Union of India (2015) 8 SCC 583** held establishment of NCLT and NCLAT valid but directed for curing defects as per dictum of R. Gandhi.

Following important issues were determined by the Supreme Court in this matter.

(i) Whether Finance Act, 2017 in so far as it amends conditions of service of persons manning tribunals could have been passed as money bill ?

Procedure of passing of money bills is different from passing ordinary bills. Council of States has limited role in passing of money bills. Money bills has been defined under Article 110 (1) which contains "only" provisions covered by sub-clauses (a) to (g). These bills can only be introduced in Lok Sabha and role of Rajya Sabha is only consultative. Under Article 110 (4) every money bill has to be certified by the Speaker of the Lok Sabha.

The Union relied on Article 110 (3) and Article 122 and contended that once money bill is certified by the Speaker the same cannot be scrutinized by the Court.

The Supreme Court relied on **Raja Ram Pal vs Speaker, Lok Sabha** wherein it has been held that immunity granted under Article 122 (1) and Article 212 (1) immunity granted is limited to "irregularity of procedure" and does not extend to substantive illegality or unconstitutionality. The Court had held that under Article 122(1) and 212(1), immunity that has been granted is limited to 'irregularity of procedure' and does not extend to substantive illegality or unconstitutionality by observing:

The Court noted that in K. S. Puttaswamy the use of word "only" was not examined and answered by the majority judgment. The majority judgment did not advert to doctrine of pith and substance. The Supreme Court referred the matter to the larger bench.

(ii) Whether Section 184 of the Finance Act, 2017 is unconstitutional on account of excessive delegation ?

The Supreme Court held that Section 184 does not suffer from vice of unguided delegation although it fails to specify eligibility qualification for members, chairpersons, chairman etc. The delegate has to mandatory follow the decisions of the Supreme Court in R. K. Jain, L. Chandra Kumar, R Gandhi and Gujarat Urja Vikas. The Supreme Court noted that in many other enactments qualifications have not been prescribed and left for the delegate to prescribe qualification. Section 184 was inserted to bring out uniformity and with a view to harmonise the diverse and wide ranging qualifications.

(iii) Whether Tribunal, Appellate Tribunal, and Other Authorities (Qualification , Experience and Other Conditions of Service of Members) Rules, 2017 are in consonance with the Principal Act and various decisions of this Court on functioning of the tribunals ?

The Supreme Court observed that Search–cum– Selection committee as formulated under rules is an attempt to keep judiciary away from process of selection and appointment of members, vice-chairman and chairman. The Supreme Court observed that in **Supreme Court Advocate-on- Record Association Vs Union of India (Fourth Judges Case)** , it has been held that primacy of judiciary is imperative in appointment of judicial officers. Executive is a dominant litigation party and it can not be given primacy in appointments of members of Tribunals.

The Supreme Court noted earlier retired judges of the Supreme Court or High Court could be the presiding members of most of the Tribunals. Under the new rules Central Government has made persons with no judicial or legal experience eligible. In some cases retired Supreme Court judge as well as retired High Court judge has been made eligible, although position of retired Supreme Court judge and retried High Court judge are not equal.

The Court also noted that members of Tribunals can not be removed without concurrence of judiciary. The Supreme Court also observed that rules would require relook as since extremely short tenure of members of Tribunals is anti-merit and has effect of discouraging meritorious candidates to accept posts of judicial members in Tribunals.

(iv) Whether there should be a single nodal agency for administration of all Tribunals ?

The Supreme Court noted the statement of Union that Ministry of Law and Justice is overburdened and can not act as single nodal agency for administration of all Tribunals. However the Supreme Court emphasized the need of financial independence of Tribunals. It directed the Ministry of Finance to earmark separate fund for Tribunals.

(v) Whether there is need of conducting judicial impact assessment of all Tribunals in India ?

The Supreme Court directed Union of India to carry out financial impact assessment in respect of all tribunals and undertake exercise to assess need based requirements and make available sufficient resources for each Tribunal established by Parliament.

(vi) Whether judges of Tribunals set up under Article 323 A and 323 B can be equated in "rank" and "status" with constitutional functionaries?

The Supreme Court observed that Tribunals are not substitutes of Constitutional Courts. State of members of Tribunals can not be equated with sitting members of Constitutional Courts. The Supreme Court directed Union of India to ensure that judges of High Courts and the Supreme Court are on a separate pedestal distanced from any other tribunal or quasi-judicial authority.

(vii) Whether direct appeal to Supreme Court from Tribunals need to be detoured ?

Statutory appeals from appellate tribunals to the Supreme Court have been provided in several enactments. The Supreme Court noted that provisions for statutory appeals to the Supreme Court is being made without any judicial impact assessment. Such provisions are bogging the Supreme Court down and inhibiting its constitutional objective. Further such appeals is against the spirit of Tribunalisation. The Supreme Court recommended Union of India for revisit of such provisions with consultation with expert body.

(viii) Whether there is need for amalgamation of existing Tribunals ?

The Supreme Court directed the Union to rationalize and amalgamate the existing Tribunals depending on case load and commonality of subject-matter after conducting judicial impact assessment. Union should ensure that circuit benched of Tribunals are set up at the seats of all major jurisdictional High Courts.

MADRAS BAR ASSOCIATION VS UNION OF INDIA

The Supreme Court in **Madras Bar Association Vs Union of India, (2020) 2 SCR 246** directed for Constitution of National Tribunals Commission. The Supreme Court also issued several directions to ensure independence of Tribunals.

Case Title : Madras Bar Association Vs Union of India
Date of Judgment : 27.11.2020
Bench : Justice L. Nageswara Rao, Justice Hemant Gupta, Justice S. Ravindra Bhat

FACTS OF THE CASE

The Supreme Court in **Roger Mathew vs South Indian Bank (2020) 6SCC 1** has struck down Tribunal, Appellate Tribunal and other Authorities (Qualifications, Experience and other Conditions of Service of Members) Rules 2017 made under Section 184 of Finance Act, 2017. The Central Government notified fresh rules under Section 184 of Finance Act, 2017. Madras Bar Association filed Writ Petition under Article 32 seeking declaration that the said rules are in violation of Article 14, 21 and 50 of the Constitution, principle of separation of powers and independence of judiciary.

FINDINGS OF THE COURT

It was contended before the Court that Search-Cum-Selection Committee did not confirm to the principle of judicial dominance. Appointment of persons without judicial experience to the post of Chairman and Members are against prior directions of Supreme Court. Terms of office of members of four years are against earlier judgments of the Supreme Court. Advocates are not being made eligible for most of the positions. Administrative control of the executive in the matter of appointment and conditions of service is in violation of principles of separation of powers and independence of judiciary.

The Supreme Court issued following important directions in this matter.

(i) The Supreme Court directed for constitution of National Tribunals Commission which will be an independent body to supervise the appointments and functioning of tribunals. Such Tribunal will also conduct disciplinary proceedings against members of tribunals.

(ii) Search-cum-Selection Committee will include - (i) the Chief Justice of India or his nominee, (ii) outgoing Chairperson, Chairman or President, in case of appointment of Chairman, Chairperson or President (or) sitting Chairman, Chairperson, or President in case of appointment of other members (or) retired Judge of Supreme Court of retired Chief justice of High Court in case sitting Chairman, Chairperson or President is not a judicial member or seeking reappointment, (iii) Secretary of Ministry of Law and Justice, (iv) Secretary of Government of India from other than parent of sponsoring department nominated by Cabinet Secretary (v) Secretary of sponsoring or parent department – without a vote.

(iii) Search -cum – Selection Committee will only recommend one name for appointment to a post.

(iv)Efforts will be made to provide suitable house to Chairman, Chairperson, President and other members. In case house is not allotted, Union of India has to pay an amount of Rs, 1,50,000/- to Chairman, Chairperson, President, Vice- Chairman, Vice-Chairperson, and Vice-President and Rs, 1,25,000/- to other members.

(v) Advocates having more than 10 years of experience will be eligible for appointment as judicial members.

(vi) The members of Indian Legal Service will be also eligible for appointment as judicial members

(vii) The recommendations of Search-cum- Selection Committee in respect of disciplinary proceedings will be final and such recommendation will be implemented by the Central Government.

(viii) Union of India has to make appointment within three months of recommendation made by Search-cum-Selection Committee.

The Supreme Court observed that dispensation of justice by Tribunals will be effective only if they function independent of any executive control. The Supreme Court noted that several directions given to the Union to ensure independence of the Tribunals, but the same have not been heeded to forcing the Petitioner to approach Supreme Court time and again.

The Supreme Court directed Union of India to strictly adhere to the directions given in this matter.

ANOOP BARANWAL VS UNION OF INDIA

The Supreme Court in **Anoop Baranwal Vs Union of India, (2023)9SCR1** directed that Chief Election Commissioner and other Election Commissioners have to appointed on the recommendation of a Committee consisting of Prime Minister, the Leader of the Opposition of the Lok Sabha and in case no leader of Opposition is available, the leader of largest opposition party in Lok Sabha in terms of numerical strength and the Chief Justice of India.

Case Title : Anoop Baranwal Vs Union of India
Date of Judgment : 02.03.2023
Bench : Justice K.M. Joseph, Justice Ajay Rastogi, Justice Aniruddha Bose, Justice Hrishikesh Roy, Justice C.T. Ravikumar

FACTS OF THE CASE

Four Writ Petitions were filed before the Supreme Court seeking a fair, just and transparent process of selection by constituting a neutral and independent body to recommend the names for appointment of the member to the Election Commission under Article 324(2) of the Constitution of India. The matter was referred to Constitution Bench for authoritative interpretation.

FINDINGS OF THE SUPREME COURT

Article 324 provides that the Election Commission shall consist of the Chief Election Commissioner and such number of other Election Commissioners, if any, as the President may from time to time fix and the appointment of the Chief Election Commissioner and other Election Commissioners shall, subject to the provisions of law made in that behalf by Parliament, be made by the President.

The Supreme Court after surveying several other authorities under the Constitution noted that Article 324 (2) is unique in its setting and purpose.

The Supreme Court observed that in catena of cases it has been held that right to vote is neither a fundamental right but a pure and simple statutory right. Even if it is treated as a statutory right, it cannot be divorced or separated from mandate of Article 326. The right to vote is of the greatest importance and forms the foundation for a free and fair election, which , in turn, constitutes the right of the people to elect their representatives

The Supreme Court in **Anukul Chandra Pradhan Vs. Union of India AIR (1997) SC 2814** has held that holding free and fair election is a basic feature of the Constitution.

The Supreme Court noted that Election Commission discharges several functions critical to democracy. Article 324 is a plenary provision clothing the Election Commission with the entire responsibility to hold the National and State Elections and carries with it the necessary powers to discharge its functions. The Election Commission under Article 324 can postpone an election on the basis of the opinion that there existed disturbed conditions in the State or some area of the State thus making of holding free and fair elections not possible. The election commission is endowed with power to recognize political parties and deciding disputes among them. Under Article 103 (2) and Article 192 (2), the President and the Governor are to act on the opinion of the Election Commission as regards the question of disqualification of the Member of Parliament and of the Legislature of a State respectively.

The Supreme Court observed that appointment of Chief Election Commission must not be overshadowed by even a perception that a 'yes man' will decide the fate of democracy and all that it promises.

The Supreme Court directed that the appointment of the Chief Election Commissioner and the Election Commissioners, shall be made by the President on the advice of a Committee consisting of the Prime Minister, the Leader of the Opposition of the Lok Sabha and in case no leader of Opposition is available, the leader of largest opposition party in Lok Sabha in terms of numerical strength and the Chief Justice of India.

Subsequent to passing of this judgment the Parliament passed Chief Election Commissioner and Other Election Commissioners Act (Appointment, Conditions of Service and terms of Office) Act, 2023. The Act provides that Chief Election Commissioner and other Election Commissioners will be appointed on the recommendation of Selection Committee consisting of Prime Minister, Leader of Opposition and a Minister of Cabinet rank.

UNION OF INDIA
VS ASSOCIATION OF
DEMOCRTIC REFORMS

The Supreme Court in **Union of India Vs. Association of Democratic Reforms, (2002) 3 SCR 696** directed Election Commission for seeking several information from candidates seeking election to Parliament or State Legislature on affidavit.

Case Title : Union of India Vs. Association of Democratic Reforms
Date of Judgment : 02.05.2026
Bench : Justice M. B. Shah, Justice Bisheshwar Prasad Singh, Justice H. K, Sema

FACTS OF THE CASE

Association for Democratic Reforms filed Petition before the Delhi High Court for implementation of recommendation made by Law Commission of India in its 170th Report. It was pointed out that Law Commission has made recommendations for debarring a candidate from contesting an election if charges have been framed against him by a Court in respect of certain offences and making it necessary for a candidate seeking to contest elections to furnish details regarding criminal cases, if any, pending against him. It was also suggested that true and correct statement of assets owned by the candidate, his/her spouse and dependent relations should also be disclosed. After considering the relevant submissions and reports as well as the view of the Election Commission, the High Court held that for making a right choice, it is essential that the past of the candidate should not be kept in dark as it is not in interest of democracy and well being of the country. The High Court directed the Election Commission to secure several information for candidates seeking election to Parliament or State Legislature.

Union of India challenged said order before the Supreme Court of India.

FINDINGS OF THE SUPREME COURT

The Supreme Court noted that it cannot give directions for amending the Act or Statutory Rules. However, it is equally well settled that when the Act or Rules are silent on a particular subject and the Authority implementing the same has constitutional power or statutory power to implement it the Court can necessarily issue directions or orders on the said subject to fill the vacuum or void till suitable law is enacted.

The Supreme Court observed that the jurisdiction of the Election Commission is wide enough to include all powers necessary for smooth conduct of elections and the word "elections" is used in a wide sense to include the entire process of election which consists of several stages and embraces many steps. The limitation on plenary character of power is when the Parliament or State Legislature has made a valid law relating to or in connection with elections, the Commission is required to act in conformity with the said provisions. In case where law is silent, Article 324 is a reservoir of power to act for the avowed purpose of having free and fair elections.

The Supreme Court observed that the members of a democratic society should be sufficiently informed so that they may influence intelligently the decisions which may affect themselves and this would include their decision of casting votes in favour of a particular candidate. If there is a disclosure by a candidate, it would strengthen the voters in taking appropriate decision of casting their votes.

The Supreme Court observed that democracy cannot survive without free and fair election, without free and fairly informed voters. Votes cast by uninformed voters in favour of X and Y candidate would be meaningless. One sided information, disinformation, misinformation, and non–information all equally create an uninformed citizenry which makes democracy farce. Casting a vote by misinformed and non–informed voter or a voter having one-sided information only is bound to affect the democracy seriously. Freedom of speech and expression includes right to impart and receive information which includes freedom to hold opinions. Entertainment is implied in freedom of speech and expression and there is no reason to hold that freedom of speech and expression would not cover right to get material information with regard to a candidate who is contesting election for a post which is of utmost importance in the democracy.

The Supreme Court directed Election Commission to call for following information on affidavit in exercise of its power under Article 324 of the Constitution of India from each candidate seeking election to Parliament or State Legislature as a necessary part of his nomination paper:

(1) Whether the candidate is convicted/acquitted/discharged of any criminal offence in the past, if any, whether he is punished with imprisonment or fine?

(2) Prior to six months of filing of nomination, whether the candidate is accused in any pending case or any offence punishable with imprisonment for two years or more and in which charge is framed or cognizance is taken by this Court of law, if so details thereof.

(3) The assets (immovable, movable, bank balances etc.) of a candidate and of his/her spouse and that of dependents.

(4) Liabilities, if any, particularly whether there are any over dues of any public financial institution or Government dues

(5) The educational qualifications of the candidates

PUBLIC INTEREST FOUNDATION VS UNION OF INDIA

The Supreme Court in **Public Interest Foundation Vs Union of India, (2018) 10 SCR 141** issued directions to contesting candidates as well as political parties   to share several material information about criminal antecedents for curbing criminalization of politics.

Case Title : Public Interest Foundation Vs Union of India
Date of Judgment : 25.11.2018
Bench : Chief Justice Dipak Misra, Justice Nariman, Justice A. M. Khanwilkar, Justice Dr, D. Y. Chandrachud, Justice Indu Malhotra

FACTS OF THE CASE

Public Interest Foundation filed Writ Petition before the Supreme Court of India seeking several directions for curbing criminalization of politics. The issue before the Supreme Court was whether disqualification for membership can be laid down by the Court beyond Article 102 (a) to (d) and the law made by the Parliament under Article 102 (e). The matter was referred to the Constitution Bench.

FINDINGS OF THE SUPREME COURT

The Supreme Court observed that it is clear as crystal that as regards disqualification for being chosen as a member of either House of Parliament and similarly disqualification for being chosen or for being a member of the Legislative Assembly or Legislative Council of a State, the law has to be made by Parliament. It is well settled in law that Court cannot legislate.

The Supreme Court observed that there is no denial of the fact that the Election Commission has the plenary power and its view have to be given weightage. That apart, it has power to supervise the conduct of free and fair election. However, the said power has its limitations. The Election

Commission has to act in conformity with the law made by the Parliament and it cannot transgress the same.

The Supreme Court noted increasing criminalization of politics and recommended to Parliament to bring out a strong law whereby it is made mandatory for the political parties to revoke membership of persons against whom charges are framed in heinous and grievous offences and not to set up such persons in elections, both for the Parliament and the State Assemblies. This would go a long way in achieving de-criminalization of politics and usher in an era of immaculate, spotless and unsullied and virtuous constitutional democracy.

The Supreme Court also issued following directions :

(i) Each contesting candidate shall fill up the form as provided by the Election Commission and the form must contain all the particulars as required therein

(ii) It shall state in bold letters with regard to the criminal cases pending against the candidate.

(iii) If a candidate is contesting an election on a ticket of a particular party, he/she is required to inform the party about the criminal cases pending against him/her

(iv) The concerned political party shall be obligated to put up on its website the aforesaid information pertaining to candidates having criminal antecedents.

(v) The candidates as well as the concerned political party shall issue a declaration in the widely circulated newspapers in the locality about the antecedents of the candidates and also give wide publicity in the electronic media.

S R BOMMAI VS UNION OF INDIA

The Supreme Court in **S. R. Bommai Vs Union of India, (1994) 2 SCR 644** held inter alia that imposition of the President Rule under Article 356 (1) is subject to judicial review.

Case Title : S. R. Bommai Vs Union of India (1994) 2 SCR 644
Date of Judgment : 11.03.1994
Bench : Justice Kuldip Singh, Justice P.B. Sawant, Justice K. Ramaswamy, Justice S.C. Agrawal, Justice Yogeshwar Dayal, Justice B.P. Jeevan Reddy, Justice S.R. Pandian, Justice A.M. Ahmadi, Justice J. S. Verma

---

FACTS OF THE CASE

Several Petitions were filed before the Supreme Court challenging the imposition of President Rule under Article 356 of the Constitution in states of Meghalaya, Nagaland, Karnataka, Rajasthan, Madhya Pradesh, and Himachal Pradesh.

The Supreme Court considered three important questions in respect of imposition of President Rule Under Article 356 of the Constitution of India – (i) Whether proclamation of President Rule under Article 356 is amenable to judicial review ? (ii) If yes what is scope of judicial review ? and (iii) What is interpretation of " a situation has arisen in which Government can not be carried on in accordance with the provisions of Constitution" ?

FINDINDS OF THE COURT

Article 356 of the Constitution provides for imposition of President Rule by proclamation by the President if the President is satisfied on the report of the Governor or otherwise that a situation has arisen wherein the government of a state cannot be carried on in accordance with provisions of the Constitution. After such proclamation the President may assume power vested in Governor or any other authority to himself except functions of State Legislature. The President may declare that legislative functions of State Legislature will be exercised under authority of Parliament.

The Supreme Court observed that conditions precedent to imposition of President Rule under Article 356 is – (i) the President should be satisfied on report of the Governor or otherwise and (ii) a situation has arisen wherein the government of the State can not be carried in in accordance with the Constitution. President's opinion has to be based on objective material. Such material should show that constitutional government has become an impossibility. Once such material is shown to be in existence, the satisfaction of the President is not open to question. If no such material exists, the satisfaction of the President is open to challenge.

It was contended by Union that the power of judicial review is narrower in Constitutional Law in comparison to Administrative Law. Judicial Review in Constitutional Law extends only if actions are unconstitutional or ultra vires. Judicial Review can be resorted to in case of infringement of separation of powers or Fundamental Rights. This contention was rejected by the Supreme Court.

The Supreme Court held that Proclamation under Article 356 is subject to judicial review to the extent of examining whether conditions precedent to the issuance of proclamation has been satisfied or not. Such examination will necessarily involve scrutiny as to whether there existed material for satisfaction of the President that a situation has arisen in which the government of the State cannot be carried on in accordance with the provisions of the Constitution. It is not personal whim, wish. view, or opinion or the *ipse dixit* of the President *de hors* the material but a legitimate inference drawn from the material placed before him which is relevant for the purpose.

The Supreme Court concurred with Sarkaria Commission Report wherein certain illustrations were given wherein President Rule can be imposed under Article 356 of the Constitution.

The Supreme Court also dispelled the contentions of the Union of India that judicial review of imposition of President Rule on advise of Council of Minister is barred as Article 74 (2) bars judicial review of any advise tendered by the Council of Ministers to the President. The Supreme Court negated this contention, firstly, on the ground that the purpose of Article 74 (2) was not to exclude any material from scrutiny of the courts but to provide that an order of the President cannot be challenged on the ground that it was contrary to the advice given by Council of Ministers or was issued without obtaining any advice from the ministers. Secondly, 74 (2) bars judicial review of advice tendered by the Council of Ministers but does not bar scrutiny of materials on the basis of which advice was tendered.

The Supreme Court held that such proclamation will be amenable to judicial review even if it has been approved by Parliament.

The Supreme Court noted that democracy, federalism and secularism is basic feature of Constitution. The Supreme Court dispelled the contention that if ruling parties in state suffer an overwhelming defeat in Lok Sabha, it will be ground for proclamation under Article 356.

The Supreme Court also endorsed the view of the Sarkaria Commission that President may issue waring to States as first measure before imposing President Rule under Article 356.

The Supreme Court held that the President cannot exercise power under Article 356 (1) (a) (b) and (c) till both the houses of Parliament have approved the proclamation. If the proclamation is declared invalid, the Court may restore the *status quo ante*.

The Supreme Court declared proclamation of President Rule in Karnataka, Meghalaya and Nagaland as unconstitutional. The Supreme Court held proclamation of President Rule in Rajasthan, Madhya Pradesh and Himachal Pradesh constitutional.

About the author

Mukesh Kumar Suman is an advocate and legal author based at Delhi. His books include *Fundamentals of Indian Constitution; Insolvency and Bankruptcy Code, 2016: A Paradigm Shift; Protection of Women from Domestic Violence Act, 2005 : A Concise Commentary; and The Industrial Relations Code, 2020 : The new Framework for Industrial Peace.* His legal articles are available at www.mukeshsuman.com.